"This book is more than a manual—it is a vessel. Within its pages, clinicians find not only the skills and insights to navigate psychedelic therapy, but also the guidance to prepare themselves as instruments of healing. From history to nutrition, from touch to silence, it offers a holistic frame where knowledge and intuition can merge. In times like these, where holding space with integrity is vital, this book equips us with the container to help clients awaken their best selves."

Mariam Dum, *PhD, author and clinical psychologist*

"This book is the real thing. It comes from a woman who has walked the path herself—not only studying and researching but living, healing, breaking, and rebuilding. She brings together science, psychology, and ancient wisdom with a clarity and compassion that makes the most complex ideas feel human and useful.

In a field that can easily get lost in hype or mysticism, Bibliowicz writes with grounded integrity. She knows the risks, honors the traditions, and never loses sight of what matters most: the human being in front of her. This book is not just about psychedelics; it is about healing, meaning, and the possibility of becoming whole again.

If you are a therapist, a seeker, or someone curious about the power of expanded states of consciousness, read this book. It is a trustworthy guide written by someone I know to be kind, wise, and deeply in it for the right reasons."

Alejandro Junger, *MD, creator of the Clean detox program*

"I have witnessed clients make a meaningful shift towards healing, self-discovery, and transformation through the supportive, non-judgmental relationship they have with Vanessa Bibliowicz. This manual makes Dr. Bibliowicz's framework available to everyone, enabling readers to integrate the science and therapeutic process of psychedelic integration theory with an understanding of the importance of inner wisdom and human connection. This book will be effective for therapists, coaches, and physicians interested in expanding their knowledge and skills working with psychedelic-assisted therapy."

Michelle Weiner, *DO, MPH, ketamine expert, researcher, and educator*

The Therapeutic Use of Psychedelics

The Therapeutic Use of Psychedelics is a comprehensive manual for mental health professionals that details the vital aspects of psychedelic integration therapy.

The book provides essential skills, tools, and insights for preparing clients for psychedelic sessions, supporting them during the experience, and aiding post-session integration for long-term benefits. Chapters describe the personal work, tools, and mindsets professionals need before they begin work in this area, and the book also covers vital topics such as proper client screening for safety, vital psychedelic psychoeducation, and the relationship between mindfulness skills, psychedelics, and other states of consciousness.

Throughout the manual, clinicians will find engaging stories and case studies, academic research, and practical guidelines to help them bridge the gap between traditional mental health practices and the emerging field of psychedelic therapy.

Vanessa Bibliowicz, DMFT, LMFT, is a licensed psychotherapist specializing in the facilitation of healing experiences through psychedelic integration, blending systemic therapy, neuroscience, and spirituality.

The Therapeutic Use of Psychedelics

Essential Skills and Insights for Psychotherapists

Vanessa Bibliowicz

Routledge
Taylor & Francis Group
NEW YORK AND LONDON

Designed cover image: Getty Images

First published 2027
by Routledge
605 Third Avenue, New York, NY 10158

and by Routledge
4 Park Square, Milton Park, Abingdon, Oxon, OX14 4RN

Routledge is an imprint of the Taylor & Francis Group, an informa business

ISBN: 978-1-032-89189-7 (hbk)
ISBN: 978-1-032-89187-3 (pbk)
ISBN: 978-1-003-54163-9 (ebk)

DOI: 10.4324/9781003541639

Typeset in Optima
by Apex CoVantage, LLC

Access the password protected support material: https://resourcecentre.routledge.com/books/9781032891873

Disclaimer

The Therapeutic Use of Psychedelics: Essential Skills and Insights for Psychotherapists presents a model for psychedelic-integrated, resource-based therapy. This approach outlines how psychedelics can enhance therapeutic work by facilitating access to the subconscious and inner wisdom.

This book is designed primarily for mental health professionals seeking to incorporate psychedelic integration into their practice. It offers foundational principles, practical tools, ethical guidance, and real-world case studies. It may also serve as a resource for individuals interested in understanding the applications of psychedelic integration therapy and its potential role in their healing journey.

This model is not a standalone method but rather an adjunct to a comprehensive therapeutic framework. It emphasizes the importance of a strong therapeutic relationship, therapist self-awareness, and careful preparation. Safety, ethics, and a deep respect for the transformative potential of psychedelics are central to this work.

The legal status of psychedelics varies by jurisdiction. This book does not advocate for or encourage illegal activity. It is intended for informational purposes only and does not constitute medical, legal, or professional advice. Practitioners should familiarize themselves with local laws and seek appropriate legal counsel, training, and supervision before incorporating psychedelics into their practice.

Although the term *therapist* is used throughout this text to refer to professionals in psychedelic integration, healing work extends beyond licensed mental health practitioners. Coaches, spiritual guides, shamans, and traditional healers also bring valuable and diverse perspectives to this evolving field.

Contents

Preface

Our sense of self is shaped by the systems we inhabit—culture, religion, socioeconomic status, and the collection of social interactions that define our place in the world. These forces create an implicit map that influences our perceptions, choices, and beliefs, often beyond our conscious awareness. We may believe we are making independent decisions with a fresh perspective; however, in reality, our choices are often shaped by the frameworks we have inherited from the world around us. These frameworks were constructed long before we were ever aware of them, and they do not exist in the abstract. Instead, they shape the way we experience the world and the roles we are expected to play within it.

My own identity reflects this interplay between personal agency and external influence. I define myself as a White, Jewish, Colombian woman—an identity layered with expectations, limitations, beliefs, and lived experiences. Although I was born into privilege, my gender, religion, and cultural background exposed me to the complexities of being a minority. Growing up Jewish in a predominantly Catholic country with patriarchal structures outlined my map with distinct boundaries and terrain. As a Jew, I was familiar with what it meant to be Othered, face both implicit and explicit stereotypes, and grapple with a sense of belonging that often felt conditional. As a woman, I internalized societal messages of compliance and self-restraint, shaping not only how I saw myself but how I related to the world around me.

For much of my early life, I followed the path that these influences laid out for me, embracing the roles I was conditioned, or constrained, to see as markers of success and fulfillment. The earliest paths on my map led me to marriage and motherhood at a young age. By 22, I was married with my first child, and over the next 7 years, I had two more. I followed the trajectory prescribed for me, guided by societal expectations and a deep sense of duty.

However, at 30, my constructed world unraveled. The map I had relied upon—one defined by societal expectations, cultural frameworks, and inherited roles—collapsed beneath me. A personal crisis propelled me into unknown territory, pushing me to deconstruct, reconfigure, and rebuild my sense of self, others, and my understanding of healing. It was during this period—one that felt like a rebirth—that I discovered psychotherapy, systemic family therapy, and later, psychedelic-assisted therapy: modalities that not only facilitated my personal healing but also profoundly reshaped my professional trajectory. These were not just tools for personal healing: They became the foundation of a new professional path.

I pursued both my master's and doctoral degrees in family therapy, a field that matched my belief in systemic thinking and relational dynamics. I came to fully see that transformation does not occur in isolation: It requires an awareness of both the individual and the larger systems that shape them. This led me to therapeutic modalities and ways of thinking that honored the deep connection between mind, body, and environment.

My first professional endeavor was in equine-assisted therapy, where I worked as an equine staff therapist during my graduate studies. Horses became my first therapeutic collaborators, revealing the depth of healing that can occur beyond verbal communication. Their ability to mirror emotions, provide grounding, and offer access to unspoken truths strengthened my understanding that therapy extends beyond cognitive work—it is a holistic process shaped by physical being and the environments we inhabit.

My passion for healing as an immersive, embodied experience naturally guided me toward modalities that access deeper states of awareness. One of these modalities, which I explored while pursuing my doctorate, was hypnosis. Under the guidance of my mentor, Dr. Douglas Flemons—a renowned Ericksonian hypnotherapist and teacher—I trained in hypnotherapy, gaining profound insights into the paradoxical complexities of the mind and the transformative power of hypnosis to reshape our relationship with these internal patterns. Simultaneously, I explored shamanic breathwork, a practice rooted in spiritual traditions that also created the possibility of an altered state. These modalities taught me that some of our greatest transformations occur not through intellectual insights alone but when we surpass the barriers of our rational minds—when we surrender control, drop beneath analytical thought, and allow ourselves to access the deeper emotional and spiritual realms where true healing can unfold.

It was within this expanding landscape of non-ordinary states that I began working under the clinical supervision of Dr. Isaac Farin, who influenced my path further. Isaac introduced me to psychedelic-assisted therapy, a developing field that resonated strongly with my interest in altered states and even a past personal experience. Several years earlier, I had my first experience with ayahuasca, which had profoundly opened a door to deeper dimensions of consciousness. Building on this powerful personal experience—and guided by Isaac's mentorship as well as the teachings of other shamanic facilitators—I explored psychedelic-assisted therapy both clinically and personally. Through this integrative approach, I witnessed firsthand how combining psychedelics with ancient wisdom within a contemporary therapeutic framework can unlock profound and lasting transformation.

In 2019, Isaac and I established Mindful Psychedelics™, a private practice dedicated to psychedelic integration therapy. Since its inception, I have worked closely with clients exploring psychedelic-assisted therapy to support their healing, self-discovery, and transformation. My approach is deeply systemic and strength-based, blending hypnotherapy, mindfulness, breathwork, and integrative medicine to promote lasting personal growth. Furthermore, recognizing the need for structured training and more clinicians in our field that work with altered states, Isaac and I later developed the Mindful Psychedelics Integration Model™ (MPIM™), through which we've trained mental health professionals seeking to thoughtfully incorporate this approach into their clinical practice.

Through the years, I have witnessed hundreds of individuals undergo profound, life-altering transformations, offering compelling evidence of the immense therapeutic potential within this emerging field. These experiences led me to recognize the necessity of sharing this multidimensional approach—one that integrates contemporary psychotherapy with time-honored psychedelic traditions—with a wider audience. This book is a direct result of that realization, bringing together the structured methodologies of my formal education in family therapy and altered states of consciousness with the wisdom of ancient healing traditions. It offers a clinician-ready way to prepare, guide, and integrate psychedelic experiences with clarity, humility, and respect for the cultures that have carried these practices.

Throughout the book, I share key concepts of our therapeutic model and the importance of the therapeutic relationship, bringing these ideas to life through real stories of transformation. These narratives highlight the deeply interconnected psychological, physiological, and existential aspects of healing in ways that theory alone cannot fully capture. My hope is that this book will serve as both a practical guide and a source of inspiration, encouraging mental health professionals and healers to thoughtfully explore the therapeutic potential of psychedelics. Furthermore, readers will be introduced to this exciting yet still-evolving field and come to understand why it is essential to pair scientific rigor with deep respect for the indigenous traditions that have long recognized the healing potential of these substances. You will not find hype here. You will find a clear, ethical map; scripts and structures you can actually use; and case work that shows how change becomes lived. If you are new, this book will orient you. If you are already in the work, it will deepen your stance and your skills.

Looking back, I feel both gratitude and a sense of wonder. This path—created through personal upheaval, academic study, and deep spiritual curiosity—has shown me that healing is not linear. It's messy, beautiful, and often surprising. Psychedelic-assisted therapy has opened doors I never imagined, not just for me but for so many of the people I've had the privilege to work with. This book is my way of offering what I've learned—an integration of science, soul, and the wisdom passed down through generations. I hope it serves as a companion for clinicians and seekers alike, sparking curiosity and offering something useful along the way. I don't pretend to have all the answers, but I do believe deeply in what's possible when we approach this work with humility, integrity, and heart. The field is still growing, and so am I. And I'm hopeful—for what's unfolding and for the many ways we can continue to show up for healing, together.

Vanessa Bibliowicz

Acknowledgments

As I write the concluding words of a book that has spanned over two years, I reflect on the many factors that made this journey possible. It's difficult to attribute the culmination of this book to a singular influence, person, or motive. Yet, there exists an inexplicable guiding force that led me, almost subconsciously, through the process without much deliberation on its meaning or implications.

This feeling reminds me of a book I read years ago by Michael Singer: *The Surrender Experiment*. In it, Singer talks about his decision to navigate life by surrendering to its unpredictable ways, always saying yes to whatever opportunities and challenges came his way. Gradually, my academic endeavor evolved into something similar—a willing surrender to life's ebbs and flows, fortified by trust that each turn would lead me exactly where I needed to be and always saying "yes." Today, as I look back, I can affirm that this intuition was correct. I find myself in a life I never imagined, but that perfectly aligns with my unvoiced dreams.

Therefore, first and foremost, I am profoundly grateful for life in all its complexity. Its beauty and hardships have been equally invaluable, and I would not change one thing, encapsulating what Friedrich Nietzsche referred to as "the eternal recurrence"—the idea that one should live life as if one will have to relive it over and over again for all eternity, without any changes whatsoever. Thankfully, I can confidently say that I would.

I am also incredibly grateful for my family, starting with my husband Mark, who has been an unwavering pillar of support, enabling me to wholly invest so much of my time in pursuits of intellectual curiosity and passion. My children, Elias, Jonathan, and Sonia, are daily inspirations, guiding me toward becoming the person I hope they will be proud of and want to emulate in the future. Their lessons on the depths of love are my greatest gifts.

My heartfelt thanks go to my mentors and colleagues—Isaac, Michael, Douglas, and Shelley. I couldn't have been more fortunate to have the opportunity to learn from some of the most brilliant minds in my field. It's something I could never have conjured, even in my most audacious dreams.

Before concluding, a special thanks to my editors. Your keen eye and dedication elevated this work beyond measure. I am very appreciative of your contributions.

In sum, this journey has been a testament to the power of saying "yes" to life, of trusting its intricate designs, and of surrendering to its majestic, unknowable course. And for that, I am eternally grateful.

Foreword

By altering the boundaries of a circumscribed sense of self, psychedelics disrupt status-quo thinking and feeling, offering efficient and compelling pathways for significant mindset resets. No wonder, then, that they can so effectively occasion a meaningful shift in a client's relationship to a traumatic past, an intractable problem, a dreaded future. But for such therapeutic potential to be safely and reliably enacted, it is best realized within the context of a supportive, nonjudgmental relationship with an informed and experienced therapist, one who is emotionally grounded, fully present, and skilled at utilizing and later processing whatever dream-like reality unfolds.

Just as clients need a trusted guide to help them navigate such psychedelic journeys, clinicians need a trusted guide to help them get up to speed on how best to offer such guidance. Enter Vanessa Bibliowicz. An astute, sensitive, and mindful systemic therapist, Vanessa is as warm and genuine in person as she is in these pages. For years now, I've been witnessing and appreciating her inexhaustible curiosity and desire to learn, coupled with her skill and ability to tease out and nurture client strengths and possibilities. In this remarkable book, she develops a comprehensive approach to psychedelic-assisted therapy, contextualizing it within both scientific research and shamanistic spiritual traditions.

Bibliowicz introduces the chemistry and history of, the relevant research on, and the clinical implications for five different hallucinogens—ketamine, psilocybin, MDMA, LSD, and ayahuasca. You'll learn how these substances decrease the activity of the default mode network (which plays a critical role in processing information about the self) and increase connectivity between otherwise separate neural networks, disrupting habitual ways of thinking and feeling and allowing novel cognitive and emotional patterns to form. But you'll also come to appreciate each of their idiosyncratic qualities and distinctive applications.

Step by careful step, Bibliowicz walks you through a three-stage therapeutic process: (1) thoroughly preparing clients for and orienting them to their impending psychedelic journey, (2) designing and providing an appropriate setting for safely supporting them through their psychedelic experience, and (3) framing and integrating what they saw, felt, recalled, endured, and discovered. To do this effectively, says Bibliowicz, you, yourself, need to have personal experience with whatever substance you are recommending for your clients. Such firsthand knowledge is a prerequisite for the guiding responsibilities you are taking on.

The ineffabilities of psychedelic experience and the mystical qualities of spiritual practices could easily lend themselves to vague gesturing and gauzy proclamations. You'll find none of that here. Bibliowicz balances a holistic sensibility with down-to-earth practicality. In so doing, she manages to inspire *and* inform. And although she embraces the potent possibilities of psychedelic-assisted therapy, there is nothing naïve or breathless about her hopeful vision. She is clear about potential dangers, and she counsels level-headed caution. This includes not only staying alert and knowing how to effectively respond to clients' fearful responses to strange and frightening visions but also staying committed to defining and maintaining clear interpersonal boundaries that ensure physical and emotional safety throughout the client's journey.

Even though psychedelics are being incorporated in a variety of clinical research and therapeutic protocols, the field is still very much bootstrapping itself into being. Whether you're trying to decide if you want to launch into what is still largely unchartered territory or you've already introduced psychedelics into your work with clients, you'll find in the pages that follow an invaluable map for finding your way, a map that is generously illustrated and vivified with compelling personal stories and client cases. I learned a lot from this timely and welcome contribution, which was no surprise, given the integrity and wisdom of the author.

Douglas Flemons, PhD
Professor Emeritus, Nova Southeastern University
Author of *Empathic Engagement in Clinical Practice* and
The Heart and Mind of Hypnotherapy

Part I

The Therapist

Introduction

Bridging Science, Psychotherapy, and Spirituality in Altered States of Consciousness

Your mind, my mind, our clients' minds—they remain shrouded in mystery. Despite remarkable advances in neuroscience and psychology, consciousness continues to elude full understanding. Our brains, with billions of neurons forming countless connections (Herculano-Houzel, 2012), constitute an intricate system that fascinates and challenges researchers, remaining one of the most complex and least understood organs in the human body. This mystery has led many to seek insight beyond empirical data, turning to spiritual and existential frameworks for the meaning and healing that science alone cannot provide. Along the way, these seemingly opposing worldviews have often clashed—dividing those who view the mind through a spiritual lens and those who insist on looking through a purely scientific one.

Psychotherapy sits squarely within this tension. It is a field deeply concerned with the mind, consciousness, and human transformation. Even the word "psychotherapy"—from the Greek *psyche* (meaning soul or mind) and *therapeia* (meaning healing or treatment)—reflects this duality. Depending on interpretation, it may suggest a process of soul healing or a more clinical treatment of the mind. This ambiguity has long reflected the broader challenge within psychotherapy and consciousness studies: the struggle to bridge scientific rigor with subjective, often spiritual, experience.

Traditional Western clinical training tends to emphasize evidence-based models, scientific explanations, and measurable outcomes, often approaching spiritual or non-ordinary experiences with skepticism. But clinical work tells a more nuanced story. Practitioners quickly learn that human suffering and transformation rarely fit neatly into diagnostic categories or linear treatment plans. Although science provides essential structure, credibility, and tools for outcome tracking, spiritual traditions offer something equally vital: a framework for meaning-making, emotional resilience, and human connection. When seen as complementary rather than conflicting, these perspectives enrich therapeutic work and expand what healing can look like.

DOI: 10.4324/9781003541639-2

Clients, after all, do not enter therapy as data points or diagnostic puzzles. They come with layered histories, emotional complexities, and existential questions—seeking not just symptom relief but deeper transformation. They are often in search of meaning, connection, and a renewed sense of wholeness. As Irvin Yalom once said, "I believe that the majority of people in therapy are there because of the absence of meaning in their lives" (Yalom, 1980, p. 448). Viktor Frankl (1959/2006) echoed this truth: "Life is never made unbearable by circumstances, but only by lack of meaning and purpose" (p. 104). It is this deeper longing that calls therapists to look beyond technique alone.

This book was written in honor of the merging of that duality. It weaves together clinical expertise, spiritual insight, and lived experience to offer a framework that is at once structured and deeply human. Whether you're a clinician, student, or seeker, what follows is a chapter-by-chapter rundown of how this work unfolds in practice: from the philosophical principles that guide it, to the tools that support change, to the deep inner shifts that psychedelic therapy can help catalyze.

This book is divided into three parts, each building on the last to offer a clear and integrated approach to psychedelic-assisted therapy.

Part I begins with what matters most: the therapist. Before learning techniques or protocols, we must understand how we show up in the room. This section introduces the foundational principles that guide this work—presence, mindfulness, unconditional positive regard, curiosity, trust in the client's inner wisdom, and a systemic understanding of healing. These are not tools to apply, but ways of being that shape everything else. Whether or not you work with psychedelics, these principles offer a grounding orientation for any therapist committed to deep, ethical, and heart-centered work.

Part II explores the history, science, and clinical use of psychedelic medicines. It begins with how these substances interact with the brain and why they can shift perception, loosen rigid thought patterns, and open new possibilities for healing. From there, it traces the history of psychedelic use across cultures, from ancient spiritual traditions to modern clinical trials. The second half of this section focuses on five specific medicines: ketamine, psilocybin, MDMA, LSD, and ayahuasca. Each chapter explores the chemistry, mechanisms of action, history, clinical research, and potential therapeutic applications of the medicine. Clinical considerations at the end of each chapter offer guidance for how to assess fit and hold space for the unique effects of each substance.

Part III presents MPIM—our practitioner-tested framework that operationalizes preparation, journey guidance, and integration with concrete checklists, scripts, and handouts you can put into practice immediately. This section walks you through preparation, the experience itself, and integration. You will learn how to help clients clarify their intentions, prepare emotionally and physically, navigate altered states with trust and presence, and turn their insights into meaningful, lasting change. Through client stories, therapeutic reflections, and session guidelines, this part of the book translates principles into action.

The final chapter returns to the bigger picture. It reflects on what it means to do this work with integrity in a field that is growing quickly but unevenly. It speaks to the beauty and power of psychedelic therapy, but also the challenges that remain—legal uncertainty, lack of access, training gaps, and cultural appropriation. Rather than offering conclusions, it offers a reminder to stay awake, stay in dialogue, and stay close to what is true.

At the end of the book, you will find an Appendix with practical tools: screening forms, preparation questions, journaling prompts, and integration resources. These can be adapted for clinical work, group settings, or personal reflection. They are offered as support, not as scripts—guides to help you and your clients walk this path with intention and care.

You can read straight through, but many clinicians move by need. If you're orienting to the field, begin with Part I to ground stance and ethics. If you're actively guiding, pair Part II's science with the day-of guidance in *The Journey*. If you're building programs or sharpening outcomes, live in Part III: adopt the intake, preparation, and integration structures and adapt the handouts to your setting.

Most importantly, this book is an invitation to think deeply, practice ethically, and hold the profound mystery of transformation with reverence. It blends structure and soul, merges science and spirit, and encourages a new vision of healing—one that is relational, systemic, and rooted in the full complexity of being human.

Chapter 1

Orienting Principles

The aim of this chapter is simple: to establish who we must be in the room—**present, loving, curious, systemic, client-centered, and resource-oriented**—so that any tool we use during preparation, journey, or integration is coherent, ethical, and effective. These qualities come alive not in theory, but in how we meet our clients. This leads to a deeper question: Who are we, truly, when we enter the room? As a therapist, what guides your process? What do you bring into the therapeutic space that you share with your clients? What are the principles that anchor your presence and shape the way you hold another's process? Discovering and knowing who you are as a therapist is foundational, as that self-awareness can help you begin integrating a wide range of tools, including psychedelics. But those tools will always remain secondary to who you are and what you bring as a therapist.

In this chapter, I'll share the principles that guide me—the ones I return to again and again, and the ones I believe create real change for my clients. Therapy isn't simply a conversation or a place to vent; it's a sacred space where transformation unfolds in the relational field between therapist and client. A good therapist doesn't offer quick advice or ready-made solutions. Instead, they hold space with presence, love, and curiosity. They honor each client's process as it reveals itself. These qualities and ways of being aren't skills in the traditional sense. They can't be taught through formulas or protocols. Instead, they are embodied states that develop through practice and reflection. Attuning to clients and creating a sacred therapeutic environment is like creating art. It involves a dynamic and relational process that layers several principles, each of which contributes distinctly to a broader whole, shaping the contours and texture of the therapeutic space.

First is the principle of mindfulness, which is the foundation of presence. It is your capacity to be here, now, with your client—not just physically, but with your breath, your awareness, your openness. If therapy is the process of creating a work of art, then mindfulness is the canvas: empty, expansive,

DOI: 10.4324/9781003541639-3

ready to receive whatever needs to emerge. It represents the background against which all other elements can take shape.

The next principle, unconditional positive regard, is the palette—the colors and textures you bring into the room through the way you see the client. Do you see them through the eyes of love or pathology? Do you trust their wholeness even when they feel lost? The way you regard your client—the light in which you hold them—will color everything that follows. These two principles, when embodied together, create a healing container. They invite the client into connection, with you, yes; but more importantly, they implicitly guide the client into deeper connection with themselves. From this love and this presence, the therapeutic space is born.

The principle of curiosity gives the work its movement and form. While mindfulness creates space and love provides safety, curiosity invites us to lean in. It allows us to stay with what is unfamiliar, what is hard to name or understand. Rather than pushing toward solutions, curiosity helps us listen more deeply. It is what allows the client's truth to gradually come into view.

The space we create as therapists when we are led by these principles allows us to walk beside our clients—not as experts, but as companions. We hand them a brush and invite them to paint; this is their work of art, after all. This leads us into three additional principles that shape the creation of a safe and sacred therapeutic space. The first is systemic thinking, which reminds us that what clients bring into the room is much more than just their individual experience—it is a map for a territory that contains family, culture, memory, trauma, and resilience. Systemic thinking reminds us that what our clients share and explore in therapy is not solely their individual experience—it is a map representing a territory made up of family, culture, memory, trauma, and resilience. To truly support someone, we must be willing to see not just the individual in front of us, but the system that shaped them in ways that are often invisible, even to them.

The next principle, the belief that the client is the expert, invites us to deeply trust that every client is full of strength and untapped resources. It guides us to walk beside or behind them. Our clients know much more about their experience than we ever could. They are the ones who live in their bodies, who carry their stories, who know what it feels like to move through their world. Our job is to offer space, attunement, and enough trust for them to experiment with new forms, try new strokes, and explore previously unimagined expressions of who they are. And when we come across blind spots, we remember that these places are not voids; they are hidden treasure troves, wells of wisdom and strength. They are forgotten truths waiting to be rediscovered.

This leads to the final principle: the unwavering belief that our clients possess more resources than they have yet accessed. Our role is not to give them power, but to reflect back to them the power they already possess.

Through our presence and the trust we create, we generate a space where they can begin to remember who they truly are. All of the interconnected principles making up this work of art are essential to what emerges. But I want to turn now to the most important element in the art of attunement, as in the art of psychedelic integration therapy: you.

Principle 1: Mindfulness

The Canvas of the Session

Before any words are exchanged, before your client begins to tell their story, before they have even settled into the space, there is presence. As Irvin Yalom has written, when we listen deeply to another person, we offer something as vital as emotional oxygen—something that allows them to breathe again, see themselves more clearly, and begin to heal (Yalom, 2002). Mindful presence begins with you. Mindfulness is not a technique or something you do between sessions and suggest to clients as a tool for helping them relax. It's the foundation of your presence as a therapist. It's how you listen, how you breathe, how you hold the room with stillness and alertness. It's the quality of your attention when nothing is being said, yet everything is being felt.

As I said before, if therapy is the process of co-creating a work of art, then mindfulness is the canvas: open, unmarked, receptive. Without it, there is no space to begin. No one there to listen. When the therapist is fully present, the client feels it. When the therapist is distracted—caught up in roles, performance, or their own inner dialogue—the client feels that too. This kind of presence can't be faked. It requires a quieting of the mind, a softening of the ego, and a willingness to open alongside the client. Mindfulness invites the therapist to move out of performance—out of thinking about what they need to "fix"—and into relationship. In psychedelic work, especially, this is essential.

In the preparation phase of psychedelic therapy, I often teach clients basic mindfulness skills: how to sit, how to notice without fixing or judging, how to return to breath when the mind begins to run. But the truth is, I know these won't mean much to my clients if I'm not embodying them myself. As therapists, our ability to hold our center is what creates safety for our clients. From that safety, transformation can take place.

Because of this, one of the first invitations I extend to participants in our MPIM model is to begin a daily mindfulness practice—not just to "do mindfulness" but to become mindful. There are many ways to begin cultivating mindfulness, and no single approach fits everyone. As a daily entry point, I often recommend Sharon Salzberg's *Real Happiness*, a structured 28-day program that introduces mindfulness as an embodied practice rather than a concept. Through a series of accessible meditations and reflections, *Real Happiness* by Sharon Salzberg (2011) offers a structured introduction to mindfulness over four weeks. The book is designed for both beginners and experienced practitioners, guiding the reader into the art of being present. It begins with the fundamentals: learning how to pause, how to observe thoughts and sensations without judgment, and how to return to the present moment. I've noticed that as people's practice deepens, they start to notice that these seemingly simple exercises are creating shifts in their internal patterns. Their nervous system settles, their awareness sharpens, and their capacity to stay with what is expands. Mindfulness influences the relational field of whoever is practicing—it shifts the ways they interact. As therapists, grounding ourselves in mindfulness helps us enter the room fully available to the presence of the person sitting across from us. Our goal is not to master mindfulness, but to achieve presence.

The practice of mindfulness can begin simply. It requires no special cushion. No timer. No app. Just breathe and attention. The work of Jon Kabat-Zinn, who's often credited with bringing mindfulness into mainstream clinical practice, has greatly influenced the way I introduce the principles of mindfulness. According to Kabat-Zinn (1994), mindfulness is simply "paying attention in a particular way: on purpose, in the present moment, and nonjudgmentally" (p. 4). His work emphasizes that mindfulness isn't about achieving a particular state, but rather *being with* what already is. As he puts it, "You can't stop the waves, but you can learn to surf" (Kabat-Zinn, 2005, p. xii). That ability—to stay steady in the presence of turbulence—is one of the greatest gifts a therapist can offer their clients.

I often encourage individuals to begin their mindfulness journey with a blend of formal and informal practices they can gently weave into daily life—not as another item on a to-do list, but as a moment to return to the body and come back to presence. One formal practice I often recommend is to spend just five minutes in seated breath awareness each morning. You can do this anywhere. In your parked car before walking into work, or outside with your feet on the ground. Close your eyes or soften your gaze. Let your attention rest on the breath—not controlling it, or changing it, just noticing. Follow the inhale, the exhale, the gentle rise and fall. When the mind wanders (and it will), notice where it went and bring it back, gently and without judgment.

As for informal mindfulness practices, there are many equally valuable ones that help develop this quality. In the most ordinary moments, mindfulness practices help you return to yourself. Washing the dishes. Brushing your teeth. Making tea. What does it feel like to truly notice the water on your hands, or the texture of the toothbrush against your gums? What happens if you make a cup of tea without doing anything else—no phone, no email, just hot water, steam, and breath? These small rituals offer something simple yet profound: the chance to be here. This is mindfulness.

One of my favorite informal practices is to create what are known as *mindful transitions*—pauses between tasks or conversations. Before a session begins or after one ends, I take a single conscious breath. That breath marks the boundary between one session and another. Other times, I wash my hands as a way to transition. Truly washing your hands—feeling the water on your skin, smelling the soap, and experiencing your breath—offers another way to mindfully transition. These breaks are especially helpful for therapists and guides, who often move from one relational space to another. Those small pockets of time give us a chance to come back to the moment refreshed, recentered, and ready to listen and explore.

Another great informal exercise for accessing mindfulness is intentionally listening to music. Choose a piece of instrumental music or nature sounds, and sit with it for a few minutes, listening as if it's speaking directly to you. Simply connect with the sounds. Let your attention follow the transitions in the music. Let it land on the furthest sound you can hear. Then the closest. Then the space in between. You are not interpreting or analyzing—you're just listening.

As therapists, our mindfulness in the moment, open and uncluttered, is the canvas upon which the artwork of therapy gets created. This intentional presence is what lets us show up without crowding the therapy room, to sit without needing to know, to listen without rushing to fix. However, we need more than just this canvas to make art. We need the palette of paints that will bring life to it. How we see our clients—the assumptions we make, the love or judgment we project onto them—bring color to the art work of therapy. As a therapist and guide, the way you see the people you work with becomes the medium through which their healing process is painted. Before a single word is spoken, your body and your gaze are already speaking. The question is: What are they saying?

Principle 2: Unconditional Positive Regard

The Colors We Paint with

Presence alone creates the space, but it is how we see the person in that space that brings the work to life. This brings us to the second principle: unconditional positive regard. This is where I, like so many therapists, began: with the teachings of Carl Rogers. His concept of unconditional positive regard, first introduced as a foundational element of person-centered therapy, was radical in its time and remains prevalent in the counseling professions today. Rogers (1951) believed that when a therapist holds a client in unconditional acceptance, without judgment or agenda, something essential shifts in the relationship. The client begins to feel safe enough to explore who they are, not who they think they should be. In my early training, this principle gave me language for something I had always intuitively felt: that the way we *see* another person has the power to transform them. Sometimes your gift becomes seeing them before they can fully see themselves.

Over time, and through my work with psychedelics and indigenous wisdom traditions, this principle began to expand in my own understanding. What Rogers called unconditional positive regard, many plant healers call *unconditional love*. And although these terms may differ, they point to the same deep truth: Healing begins not with insight or interpretation, but with how we hold another in our gaze—with the energy we transmit before exchanging a single word.

To form the essential foundation of good therapy—which is that strongly bonded human connection between our clients and ourselves—we need to hold them in sincere positive regard. With my own clients, I establish and observe my connection with them by focusing attention on the genuine, unconditional positive feelings I experience toward them. In session, I often check in with myself about how I feel about the person in front of me, whether I'm feeling love and acceptance toward them. If I'm not, I get curious about what I'm not seeing or understanding about them. Then, I become more curious, asking questions that may help me gain a clearer understanding of their experience, their perspective, and the thoughts and emotions that guide their choices. If through further exploration I can't arrive at a feeling of love and acceptance, I know I have to refer this person to someone else. Because, as I said previously, I understand that how I see them will shape the therapeutic space and influence what's possible in the therapeutic process.

As I mentioned previously, positive regard, in the world of plant healing and shamanism, is referred to as *unconditional love*. Many believe and teach that love is the only thing that is real. It is the basis of who we truly are, and who we have been since we first came into the world. According to these healers and shamans, feelings of fear, hate, and anger—along with all other negative emotions, ideas, intentions, and actions—are unnatural. People learn them over time through difficult and traumatic experiences. In this tradition, one important prerequisite to healing is being able to see greatness in another, no matter who they are or what they have done: "Love is our capacity to appreciate the complexity of the other in all their dimensions" (Bourzat & Hunter, 2019, p. 75). Our primary job as healers and therapists is to return to that unconditional love. From there, we can become healers for ourselves, others, and ultimately the world.

To exemplify this idea, I'd like to share a personal journey I had in a psilocybin group ceremony, during which I experienced the power of unconditional love in a way that changed my work with clients. My intention in this journey was what it often is: to grow and improve as a psychedelic integration therapist. However, this time, the message of growth was love. Though the message was simple, I understood it to be everything.

I was outside, lying directly on a patch of grass surrounded by trees, and although I had taken a large dose of psilocybin, I was present enough to know who I was, where I was, and what I was doing. However, I was also experiencing something I never had before. As I lay on the grass, I felt like I had merged with the land. There was no separation between it and me; I could not tell where my body ended and the grass began. As I lay there, the land began communicating—not in language, but through vibration. It is hard to make sense of what followed, but I instinctively knew the vibrations were what I subjectively labeled and understood as love. Energy flowed through me as electricity. There was no way of stopping it, and I didn't want to. Tears of gratitude ran down my face as a feeling of tremendous honor for the opportunity to experience something powerful swelled inside of me.

Midway through the journey, I turned and looked at the woman next to me. She was shaking uncontrollably, and I could tell she was having a terribly challenging time. I still felt the electricity flowing through me, so I put my hand on her leg and felt the energy radiating from me to her. Then, I whispered to her, "Just feel. Quiet your mind and feel." I noticed she began to calm down and then became utterly silent and still. Hours after the ceremony closed, she approached me and thanked me. What she said next left me completely dazed. She said that when I touched her, it was not my hand on her leg but something much greater radiating through her. When I told her to feel, she immediately started to experience what felt like love radiating through me to her. This comment left me feeling overwhelmed that a stranger had validated the experience I had yet to understand myself.

This encounter challenged my relentlessly rational mind not to label the psychedelic experience as some sort of nonsense—something it, unfortunately, still often does. It brought to mind Virginia Satir, one of the pioneers of family therapy, who spoke and wrote about what she called the *individual life force* or *energy field* (Satir et al., 1991). She believed that humans possess a positive manifestation of life energy and are, therefore, sacred (Satir et al., 1991). Furthermore,

she explained that through touch, individuals can transfer energy with the potential to heal. According to Satir (1980), the hands are channels for giving energy. That was what I felt during the psilocybin journey—my hands were a channel of energy through which love could be transferred and used to heal.

It took me many days and numerous conversations with friends and colleagues to integrate and make sense of everything that happened. Ultimately, I came to perceive that the psilocybin medicine was teaching me what I had asked for through my intention to become a better therapist. My job was to practice loving unconditionally, first myself and then others. It also gave me a new understanding of what Satir referred to as the human life force and the power of touch. After that journey, my belief in therapeutic unconditional positive regard expanded to include the practice of loving anyone and everyone unconditionally. Afterward, I found myself connecting with clients on a deeper level and stepping onto their maps with much more empathy. Now, I believe in the concept of unconditional love more passionately. I bring it into my work and believe that it significantly impacts my clients, specifically throughout their psychedelic journeys. Furthermore, I believe that any individual or therapist is capable of tapping into that love. Individuals who aim to work as therapists in this field and with these substances would benefit significantly from exploring and growing this love for themselves and, of course, for humanity—a practice that has the potential to promote profound healing.

Principle 3: Curiosity

The Invisible Architecture Beneath the Image

Returning to the metaphor, if mindfulness is the canvas and unconditional positive regard the palette, curiosity is the movement of the brush. Curiosity is what moves us forward. It invites us to lean in and discover. It embodies the posture of a therapist who trusts that even in darkness, there is something valuable to uncover, and that clients' emerging insights carry the deepest healing potential.

The goal is to create a therapeutic space that is free of moralizing judgments and rigid expectations—one that avoids imposing predetermined outcomes or interpretations onto clients' lived experience. It's a space where clients feel genuinely accepted and safe to express their authentic selves. Experiencing this kind of unconditional presence helps clients begin to cultivate self-acceptance within themselves. For this process to unfold naturally, compassion and curiosity must remain central, particularly in moments when the work feels difficult or stuck. Rather than pulling away or becoming directive in response to discomfort, the therapist remains curious: What might this discomfort reveal? How might holding steady in this uncertain place open pathways toward deeper healing?

During my training at Nova Southeastern University, I participated in supervised therapy sessions observed through a one-way mirror. A team of students and a professor would sit behind the glass, watching and listening to live sessions as part of our learning. One day, I was asked to work with a father who had been court-mandated to attend therapy following an accusation of sexual abuse from his daughter—a story I had just heard from her earlier that day. I felt a visceral wave of dread. How could I sit with this man? How could I stay present and nonjudgmental?

Sensing my hesitation, my supervisor offered a simple instruction: "Get really curious." Those words became my anchor and my posture. In session, I didn't interrogate the accusation or try to solve it. I slowed down. I asked about mornings in his house growing up—who his support system was, what his room looked like, and what affection was like in his home. I asked: When things were hard growing up, who felt steady to you? Who noticed you without you having to ask? If you needed something—comfort, advice, a ride—who did you find yourself going toward, even a little? As he spoke, a map came into view: a boy raised inside confusion and threat, improvising ways to survive that hardened into adult patterns.

Curiosity didn't excuse what he was accused of, and it didn't eclipse his daughter's pain. It widened the frame. I could hold two truths at once: harm requires accountability, and the person who causes harm is more than the harm. That stance kept my boundaries intact while softening my nervous system from judgment to listening. It let me see not just his story about what happened, but the structure that shaped how he learned to be in the world.

What changed in the room was subtle but decisive. He stopped performing a defense and started remembering. The pace shifted. His language grew less certain, more honest. He didn't become innocent; he became human. And that is where therapeutic work can begin—not in collusion or denial, but in fuller contact with reality. Curiosity is not a loophole around ethics; it is the discipline that lets us meet the whole person while staying oriented to repair. Sometimes healing begins precisely there—when someone is fully seen, even in the shadow, and invited to choose differently.

Curiosity is an antidote to judgment. When we wonder about a client's story—even when it challenges our values—we open the door to understanding and the possibility of transformation. Without that space, people who have caused harm are more likely to remain stuck in shame, defensiveness, and repetition. With curiosity, there is movement. There is the potential for something new. As Carl Jung (1979) wrote, "No tree, it is said, can grow to heaven unless its roots reach down to hell" (p. 43). In therapy, we do not shy away from the darker parts of human experience. We welcome them with care, helping clients move toward wholeness—not by cutting off the parts they fear, but by making space for all that they are.

My work with John, a 27-year-old medical student, illustrates this kind of exploration. John came to therapy feeling depressed and unable to maintain long-term relationships. He described his past girlfriends warmly, but said things always ended suddenly and badly. At first, his explanations were vague. I sensed there was more he wasn't saying. After three sessions, he blurted out, "The problem is, I'm a pervert." He told me he had a fetish for extremely large breasts. As a devout Muslim who dated modestly dressed women, he often didn't realize their breast size until they were physically intimate. When they didn't meet his expectations, he lost his erection—sometimes even vomited—and would abruptly leave. The breakups that followed these encounters were painful and confusing for everyone involved.

Rather than pushing John to change or pathologizing his desire, I got curious and invited him to join me in this curiosity. Together, we explored his associations and memories. One that stood out was a childhood painting in his home of a woman breastfeeding a child—a symbol that had embedded itself deep in his psyche. I offered the idea that early attraction to breasts is normal, rooted in survival and attachment. What mattered was not the fixation itself, but whether it could evolve. Together, we explored the possibility that his desire didn't need to be rejected. Instead, it could grow in depth and complexity, just as a child's food source and palate mature over time. Could he learn to appreciate the whole woman, rather than beyond that single feature?

Months passed before I heard from John again. He reached out to say he had reconnected with a former partner, shared his story, and found the courage to be intimate again. This time, he was finding that his desire extended beyond his partner's physical attributes. He was able to remain present. He didn't lose his arousal or feel sick when it came to this part of his relationship. He felt connected.

Staying curious with John required me to notice my own internal reactions. It would have been easy to label his fixation as objectifying or immature, to jump into a corrective stance or communicate disapproval. But that would have shut the door on something more important: his story, his beliefs, and where those beliefs came from. Instead, I asked questions with the intention of understanding. What did this obsession mean to him? Where had it begun? How had it shaped his relationships and sense of self? As I listened, I began to see that his desire wasn't just about the other person's anatomy; it was about his own attachment and his own associations with sexuality as a young boy. Curiosity helped him stay open and move beyond judgment, making deeper contact with the parts of himself he couldn't see before. When we meet clients with curiosity and nonjudgment, we help them build that same capacity within themselves. That then opens the door to growth, connection, and healing.

Principle 4: Systemic Thinking

The Invisible Architecture Beneath the Image

The metaphor of art helps illustrate that there are visible dimensions of the therapeutic process, but equally important are the invisible elements that influence what transpires. Systemic thinking is one of these invisible elements. It is the underlying architecture that structures and shapes the image that gets created in therapy without a systemic lens; we risk seeing diagnoses instead of adaptations to pain, and we miss the bigger picture. A foundational idea in systemic therapy is that even when there's only one person in the room, our clients never come in alone. They carry with them an entire field of relationships, belief systems, cultural norms, and inherited expectations. Every story they tell, every symptom they describe, is shaped by the context they come from. As I've written before, the question "Who am I?" is never answered in isolation—it is always shaped by the systems that surround us: family, culture, religion, race, gender, class, education, and the social expectations embedded within each of these. These systems offer not only identities and roles, but also meaning. They influence how we see ourselves, what we believe is possible, and how we relate to others.

In therapy, a systemic lens helps us recognize that the problems or diagnoses our clients present with are never separate from the context in which they arise. Personal narratives, coping strategies, and problems are responses to broader social conditions. Someone raised in a family that prioritized achievement above all else might struggle to rest or feel unworthy if they aren't being productive—not because they're truly not good enough, but because the system around them equates value with output, leaving little room for anything else. Or consider someone who grew up in a home where strength meant never showing emotion: They may arrive in therapy unable to cry or feel—not because they're inherently resistant or shut down, but because they were never given permission to explore emotion without judgment. That wasn't part of the map they were handed.

When we understand how these invisible maps are drawn, we begin to see clients with a clearer, wider lens. We understand that problems don't live inside the person—they live in the relationships, patterns, and systems they're part of. As Salvador Minuchin, one of the founding fathers of family therapy, wrote, "the symptom bearer is not the problem; the family is the patient" (Minuchin, 1974, p. 10). As therapists, we don't treat single individuals; instead, we indirectly step into whole systems and work from there. The following case offers a clear example of how symptoms that appear to be individual and internal can often be traced back to deeper systemic roots.

Daniela came into therapy stating that she struggled with intense anxiety around socializing. A previous therapist had diagnosed her with social anxiety, and she was hoping I could offer tools to help her manage it. She explained that she felt comfortable only around a small handful of people, and even then, she often left conversations feeling ashamed or unsure. She described herself as "overly sensitive" and expressed frustration with how often she second-guessed everything she said, if she said anything at all. In session, these patterns were immediately visible. Her voice was soft, her posture apologetic. After nearly every sentence, she would ask, "Does that make sense?" or say, "Sorry, that probably sounded stupid." Her words were cautious, her tone a whisper.

During our early sessions, Daniela shared that she was born in San Francisco, but her parents had immigrated from Lebanon, and she was raised in a conservative Muslim household. As she spoke about her childhood, it became increasingly clear that this wasn't simply a case of social anxiety. What she was describing was a learned behavior—one that had protected her in an environment where silence equaled safety. In her family, conflict was avoided, and girls were expected to be modest, agreeable, and quiet. Her father was often verbally and physically violent toward her and her sisters when he felt disrespected, even if the perceived offense was something as benign as answering back in a neutral tone. In that context, speaking freely wasn't just discouraged—it was innately dangerous.

What stood out even more was that Daniela didn't label her father's actions as abusive or violent. She spoke of them as normal parental responses or discipline. Her internal map had been shaped to normalize aggression as part of fatherhood. Once I began to understand the environment she grew up in, her fear of speaking made perfect sense. Seen through this lens, Daniela's "anxiety" no longer appeared as a disorder but instead as an intelligent, embodied survival strategy. Her nervous system had learned to associate speaking with danger. Her quietness wasn't a flaw; it was a response to trauma, internalized so deeply that it had become her default way of being.

Therapy, then, was not about teaching her skills to overcome social anxiety but about helping her recognize the deeper system that had silenced her. It was about offering her a new relational experience—one in which her voice was not just tolerated, but invited and safe. One in which she could begin to see that her symptoms were not signs of dysfunction, but evidence of how intelligently she had adapted to keep the peace in her own system.

Of course, I had to be careful about how I communicated these insights. Daniela didn't see her father as abusive. She respected him deeply, and I knew that naming these dynamics too directly could threaten the trust we were building. From a systemic lens, it's essential to remember that therapists are not neutral observers. We are part of the relational field, and clients are always perceiving us through their own histories. I'm not part of Daniela's culture or religion. I'm a Latin Jew, and that alone could have introduced unspoken tensions, especially given the complex historical relationship between Muslims and Jews. I was aware that even my concern for her well-being could be misread as a judgment of her family or faith. I needed her to feel that I wasn't criticizing where she came from, especially not her father. My intention was only to honor the wisdom of her adaptation while slowly offering the idea that other ways of being were possible now.

As trust grew, Daniela began to explore her childhood with more openness. She felt safe speaking about her father in a more assertive tone, knowing that I wasn't judging her father's upbringing. This work wasn't about blaming the past: It was about understanding how it shaped her. I introduced the idea that staying quiet had been a form of protection and that it made sense she had learned to remain on the outside and to disengage. Slowly, she began to realize that the problem wasn't who she was. It was the story she had inherited about what it meant to take up space, and that story was no longer serving her.

What Daniela's case shows is that identity does not form in a vacuum. Her anxiety was not a personal flaw or diagnosis, but a patterned response to a specific system of meaning and survival. When we see our clients through this lens, our work changes. We stop treating symptoms in isolation and start honoring the stories—and systems—that shaped them. And in doing so, we help our clients not just cope, but reclaim parts of themselves that have long been silent. This lens becomes especially important when working in non-ordinary states of consciousness.

Psychedelic experiences often dissolve the filters of everyday awareness, bringing to the surface long-held beliefs and internalized narratives. Clients may suddenly feel overwhelmed by guilt around rest, tracing it back to a family legacy that equated worth with productivity. Others may confront painful messages about their gender, identity, or value—messages shaped by cultural expectations and unexamined histories. Psychedelics can bring these deeper truths into sharp focus, often without the protective buffers of logic or language.

This is why a systemic lens is essential in psychedelic-assisted therapy. When clients begin to rework core aspects of their identity, they need a therapist who can hold space for both the personal and the collective. Someone who understands that what's surfacing may not belong only to the client, but to a family, a culture, or a generational story. A therapist who can stay curious, attuned, and aware of their own position in the relational field.

Ultimately, this principle calls us to meet our clients within their full systemic context, as individuals shaped by a web of relationships, cultural narratives, and survival strategies. When we hold this perspective, we create space for our clients to step into new possibilities, drawing on strengths and inner resources they may not have realized were there. The next principle explores exactly that.

Principle 5: The Client Is the Expert

The Hand That Holds the Brush

If mindfulness is the canvas, unconditional positive regard the palette, and systemic thinking the architecture beneath the image, then trusting the client as the expert is the hand holding the brush. No matter how much training or insight we have as therapists, the client must ultimately paint their own way forward. We can witness, reflect, and offer new perspectives, but the clients themselves are the ones living inside their story. They have walked every step of their journey.

Recognizing clients as experts of their own lives is fundamental to therapeutic work. Therapists, regardless of their experience, haven't lived their client's reality. Even clients who feel fragmented or uncertain have spent every moment inside their own experience. This understanding shifts our role significantly. It's not about providing the right answers; it's about creating a space where clients can uncover those answers themselves. Our job is not to lead from the front, but to walk beside or behind them, with curiosity and presence. Clients always have knowledge. Even amid confusion, something within them is trying to speak. Often, they've come to believe that their knowing doesn't count—that they're too reactive, too disorganized, too damaged. But recognizing them as experts empowers them to find solutions and new ways of being within themselves.

This perspective has deep roots in systemic thinking. Therapists like Harlene Anderson and Harold Goolishian (1992) challenged the conventional notion of the therapist as the all-knowing expert. They proposed something radically different—that true healing emerges through shared curiosity. They termed this the "not-knowing" stance to connote the therapist's refusal to let their knowledge obstruct discovery. It's a stance of humility, predicated on the idea that meaning emerges through collaboration between therapist and client. Leading with a not-knowing posture, the therapist makes space for the client's voice, resisting the urge to interpret prematurely or offer solutions too quickly. Each session becomes a collaborative unfolding rather than a correction, and listening becomes an act of reverence. This approach requires therapists to step off the pedestal and into the relational field, side by side with clients, open to being changed by what they hear.

Douglas Flemons (2002) reminds us that insights discovered by the client, rather than handed to them, foster more lasting change. When clients arrive at answers through their own process, those answers feel earned and embodied, becoming powerful evidence that they already possess what they need. Our role is simply to help them remember how to listen. The notion that clients are the experts of their experience is not new—it's ancient wisdom we've forgotten. Sometimes, the hardest part isn't just honoring the client's expertise, but stepping down from the pedestal they may have placed us on.

I once worked with a woman named Alma who had been in therapy for nearly two decades with the same therapist in Mexico. When she relocated to the United States and began sessions with me, it quickly became clear that she was seeking more than a new therapist; she hoped to recreate the dynamic she had depended upon previously. She spoke of her former therapist with deep reverence, describing how she always gave Alma specific advice about what to do, how to feel, and how to move forward. Alma carried considerable anxiety about losing that authoritative guidance and was looking to me to provide it.

Initially, I felt deep compassion for Alma, In trying to help her client, that therapist had inadvertently created a dependency that left Alma disconnected from her own inner wisdom. Alma had learned to rely on external expertise rather than trusting herself.

In those early sessions, I sometimes felt tempted to assume the role of expert myself—to soothe Alma's anxiety by providing clear direction. But doing so would have replicated the very pattern that made her feel powerless. Instead, I slowed the process down. I reminded her continually that we were walking together, and that she was holding the map. When she asked me what to do, I gently returned the question: "What do you sense is needed?" When she pleaded, "Just tell me what's right," I'd ask: "What feels right in your body?"

At first, Alma was frustrated by my insisting that she look inward for her answers. She felt exposed and unsupported. But she continued to return, gradually opening to the possibility that answers might exist within her. Over time, Alma came to recognize all the places in her life—not only in therapy, but also in her marriage, work, and family—where she had consistently deferred authority to others. For the first time, she began questioning these external voices. This process stirred significant change within Alma and was sometimes painful, especially within her marriage, where she'd come to rely heavily on her husband's opinions. Yet, despite her discomfort, Alma gradually learned what it felt like to make her own choices, develop her own solutions. From the beginning to the end of our work together, her transformation profoundly moved me, particularly the strength and clarity that emerged as she reclaimed her voice.

The not-knowing stance requires patience, trust, and courage. It requires us to hold space while clients find their way. It asks us to resist the impulse to position ourselves as experts, even with good intentions, because doing so diminishes our clients' sense of agency. In psychedelic work, this principle becomes even more critical. Clients may emerge from their journeys emotionally raw and disoriented, seeking external interpretations for what they've experienced. Yet, when we trust their inner capacity to integrate their experiences, we align with this fundamental belief. We become mirrors rather than interpreters.

Good therapy is not about delivering new truths; it's about helping clients reconnect with the truths they've always known but perhaps forgot. By relinquishing the role of expert and all the expected answers attached to it, we encourage our clients to rediscover their own wisdom. This is genuine empowerment. As clients learn to trust their voices, they reclaim them. Recognizing clients as the artists of their healing process ensures that the art remains uniquely theirs. However, good therapy doesn't end with seeing clients as experts. This simply opens the door to something deeper: the understanding that clients are not only wise, but inherently resourceful. Even in their most challenging moments, they hold greater strength and resilience than they realize. Based on this notion, the next principle invites us to recognize and nurture our clients' power.

Principle 6: Inner Resources

Seeing What's Already There

We come now to the final tool in our therapeutic work of art—the color already held within the brush. This principle centers on the belief that clients possess more resources than they may realize, even if these resources remain unseen or forgotten. Our role as therapists is not to supply new strengths or capacities, but rather to help clients recognize and reconnect with the wisdom and resilience they already carry within themselves. Therapy is not about filling in what's missing. It's about revealing what's already present that has gone unrecognized.

Clients often come to therapy believing they are broken, empty, or lost. But in my experience, there is always something intact in each person, even in their most disoriented state. There is always something quietly working toward wholeness. Our job as therapists is to trust that. To see what our clients cannot yet see. To sit in the quiet spaces and know that something important is already there.

One of the most common questions I get as a therapist is why I use the word "client" instead of "patient." Many assume the difference is trivial—a matter of preference rather than meaning—but that's far from the truth. Language carries weight. It shapes perception. Whether consciously or not, the words we choose reflect how we see the people in front of us. The word "patient" comes from the medical model. It implies someone who is sick, someone in need of treatment, someone to be fixed. But the philosophy that grounds my work does not see people as broken. It's the opposite. Clients come in with much more than they know. They carry stories, tools, insights, and resilience that often lie just beneath the surface, waiting to be remembered. In calling them clients, I am naming that capacity. I am saying, "Even when you can't see it yet, I do. And I will sit with you in that white space until you can see it, too."

This way of seeing people draws deeply from the work of Milton Erickson (1980), who believed that each individual possesses an unconscious mind that is always striving toward health and resolution. He viewed symptoms not as evidence of damage, but as attempts—however disorganized—to solve something. He taught that the therapist's role is not to impose change, but to create the conditions for a client's inner wisdom to emerge. Erickson (1980) profoundly believed that the client already has the solution; they just don't know that they know it. This belief is foundational to how I work. I trust that something inside each person is already moving toward healing. My role is to help them pause, notice, and reconnect with that movement.

The principle of trusting the client's inner resources and inherent wisdom is perhaps best illustrated by a clinical example from my practice. Martin was 70 years old when he first came to see me. He had been in and out of therapy for decades, carrying a diagnosis of obsessive-compulsive disorder (OCD). He had worked with many therapists, explored various modalities, and was prescribed multiple medications, but nothing had seemed to reach the heart of his suffering. The obsessive thoughts persisted relentlessly, but over the years, he had learned to mask them. Out in the world, he was kind, restrained, soft-spoken, but inside, he lived in fear of his own mind.

In our second session, he told me with a trembling voice that he had almost canceled. "You're going to think I'm dangerous," he said. "You'll probably call someone." I reassured him I wouldn't. He exhaled sharply and looked at the pen on the table between us. "I imagined stabbing you in the neck with that," he said, his voice cracking. "I would never do it. I don't want to. But I saw it, and now I feel like a monster."

This was not new for him. He had intrusive thoughts like this all the time—at the grocery store, around children, during dinner with his wife. Thoughts of pushing someone, shouting obscenities, setting something on fire, harming someone he loved. His life had become a constant battle to suppress them. He had tried exposure therapy. He had tried medication. He had tried mindfulness techniques. But no one had helped him understand the thoughts in a way that actually gave him relief.

I asked him what happened inside him when a thought like that occurred. I wanted to understand his emotional reaction to the thought. "It's horrible," he said. "I feel sick. I feel ashamed. I try not to think it again, but then it comes back." I asked him what that reaction said about him. "That I'm not okay," he answered. I paused. "Or," I offered, "that you're someone who is deeply committed to never causing harm." He didn't respond at first. So, I asked again, gently: "What kind of person gets sick at the idea of hurting someone?" He looked at me, quietly. "Someone who never would." And there it was.

Martin didn't have a violence problem. He had a kindness problem in that he couldn't see how central his kindness was. He didn't have a safety issue. He had a misunderstanding about how the mind works. His thoughts were not predictors of harm. They were the brain's vivid way of confirming that harm wasn't happening. The way he knew he was safe, the way he knew he would never stab someone, was by having the thought and then not doing it. His mind gave him a terrifying image, and his body responded with horror, grief, and deep moral pain. That cycle wasn't evidence of danger. It was evidence of integrity.

I explained it like this: The mind doesn't always speak in language that's linear or logical. Especially not when it belongs to someone vivid, creative, and emotionally alive. The thought of harm is not separate from the thought, "I would never." It is the shape that "I would never" sometimes takes. For someone like Martin, the vividness of the image wasn't the problem. It was his superpower. But he had spent years trying to shut it down—thinking that the goal of therapy was to make the thoughts go away. The real goal was to change the way he understood them.

We practiced together. When a thought came up, instead of pushing it away, we stayed with it. We tracked how quickly his body moved from terror to compassion—from "What's wrong with me?" to "Oh, this means I care." With time, he began to see that the horror he felt wasn't a symptom of instability; instead, it was a signal of his moral clarity. His capacity for empathy was not a weakness. It was his anchor. The thoughts he feared weren't proof that something was wrong with him. They were reflections of how deeply he was wired to protect life and to do no harm.

He started naming the shifts himself. When a new image would arise, he would say, "There it is." He would then take a breath and remind himself what it meant. "This is my mind's way of telling me I'm safe. That I would never." What used to spiral into hours of shame began to dissolve in moments of understanding. With time, he opened to the possibility that he was sensitive and ethical, and that he could trust himself. He began to recognize that his imagination wasn't a threat—it was a gift. The same vividness that produced sharp, disturbing images was also what had made him a devoted father, loyal friend, and thoughtful listener. It was the same quality that had given depth to his relationships and care to the way he moved through the world. Slowly, he stopped being afraid of it.

Martin didn't leave therapy with a cure for his intrusive thoughts. He left with something better: a new relationship with himself. He knew how to recognize the signals his mind sent him, and how to translate them into what they had always meant: that he cared, that he was safe, and that there was nothing wrong with him. The strength was always there. It was never about building something new. It was about remembering what had always been intact.

This is the heart of the final principle. Clients are not empty. They are not missing something essential. Even when they feel lost, the compass is inside them. Our job is not to fix, fill, or repair. It is to trust what's already there. To sit with them in the white space between the lines, knowing it's not empty. It's full of meaning, insight, and the quiet return of self. Healing, at its core, is not about making someone new. It's about helping them remember who they already are.

These principles—presence, love, curiosity, a systemic lens, the positioning of the client as the expert, and a trust in what's already there—are what I return to again and again. More than techniques or interventions, they are foundational ways of being that shape how I sit with people, how I listen, and how I stay when things get hard. Psychedelics may be powerful tools, but they are never the heart of the work. You are. The space you create, the way you see your clients, the way you hold their stories—that's what heals. If you can bring your full self into the room and stay rooted in these principles, everything else will follow. So, before we go any further, before we talk about medicine or altered states or integration, I want to start here with you. Because you are the medicine, too.

Chapter 2

From Principles to Practice

Core Tools for Therapeutic Change

Therapists often ask: What should I do in the room? What's the right intervention, the correct modality, the best technique? But the truth is, if you're grounded in the principles from Chapter 1—presence, love, curiosity, systemic awareness, positioning the client as the expert, and trust in the client—you already have an abundant foundation. This chapter isn't about adding more; it's about showing how those principles take shape in practice.

The practices in this chapter are natural extensions of the core principles. They are ways of showing up—of embodying presence, love, curiosity, and trust in the room with the client. Presence expresses itself through mindfulness and the therapeutic use of expectancy. Love finds form in the practice of turning toward pain and the ethical use of touch and boundaries. Curiosity becomes the art of utilization—working with whatever shows up in the room. Systemic awareness informs how we make space for the client's relational, cultural, and intergenerational context. And trust in the client manifests through breathwork and attunement to the subconscious.

While these practices are foundational in any therapeutic setting, they are particularly significant in psychedelic-assisted therapy. Psychedelic states often dissolve typical defenses, expand awareness, and surface deeply held material in nonlinear and emotional ways. Consequently, foundational therapeutic approaches become even more essential in these altered states, helping clients feel safe enough to surrender to the medicine and grounded enough to integrate their experiences.

Practice 1: Mindfulness Skills for the Client

Mindfulness

As discussed in Chapter 1, mindfulness is a foundational principle in creating therapeutic space. In this chapter, we shift the focus to mindfulness as an essential skill for clients to cultivate and integrate into their daily lives.

DOI: 10.4324/9781003541639-4

In my experience, the more I invite clients to engage with daily mindfulness practices, the more quickly and sustainably meaningful change takes root. The ability to be fully present—to truly see, hear, and feel life—is one of the most powerful indicators of well-being. As Marcel Proust famously wrote, "The real voyage of discovery consists not in seeking new landscapes, but in having new eyes" (Proust, 1923/1913–1927, vol. 5, p. 237). Clients are often unaware that their lives, viewed through a different lens, could become a source of joy—yet they miss it because they aren't present enough to notice what's already before them. Guiding clients to witness and appreciate the richness already present in their lives is one of the most significant gifts we can offer.

When it comes to psychedelic integration therapy, mindfulness isn't optional—it's essential. It supports clients during the psychedelic journey, as well as during preparation and the critical integration phase afterward (Brendan & Belser, 2022; Gorman et al., 2021). Both mindfulness and psychedelics evoke altered states of consciousness in which the rigid boundaries of self begin to dissolve (Milliere et al., 2018). This ego dissolution—a hallmark of many psychedelic experiences—reveals significant experiential overlap between contemplative practices and psychedelic states. Mindfulness practices such as meditation cultivate openness, curiosity, and non-judgmental presence—qualities that become powerful allies in navigating psychedelic spaces. Clients grounded in mindfulness can approach uncertainty with presence rather than panic, track their inner experiences, and maintain a witnessing stance amid intense emotions. Similarly, psychedelics quiet the mind's habitual filtering mechanisms by significantly reducing activity in the Default Mode Network (DMN), a brain region associated with self-referential thinking and rumination. As DMN activity decreases, clients often experience enhanced openness and receptivity, creating fertile ground for therapeutic insights. When integrated thoughtfully, mindfulness and psychedelics amplify each other's potential, offering clients transformative tools that are simultaneously mystical and neurologically grounded. In my practice, I've consistently observed that clients who enter psychedelic experiences already grounded in mindfulness navigate the emotional intensity more skillfully and integrate their insights more effectively afterward.

This alignment between mindfulness and psychedelics is deeply informed by the foundational teachings of Jon Kabat-Zinn, whose work has significantly shaped contemporary Western approaches to mindfulness. Kabat-Zinn defines mindfulness as "awareness that arises through paying attention, on purpose, to the present moment, non-judgmentally" (Kabat-Zinn, 2012, p. 17). He observes that we often become caught in self-centered narratives of "I," "me," and "mine"—which correspond neurologically to activity—disconnecting us from the richness of the present. Mindfulness, therefore, is not merely a philosophy but a practical way of being and relating to the world (Kabat-Zinn, 2021). Approaching a psychedelic journey from this state of grounded presence creates a stable foundation for deep inner exploration.

To practically embody this presence, Kabat-Zinn outlines eight core attitudes of mindfulness: beginner's mind, non-judging, acceptance, letting go, trust, patience, non-striving, and gratitude. In my therapeutic work, these aren't abstract ideals, but concrete practices that clients intentionally cultivate. I introduce them during preparation sessions, encouraging clients to explore each element through their lived experience and daily routines.

Below, I briefly outline -Kabat-Zinn's (2013) eight attitudes of mindfulness. In later chapters, we will revisit these in greater depth, exploring their direct application in both psychedelic therapy and traditional therapeutic contexts. When integrated into therapeutic practice, these attitudes help clients approach their inner experiences with curiosity, resilience, and presence. Mindfulness, then, isn't merely preparation for specific interventions or journeys. It is itself a foundational journey toward greater self-awareness, emotional regulation, and transformative growth.

Beginner's Mind

A beginner's mind is a mind that sees all things as if for the first time. Rather than passing life and its experiences through the lens of previous perception, the beginner's mind views them through a fresh new lens. This practice is helpful because, in the mind of an expert, there are very few possibilities (Suzuki, 1970), and it is easy to get stuck in pre-established ideas and opinions. Alternatively, a beginner's mind is full of possibilities, and in those possibilities, there is potential to transform every one of life's experiences.

Non-judging

A nonjudgmental state is one in which the person is paying attention to or becoming aware of what is in their mind, without any judgment. A space of judgment is limited by the duality of good and bad, black and white, wants and don't-wants; it offers a limited view of reality. Conversely, a state of nonjudgment allows one to see what is genuinely happening in each experience. The practice is to become aware of how judgmental one truly is, without judging that new awareness; hence, not judging the judging.

Acceptance

Another fundamental mindfulness practice is the ability to meet reality with acceptance. This practice involves recognizing that things are the way they are, and not resisting this. When one does not accept things as they are—particularly things beyond their control—they will try to force things to be as they are not, ultimately leading to suffering. A quote that encompasses this principle well is, "Whatever the present moment contains, accept it as if you had chosen it . . . . This will miraculously transform your whole life" (Tolle, 2001, p. 37).

Letting Go

Letting go is a powerful practice that can flow from acceptance. One often clings to what they want or pushes away what they don't want. As a result, they are caught up in their desires, which can be very painful. Learning to let go of controlling those things one labels as wants or not-wants becomes the gateway to freedom.

Trust

Individuals practice trust much more than they realize. For example, they implicitly trust their body's wisdom in moving the breath in and out on its own. This fact can be used as a gentle reminder to trust one's life the same way they trust their body and breath. Life can be trustworthy.

Patience

Practicing patience involves understanding that certain things cannot be hurried. It requires learning that things evolve in their own time.

Non-striving

Non-striving is allowing things to be as they are, without trying to achieve a special state. There is no agenda other than just being. There is no need to feel something special or escape something unwanted. Non-striving means being with whatever the moment delivers. That is always enough.

Gratitude

The practice of gratitude involves bringing awareness to what one has, instead of what one doesn't. Through the deliberate practice of looking at life through grateful eyes, one comes to see that every moment can be met with gratitude, and nothing should be taken for granted.

These eight attitudes are powerful when integrated into the therapeutic process. Furthermore, in altered states, beginner's mind and non-judging keep curiosity open as reality shifts; acceptance and letting go support surrender when the intensity rises; trust and patience steady the nervous system through long swells and the comedown; non-striving prevents grasping for answers mid-journey; and gratitude helps anchor what's helpful during and after, turning brief insights into lived practice. I return to this theme in Chapter 7, where I explore it more fully.

I often invite clients to choose one or two attitudes each week to observe intentionally in their daily lives. Keeping a *mindful noticing* journal, clients note moments each day when they witness these attitudes in themselves or others. This practice anchors mindfulness in everyday experiences, strengthening the very capacities essential for deep therapeutic work.

To support this process with their own clients, therapists should consider how they can authentically embody mindfulness principles themselves, naturally modeling them during sessions. Offering a variety of mindfulness approaches—both formal and informal—alongside carefully selected readings, documentaries, and guided practices is another way to encourage clients' development and accommodate their individual needs. Additionally, it can be helpful to dedicate session time to directly practicing mindfulness exercises, fostering deeper presence and self-awareness.

Some recommended resources include:

Books:

- *Wherever You Go, There You Are* by Jon Kabat-Zinn (2005)
- *The Power of Now* by Eckhart Tolle (2001)
- *Zen Mind, Beginners Mind* by Shunryu Suzuki (1970)
- *The Miracle of Mindfulness by* Thich Nhat Hanh (1987c)
- *The Surrender Experiment* by Michael A. Singer (2015)
- *Be Here Now, Remember.* by Ram Dass (1978)
- *Siddhartha* by Hermann Hesse (2000)

Documentaries and Videos:

- *From Stress to Happiness (2020)*
- *Ram Dass, Going Home (2017)*

Lastly, I encourage clients to maintain a gratitude journal, making daily entries about what they're thankful for that they can later reflect on in our sessions. Cultivating gratitude helps clients recognize and appreciate the abundance already present in their lives, nurturing deeper contentment and resilience. Through consistent mindfulness practice, clients naturally develop a heightened capacity for self-observation and present-moment awareness, engaging fully with life through all their senses. As Kabat-Zinn beautifully expresses, mindfulness helps us shift from being "human doings" to embracing our authentic nature as "human beings" (Muelrath, 2018).

With this foundation of mindful presence firmly established, clients become well-positioned to explore another potent therapeutic force: the power of expectancy. By intentionally directing their attention toward positive expectations, clients can significantly influence therapeutic outcomes and actively participate in shaping their journey toward healing.

Practice 2: The Power of Expectancy

The power of expectancy lies in a person's belief or anticipation that something might happen, which serves to influence their behavior and outcomes. In my experience facilitating psychedelic therapy, I've observed how clients' expectations significantly shape the outcomes of their therapeutic process. What we anticipate impacts what we notice. Mindfulness, as discussed earlier, becomes a vital tool in this context. It enhances clients' awareness and allows them to perceive subtle shifts, quiet synchronicities, or meaningful dreams that might otherwise pass unnoticed. These small recognitions strengthen their sense of expectancy and create a self-reinforcing loop in which anticipation fuels behavioral and perceptual changes.

I often remind clients that transformation can begin before they ever touch the medicine. During our early sessions, I ask what changes they might expect to see in their everyday lives if the healing they desire were already underway. I invite them to stay alert to anything that feels different or special, whether it's a passing moment of peace, a curious coincidence, or an inner movement they can't quite explain. This helps them recognize that something meaningful may already be in motion.

I also share my view that the world contains many kinds of magic—not only in the mystical sense, but in the way attention, intention, and perception shape experience. This is one of the places where science and spirituality meet. While I deeply value divine synchronicities, I also understand that the transformative power of belief is not merely a spiritual idea. Psychological research into expectancy and placebo effects has shown that belief itself can lead to measurable biological and emotional changes. A shift in mindset can have ripple effects throughout the body and psyche (Kirsch & Lynn, 1999).

This concept echoes the principles behind the miracle question technique developed by Insoo Kim Berg and Steve de Shazer. The technique invites clients to imagine waking up tomorrow and finding that their presenting problems have resolved (de Shazer & Berg, 1997). They are then asked to describe, in vivid detail, how this change would show up in their daily lives. It's a gentle but deliberate reorientation of attention, away from pain and toward possibility. A couple I once worked with came to therapy describing feeling distant from each other every morning. When I asked the miracle question, one partner said their miracle would be waking up to see the other smiling. That smile, they said, would create a feeling of warmth and ease, prompting a smile in return. As we explored this further, the partner asked,

"What if I chose to smile first?" That simple reflection led to an experiment: They began smiling upon waking, even slightly. In subsequent sessions, they described noticing subtle shifts—brief smiles exchanged, a little laughter, an unexpected sense of closeness. What they had overlooked before began to take on new meaning, and each small change fueled a sense of hope and momentum. Something so small created positive change.

This is the essence of expectancy in therapeutic work. When clients turn their attention from what's missing to what might be possible, they begin to engage with the world differently. Their perceptions shift, and these shifts create the possibility for new experiences to emerge. The psychological literature refers to this as a self-fulfilling prophecy, wherein beliefs influence actions and, ultimately, shape outcomes (Kirsch & Lynn, 1999).

Psychological research into expectancy and placebo effects highlights the remarkable influence of belief, showing how expectations alone can prompt measurable biological and emotional shifts. For instance, meta-analyses comparing antidepressants with inert placebos reveal that a significant portion of observed therapeutic effects (ranging from 73% to 93%) may result from clients' beliefs about treatment efficacy, rather than the medication's chemical properties (Greenberg & Fisher, 1989; Joffe et al., 1996; Kirsch & Sapirstein, 1999; Walach & Maidhof, 1999). Kirsch and Lynn (1999) further illuminate how expectancy initiates a cascade of interconnected changes. Psychologically, expectancy directs perception, helping individuals notice improvements and discount setbacks. Physiologically, belief can activate the body's intrinsic healing mechanisms, triggering mood-enhancing neurotransmitters such as dopamine and endorphins. Behaviorally, individuals expecting improvement are more likely to engage in supportive actions like self-care and consistent therapy participation. Thus, expectancy is not merely a mindset; it is an active mechanism for sustained therapeutic transformation.

In psychedelic therapy, this principle becomes especially potent. When clients consciously direct their focus toward transformation, they become more attuned to inner and outer signs of change. They enter the journey with a sense of openness and possibility. Still, while expectancy can open doors, walking through them requires courage. The next essential practice, *turning towards*, invites clients to face the very discomfort they might otherwise avoid. This movement toward pain, rather than away from it, marks a threshold in the healing process, where insight becomes integration.

Practice 3: Turning Toward, Acceptance, and Letting Go

In certain parts of Asia, an old parable is often told about how to trap a monkey. A hunter carefully hollows out a coconut, carving an opening just wide enough for a monkey's empty hand. The coconut is securely chained to a tree, and a banana is placed inside. Attracted by the sweet aroma, the monkey eagerly slips its hand through the hole to grasp the fruit. Yet, with its fist clenched tightly around the banana, the monkey cannot pull its hand out. Freedom is simple—let go—but the monkey, unwilling to relinquish its grip, remains trapped by its attachment.

This parable vividly illustrates a common human predicament: holding tightly onto something that once served us well—a belief system, relationship, or familiar circumstance—but has come to hold us captive, becoming a source of pain and suffering. As our pain intensifies, we often cling even more tightly, believing that letting go would mean losing control, security, or even identity.

At the heart of human suffering lies resistance—to discomfort, to letting go, to fully experiencing what is present. Many clients come into therapy burdened by intense pain. Some are overwhelmed by it, while others numb themselves because the pain feels intolerable. In these difficult moments, practices like mindfulness or positive expectancy are often insufficient on their own. Introducing these tools prematurely can even feel dismissive or destabilizing. Clients in profound distress require us to first meet them exactly where they are, without bypassing or minimizing their suffering.

This essential therapeutic skill demands that therapists develop a strong tolerance for discomfort—their clients' as well as their own. If we cannot comfortably sit with pain and distress, we risk attempting to fix or rescue our clients from their experience. Such premature efforts can inadvertently communicate that something is wrong with their pain or that their emotions are too intense, creating further resistance, misunderstanding, or even ruptures in the therapeutic relationship.

In psychedelic therapy, the ability to hold space for discomfort becomes especially critical. Psychedelic journeys often surface intense emotions such as grief, fear, or deeply embedded trauma. At these moments, the therapist's capacity to remain calm and supportive, allowing the client to fully experience their discomfort without interruption, becomes paramount. Attempting to prematurely rescue a client from these difficult experiences can disrupt the natural healing process, unintentionally signaling that their pain is problematic or excessive. These challenging moments frequently yield the most profound therapeutic breakthroughs, as they encourage clients to courageously stay present, supported by a therapist who can compassionately hold space.

Resisting pain inherently amplifies suffering. Struggling to avoid or change the present moment fuels frustration and distress. Mindfulness teacher Shinzen Young (2010) succinctly captures this dynamic with the formula: Suffering = Pain × Resistance. If resistance can be reduced or eliminated, suffering diminishes dramatically. Even intense pain becomes manageable when we stop resisting it, transforming from a prolonged battle into a transient experience we can witness and move through. Pain, I often remind clients, is an energy that naturally arises and moves through the body, whereas suffering emerges in the mind through repetitive, resistant thought patterns.

Douglas Flemons (2002) insightfully expands upon this idea, explaining that when therapist, client, and problem share a space openly and authentically, a remarkable harmony emerges. Within this shared space, the perceived power of the problem diminishes. The mind, previously fixated and resistant, begins to soften and expand, opening to new insights and perspectives. Often, the issue itself loses significance—not because it has been logically resolved, but because the meaning clients attach to it fundamentally transforms.

On a spiritual level, the power of turning toward pain is a concept that Buddhist teacher Pema Chödrön (2000) has explored with great depth. In her book *When Things Fall Apart*, Chödrön suggests that our deepest suffering can also serve as our greatest teacher. Instead of acting as something to fear or avoid, pain becomes a doorway, inviting us toward deeper self-awareness and wisdom. By compassionately embracing discomfort, we create openings within ourselves—tender yet resilient spaces where empathy and growth take root. Thus, turning toward pain rather than away from it doesn't merely heal; it awakens and transforms us.

My client Sara came to me carrying profound grief and anger after losing her daughter more than 20 years earlier. She shared that she had been in therapy several times before, but her loss had led her to conclude that life was unfair, and that she would suffer deeply for the remainder of it. As Sara spoke, I felt the immense weight of her sorrow. There was truth in her belief that losing a child would always be painful, yet I also recognized that the intense suffering she endured daily wasn't inevitable. I sensed that Sara resisted accepting her daughter's death, tightly holding on to her grief, because she felt this suffering was the only meaningful way to remain connected to her daughter.

Over numerous sessions, I held space for Sara's sorrow, listening as she shared memories and stories, allowing her pain and anger to exist in the room. Gradually, once the trust between us deepened, I introduced the distinction between pain and suffering, carefully inviting her to consider acceptance—acknowledging the reality of her loss without attempting to resist or control the depth of her grief. Additionally, I introduced the concept of letting go, clarifying that this wasn't about relinquishing her love or memories of her daughter, but rather about releasing the heavy burden of suffering she had come to equate with honoring her.

With openness and courage, Sara began to gradually accept her daughter's passing. She experimented with small rituals and symbolic gestures, such as journaling and sharing stories about her daughter's life within an online grief community. Through the process of acceptance and these intentional practices, Sara discovered moments of relief and calm amidst her persistent sorrow. Over time, she reported experiencing her grief as less overwhelming and more manageable. Although Sara's pain never completely disappeared—and she did not expect it to—she found comfort in realizing she could honor her daughter's memory without carrying the constant weight of suffering. Her therapeutic journey provided a gentler, more compassionate way of relating to her pain, accepting what is, and gradually allowing her daily life to feel lighter, more meaningful, and hopeful.

Sara's experience demonstrates the transformative power of courageously turning toward pain rather than resisting it—a courage frequently evoked by psychedelic experiences that uncover deep layers of suppressed emotion. When clients consciously face their inner challenges, they cultivate resilience, approaching their inner world with openness, curiosity, and courage. Ultimately, turning toward discomfort unlocks profound potential for authentic healing, lasting growth, and spiritual insight

Practice 4: Ethical Use of Touch and Boundaries

In therapeutic work, the container is everything. It's the space in which deep healing unfolds, and that space must feel both safe and human. At the heart of this container lies the therapist's ability to maintain ethical clarity while offering genuine connection. Boundaries are not barriers; they provide the essential structure that holds the therapeutic space. Without clear boundaries, there can be no safety; without warmth, there can be no healing.

Establishing a strong therapeutic bond requires a delicate balance of presence, trust, and care. In psychedelic-assisted therapy—where clients enter vulnerable, altered states—that bond must be especially cemented. Closeness within the therapeutic relationship can evoke powerful emotions like love, dependency, or idealization, which can become destabilizing without clearly established and communicated boundaries. Therapists need to explicitly discuss these boundaries beforehand and remain consistently transparent and attuned during the therapeutic process. Boundaries, therefore, are not about distancing—they are about fostering consistency, clarity, and emotional safety. They allow clients to feel secure enough to fully enter and explore their inner experience.

In my experience, many therapists err on the side of being too rigid. Early in my training at the Brief Therapy Institute, I witnessed this often. Many of the therapists in training, uncertain of their competence or emotional safety, would default to a distant, clinical style. Their sessions became procedural, reducing human connection to checklists and interventions. While their intentions were good, the therapists who adopted this overly professional stance often created emotional distance from their clients, who were less likely to open up. As a result, the work remained surface-level. Over time, and often as a function of their own healing, therapists begin to soften these defenses. As we become more grounded in ourselves, we can offer more presence, compassion, and flexibility without losing our professional center.

On the other side of the spectrum are therapists whose boundaries become too porous. Here, emotional enmeshment or unacknowledged transference can blur the lines of the therapeutic relationship. Clients may begin to see their healing as entirely dependent on the therapist's presence, and therapists may unconsciously reinforce this belief. In psychedelic therapy, where the experience of deep connection is often amplified, it is especially important to reflect the client's growth back to them. One of the most healing messages we can offer is: This came from you—from your courage, your wisdom, your work. The love clients often feel in therapy is real, but it must remain within the frame of a professional, respectful, and platonic relationship.

Boundaries aren't just emotional, they're also physical; and few topics evoke more ambivalence in the field than the question of therapeutic touch. In many traditional training programs, therapists are taught to avoid physical contact altogether, out of concern for ethical violations. This caution is understandable, but it can also leave therapists unprepared for moments when words are insufficient, and the body must speak.

I first encountered this early in my career, while working with a Haitian client in her late 50s who had recently been diagnosed with breast cancer. At the end of an emotional session, I instinctively offered her a hug; and as soon as I did, I felt a wave of panic. I suddenly remembered that my supervisor and classmates were watching my session behind the one-way mirror. Instantly, I was flooded with anxiety about potentially crossing professional boundaries. In supervision, I explained that the gesture came from a place of cultural and emotional authenticity. In my Colombian upbringing, physical affection was a natural and familiar expression of care. My supervisor responded with curiosity and caution. She acknowledged that although my gesture was well-intentioned, in other contexts, it could be misinterpreted or even cause harm. That conversation stayed with me.

For a long time after that session, I avoided initiating touch with clients. But gradually, my understanding began to shift. Over and over, I found myself in session with clients who were grieving, dissociating, or seeking a sense of physical grounding. One such moment came with a client named Bernice, who was navigating the early weeks of widowhood. As she described waking up alone for the first time in decades, her face collapsed, and her hand instinctively reached out—not to me, specifically, but to the space between us. I gently placed my hand on hers. She later told me it was the first time in weeks she had felt someone who could hold it.

These moments taught me that healing is somatic and relational. The question isn't whether touch belongs in therapy, but rather *how* and *when* it does. Therapeutic touch must always be consensual, attuned, and purposeful. It must arise from the client's needs, not the therapist's impulses. When offered with integrity, clear communication, and deep respect, touch can become an extension of presence—grounding, regulating, and profoundly healing. Examples of appropriate therapeutic touch might include holding a client's hand during intense emotional release; gently placing a reassuring hand on their shoulder or upper back; or offering supportive, grounding contact to their feet or hands if they feel dissociated or overwhelmed. Such touch should always be clearly explained and explicitly consented to in advance, ideally within a broader conversation around boundaries and comfort.

Of course, discernment is essential. Therapists must be attuned to the clinical context, as well as to their own histories, cultural backgrounds, and potential blind spots. We must continually ask ourselves critical questions, such as: Who is this touch for? What meaning might it carry for this client? How might it be interpreted, or misinterpreted? When we approach touch with this level of care and awareness, it becomes a conscious tool for connection rather than an impulse to rescue or an unconscious reaction to our own discomfort.

Ultimately, boundaries are about trust. They shape the relational field, allowing safety and intimacy to coexist. In psychedelic therapy especially, where clients may enter states of profound vulnerability, our ability to hold boundaries with kindness and clarity is foundational. When we remain grounded in the delicate balance between closeness and professionalism, we create a therapeutic container that is spacious enough for profound transformation, and strong enough to safely hold its complexity.

Practice 5: Utilization-Based Psychotherapy

You use what the patient brings you.

—Milton Erickson (1980, p. 224)

Milton Erickson's principle of utilization remains one of the most radical and deeply respectful approaches in psychotherapy. Rather than trying to change a client by confronting their defenses or correcting their thinking, utilization invites us to work with what is already there—their stories, symptoms, values, contradictions, and even their resistance.

Steve de Shazer (1988) described utilization as a method of using "whatever the client does that is somehow 'right,' 'useful,' 'effective,' or 'good,' for the purpose of developing a solution" (p. 114). This principle rests on the foundational belief that clients already contain the raw material for transformation. Our role is not to impose insight from the outside, but to create space for their inner wisdom to surface and become usable.

This is especially critical when clients are caught in ambivalence, stuck between deeply held values that are trying to pull them in opposite directions. Attempting too quickly to resolve these tensions often backfires. Instead, utilization invites us to listen to the conflict and help the client follow its intelligence.

One example of this that I encountered in my practice was Rebecca, a mother of two who was navigating a painful marriage. She came to therapy torn between two vital instincts: her commitment to protecting her children's stability and her longing to reclaim a sense of self in a relationship that had drained her. These were not abstract dilemmas. They were values in conflict—loyalty versus aliveness, safety versus truth. Recognizing her bind, I knew that if I pushed her toward a decision, she might retreat. She didn't need answers from me. She needed help hearing the ones already inside her.

Instead of challenging her hesitation, I leaned into the value behind it: her fierce love for her children.

"What do you hope your children learn about relationships from watching yours?" I asked.

She paused. "Mutual respect," she said. "That love should feel safe."

"And what do you think they're learning now?"

Her silence spoke volumes. She physically shifted, clearly seeing the gap between what she wished for her children and what they actually experienced.

Then I asked, "If your child were in your exact position twenty years from now, what would you want them to do?"

Without hesitation, she replied: "I'd want them to leave."

"Why?"

"Because they deserve better."

I said nothing after that. The clarity she came upon didn't come from me; it came from her own inner compass, which had been buried under fear and guilt. My role was not to direct Rebecca, but to reflect and respect the values already guiding her process.

This moment with Rebecca illustrates a key tenet of Ericksonian utilization: meeting the client where they are and using their existing values and language to facilitate change. Rather than challenging her fears or presenting external solutions, I followed the thread of her internal conflict. By staying with the value that underpinned her hesitation—her love for her children—I helped her access her own wisdom. In this way, the ambivalence wasn't a barrier to overcome. It was the very material out of which clarity emerged.

Utilization means trusting the client's internal complexity. It means giving up our attempts to override resistance and, instead, starting to work with it. Viewed through this lens, a resistance is a form of protection, creativity, or even devotion. When welcomed and explored, it becomes the basis of transformation.

Another client, Daniel, came to therapy to address his intense insecurities at work. Despite being bright and capable, he second-guessed himself constantly. He hesitated in meetings, stumbled during presentations, and suffered from a deep fear that his self-doubt might jeopardize his job. As we traced the roots of this pattern, Daniel revealed a painful history: his father left when he was five, and he was later sexually abused by a trusted family friend. These experiences left deep imprints of shame, confusion, and fractured identity.

For much of his adult life, Daniel lived under the weight of this history. But during one session, almost offhandedly, he mentioned his time in the army. His voice shifted. He described being selected for an elite leadership position that required him to confidently and competently lead complex missions, and he shared that his unit had thrived under his direction. "That time in my life felt like a different reality," he said. "There, I knew who I was." This disclosure became a turning point in the therapeutic process. We didn't focus on fixing his insecurity. We focused on remembering the version of himself who already knew how to lead.

What made that time different? For one, the army offered him a clean slate. There, it was his performance—not his pain—that determined his experience. And he excelled. Together, we worked to anchor that confident self. We explored how he carried himself then, what internal dialogue supported him, and what rituals helped him feel strong. He began using imagery, breath, and physical cues to tap into that version of himself before walking into meetings. He even removed a pin from his army uniform and kept it in his workspace, as a symbol of the courage and confidence already living inside him.

This work didn't erase Daniel's trauma or deny the reality of his pain. But it reconnected him to a deeper truth—that his strength wasn't something he had to construct, it was something he got to reclaim. For Daniel, utilization meant drawing from a version of himself he had once fully embodied, but no longer recognized. Rather than trying to eliminate his insecurity, we focused on amplifying what was already inside him. As Erickson emphasized, the work of therapy is often in helping clients access what they already do well, even if only unconsciously. My goal was to help Daniel re-engage a forgotten capacity and integrate it into his present circumstances. His old army confidence could be remembered and restored—brought back into relationship with the version of himself living in the here-and-now.

Utilization demands precise listening and deep attunement. We pay attention not only to what clients say, but to how they say it. We notice what softens them, what lights them up, what doors may already be open inside them. This approach is fundamentally about humility. We do not fix or direct clients; instead, we navigate alongside them. Resistance becomes meaningful information, ambivalence holds hidden wisdom, and symptoms serve as important signals. The client's story, therefore, is not an obstacle; it's the very path along which healing unfolds. When we center utilization in our therapeutic conversations, we allow clients to appreciate and work with their story, building from within, and drawing from what they already have.

Practice 6: Foundational Framework: Holistic Integration of Body, Mind, and Soul

At the heart of deep therapeutic work lies a truth that is both ancient and, increasingly, backed by modern research: we cannot heal the mind without also tending to the body and the soul. True transformation—the kind that lasts beyond the lightbulb moment—arises when all parts of a person are invited into the room.

In my work, especially with clients moving through psychedelic integration, I have found that it isn't enough to work only with thoughts or behaviors. Clients may have insight into their trauma, but if they feel disembodied and dysregulated, they will struggle to integrate it. They may understand their patterns intellectually, but feel directionless or numb. They may seem high-functioning from the outside, but carry an aching void inside. Healing begins when we begin to see, and work with, the whole person.

Trauma lives in the body. It's the place where anxiety surges, and the place where inner balance can begin. The mind is where we construct meaning, creating interpretations and narratives to make sense of our experience. The soul, a bit harder to define, is where we anchor our sense of purpose, our longing to belong, and our vision of what matters most. Therapy that honors all three dimensions—body, mind, and soul—creates a kind of coherence that no single approach can achieve on its own.

Somatic engagement is foundational to effective, impactful therapy. Advances in neuroscience and trauma-informed therapy make clear that the body must be included in the therapeutic process in order for a person to integrate their insights—to experience in their bodies what they understand in their minds (Porges, 2011; Van der Kolk, 2014). For clients living in states of chronic anxiety, disconnection, or trauma activation, the process of achieving regulation must begin below the neck. Grounding practices like breathwork, movement, and interoceptive awareness help stabilize the nervous system and prepare the client for deeper work (Critchley & Garfinkel, 2017; Dana, 2018).

The mind, with its capacity to reflect, make meaning, and create stories, organizes what the body feels into language. Clients who learn to identify their patterns, question their narratives, and reflect on their values begin to reclaim authorship of their own lives. Journaling, cognitive reframing, and mindfulness-based practices help give structure and coherence to internal shifts (Beck, 1979; Pennebaker & Smyth, 2016; Segal et al., 2018).

But it is the soul that makes healing matter. The soul is the part of us that asks: What is this all for? As Viktor Frankl's (1959) remarkable teachings remind us, a sense of meaning can sustain us, even in suffering. And current research confirms that spiritual engagement and existential clarity are vital sources of resilience and well-being (Park, 2010; Steger, 2012; Wong, 2017). In my work, this can take many forms. It might show up as helping a client reconnect with ritual, ancestry, faith, nature, or a sense of calling. Or it might look like integrating psychedelic insights into everyday life, with reverence and intentionality.

My work with Ryan, a 16-year-old high school junior, exemplifies the need for a whole-person approach. He came to therapy to address escalating anxiety, panic attacks, and crushing self-criticism. Diagnosed with ADHD, and a perfectionist by nature, Ryan believed that his struggles were the result of personal failure. Since he thought he was failing, he thought the solution was to try harder. But the more he tried, the more overwhelmed he became.

My conversations with Ryan weren't focused on time management or positive thinking, but on his body. His nervous system was in chronic overdrive. I started by introducing grounding practices, including extended exhalation for panic, progressive muscle relaxation before studying, and movement breaks to discharge excess tension (Ratey & Hagerman, 2008). As Ryan learned to regulate physiologically, he became more available to cognitive and emotional work.

From there, we explored his thought patterns. His worth was tied to achievement, and experiences that he deemed failures were a trigger for deep shame. We began to work with Ryan's performance-based identity, helping him to gradually engage with life in a more values-based way. He reflected on what he enjoyed about learning, what challenged him, and how he could move through tasks with curiosity rather than fear. We used journaling to track emotional patterns and invite a gentler internal dialogue.

Finally, we explored his identity. Ryan felt broken, as if his ADHD defined him. Together, we reframed this. What if his brain was wired for depth, creativity, and focus—just in a different rhythm? He began identifying moments when his unique thinking style had been a gift. He stopped seeing himself as defective and started to honor that he was someone who required different tools, and whose journey had value.

By engaging body, mind, and soul, Ryan's therapy became about much more than symptom reduction. It became an act of self-reclamation. Within a short amount of time, his panic attacks subsided. He still experienced stress, but he no longer interpreted it as a sign of failure. He felt more grounded, more present, and more himself. As I've emphasized throughout this chapter, therapeutic work isn't about fixing. It's about restoring coherence. When therapy includes the full spectrum of the human experience, clients begin to feel whole again. Having addressed body, mind, and soul, we now return to the most accessible and fundamental entry point connecting all three—the breath.

Practice 6: The Power of Breath

> *Breathing is so much more than just getting air into our bodies. It's the most intimate connection to our surroundings.*
>
> —*James Nestor (2020 p. 38)*

As a therapist and human being, I have learned, over and over again, that breath is a bridge between body and mind, between fear and regulation, and between this moment and what lies beneath it. If I were to write another book, it could easily be dedicated entirely to breathwork, given its profound depth and diversity. But here, I want to offer a doorway. This section is an introduction to something I believe every client and therapist can benefit from. The breath, after all, is always with us. It is perhaps our most underutilized tool for becoming present, regulating our nervous systems, and experiencing transformation.

Breathing is more than a basic biological function; it intimately connects the body and mind, linking us directly to our inner world and our surroundings. Throughout history, breath has been revered as more than just a physiological necessity. It has been seen as a source of wisdom, healing, and transformation. In both Latin and Hebrew, the word for breath also means spirit—*spiritus* in Latin, and *ruah* in Hebrew. Across cultures and traditions, the act of breathing has been associated with life force, consciousness, and even divinity. It is no surprise, then, that breathwork has become a powerful practice in modern healing, psychotherapy, and self-exploration.

Breathwork exercises have been widely recognized for their profound effects on emotional regulation, stress reduction, and overall well-being. Scientific research has shown that controlled breathing techniques can lower cortisol levels, activate the parasympathetic nervous system, and promote relaxation, helping individuals cultivate greater emotional resilience and inner balance (Maniaci et al., 2024; Saoji et al., 2019). In psychotherapy, breathwork can be used to help clients regulate anxiety before difficult disclosures, anchor during emotionally intense moments, or create a bridge between talk-based insight and embodied integration. In trauma therapy, breathwork plays a particularly vital role in helping individuals access and release suppressed emotions. By focusing on intentional breathing, people can create a safe and embodied way to process unresolved experiences, allowing for greater self-awareness and emotional healing (Van Der Kolk, 2014).

Some breathwork practices go even further, facilitating deep introspective states that lead to profound psychological insights. One such practice is holotropic breathwork, a technique developed by psychiatrist Stanislav Grof. This method involves rhythmic, intentional breathing that can induce non-ordinary states of consciousness, unlocking deep emotional processing and self-discovery (Grof & Grof, 2010). Grof initially developed this practice as a therapeutic tool, recognizing its potential for surfacing buried emotions and offering a structured way for individuals to release unresolved psychological material. Those who practice holotropic breathwork often describe having powerful experiences—waves of emotion, vivid imagery, or sudden realizations about their past or present. It isn't uncommon for individuals to cry, laugh, or make any number of vocalizations during these sessions, as they process and release deeply held emotions. Due to its intensity, holotropic breathwork should only be facilitated by trained, experienced professionals. However, breathwork as a whole remains an accessible and transformative practice that anyone can integrate into their daily life.

An in-depth study of breathwork would require an entire textbook, but its effects can be felt through even the simplest practices. A few foundational techniques can provide immediate and lasting benefits. One of the simplest yet most effective of these is the 4–7–8 breathing technique, developed by Dr. Andrew Weil. This method, often described as a natural tranquilizer for the nervous system, helps regulate stress and promote relaxation. The process is simple. First, you place the tip of your tongue gently behind your upper front teeth. Then, you inhale slowly through the nose for 4 seconds, hold the breath for 7 seconds, and exhale completely through the mouth for 8 seconds, making a soft "whoosh" sound. Repeat this cycle a total of four times, and you'll likely start noticing a sense of calm. Dr. Weil (2022) recommends practicing this technique twice a day for the first month, cautioning that mild lightheadedness may occur initially, but typically subsides with regular practice. Many individuals find this breathing method particularly useful before bedtime, as it facilitates relaxation and quiets the mind, making it easier to fall asleep. Others incorporate it into their daily routine as a way to manage stress and maintain emotional balance.

Another foundational breath practice, often used in Zen meditation, is breath counting. Though seemingly simple, it requires sustained focus and serves as a powerful tool for mindfulness. The practice begins by silently counting "one" on the first exhale, then "two" on the next, continuing up to "five." Once reaching five, the count starts over at one. The key is to never count beyond five and only count on the exhale. If the mind begins to wander or counting extends beyond five, simply return to one and restart. This technique helps strengthen focus, regulate breathing, and bring awareness to the present moment. Many people who struggle with traditional forms of meditation find breath counting to be a useful entry point into mindfulness practice, as it provides a structured yet accessible way to train one's attention.

Recent scientific research has further emphasized the impact of breathwork on the nervous system. Dr. Andrew Huberman, a neuroscientist at Stanford University, has studied the effects of various breathing techniques on stress regulation. His research indicates that the physiological sigh—a specific pattern of breath—can quickly reduce stress and promote a sense of calm (Balban et al., 2023). This technique involves taking a deep inhalation through the nose, followed by a second, shorter inhalation before exhaling slowly and completely through the mouth. The physiological sigh is particularly effective because it maximizes oxygen intake while facilitating the release of excess carbon dioxide, leading to an immediate calming effect. Many individuals report that just two or three cycles of this breath pattern are enough to shift their emotional state and restore equilibrium. Unlike some breathwork techniques that require extended practice, the physiological sigh can be used in high-stress situations to regulate emotions in real time.

Breathwork is an ever-present and accessible tool for self-regulation and transformation. Whether used for relaxation, emotional processing, or deep self-exploration, these techniques offer an immediate and profound way to cultivate inner balance. Many people find that incorporating even brief breathwork sessions into their daily routine leads to noticeable improvements in mood, focus, and overall well-being. Although certain breathwork modalities, such as holotropic breathwork, require professional guidance, many other techniques can be practiced independently, providing long-term benefits with minimal effort.

For those who wish to deepen their breathwork practice, a wealth of resources and training programs are available to explore it further. Therapists and practitioners who integrate breathwork often find that it enhances their clients' ability to navigate emotions, regulate stress, and cultivate deeper self-awareness. Ultimately, breath is an ever-present ally, offering a direct pathway to healing, clarity, and emotional resilience. Whether used in moments of crisis, quiet reflection, or deep self-inquiry, conscious breathing reminds us that healing is not something we must seek outside of ourselves—it is something we can access with every breath we take.

Part II

Exploring the Inner Landscape

Neuroscience, History, and the Clinical Use of Psychedelics

Chapter 3

The Role of Personal Experience in Psychedelic Therapy

Unraveling and Becoming: An Initiation into Psychedelic Consciousness

It was almost dusk. About 20 of us sat quietly near a fire pit surrounded by trees, stones, and the sound of a gently gurgling creek a few steps away. As I sat there, chilled by a cold breeze, I became engulfed by a series of emotions. Fear, excitement, confusion, and doubt flowed through me as I unsuccessfully tried to bring my awareness back to my breath, hoping that my heart might slow its pounding and my body calm its tremoring. The night before, I boarded a flight from Miami to San Francisco with a family friend. He offered to take me to an Indian reserve a few hours away from the airport, where he had previously attended several Ayahuasca ceremonies and grown closely acquainted with the head shaman[1] of the tribe, known as "El Abuelo" (The Grandfather).

Before I continue my story, I think it will help if I offer some context for how I ended up in an Ayahuasca ceremony in the first place and why, as I'll propose later in this chapter, I've come to believe that therapists working in the world of psychedelics must have direct, personal experience with these medicines.

Just a few months before my trip to California, I heard the words *ayahuasca* and *shaman* for the first time, from my old friend Cindy B., whom I was seeing for the first time since childhood. As soon as Cindy started sharing her experience, I was intrigued. But it was in the way that a person might be intrigued about going to space—marveling at it, but never believing they'll go there themselves. Soon after my conversation with Cindy, my curiosity led me in pursuit of websites, documentaries, books, and any other information I could find about this interesting drink/brew/spirit and the spiritual guides who conduct ceremonies with it.

The more I learned about Ayahuasca, the less I thought I would ever experience it firsthand. The way I saw it, Ayahuasca was a drug, and—given that the "Say No to Drugs" movement of the late 1990s had made a strong

DOI: 10.4324/9781003541639-6

impression on my vulnerable adolescent mind—I had no interest in exploring drugs. So, when I heard Cindy's account of this mysterious intoxicant, I tucked the idea of doing it myself into the recesses of my mind. Occasionally, though, I would recall a confusing warning Cindy had given me at the end of our conversation: In time, she said, "Aya" would call me to "her," and it would then be my turn to ingest the psychedelic. This puzzled me. Why would Aya call *me*, and what exactly would it mean if she did?

Around that same time, I was enrolled in a doctoral course titled Thinking Systems that centered on systemic ideas found in Taoism, Zen, and the writings of cybernetic philosopher Gregory Bateson. Bateson was an English anthropologist and social scientist whose work led to much of what is known today as systems theory. Bateson's influential ideas, such as the double bind theory for schizophrenia, made a significant impact on the field of mental health. I quickly came to understand why Bateson was regarded as one of the least understood thinkers of the 20th century—it was a rigorous and exhausting cognitive exercise to understand his teachings.

Bateson often conveyed his ideas with stories and metaphors, along with abstract theories and absurdities intended to challenge the Western framework of good versus bad, right versus wrong. As a student in the course, I explored Bateson's concepts of "the Mind" and "its information" with fascination, slowly beginning to rethink everything I think I know about thinking, and to reconsider everything I thought to be true. I discovered the truth in Bateson's (2002) words, that "those who lack all idea that it is possible to be wrong can learn nothing except know-how" (p. 24). I was determined to learn more. However, as determined and intelligent as I tried to be, I was far from understanding. The concepts I was learning in class weren't fitting into my mind's compartmentalized categories, and my presuppositions were filtering and admitting only a trickle of the information. Week after week, I struggled to make sense of what Bateson wrote and what my professor, Dr. Douglas Flemons, was patiently trying to convey. I couldn't explain these riveting ideas, even to myself.

Midway through the semester, while reading the transcript of a lecture Bateson gave in 1970, I learned of the time he ingested LSD and experienced something he'd always deemed vital to our survival: the disappearance of the self (Bateson & Bateson, 1972/2000). Reading this, I began, for the first time, to consider the nature of the self, and to wonder how I might relate to or experience it. This philosophy, which I had previously overlooked, soon generated a profound paradigm shift.

Bateson and Bateson (1972/2000) were adamant that we, humans, need to fundamentally rethink our understanding of ourselves and others, as our current perception of the world is flawed. He cautioned that people tend to see themselves as separate from, and even in opposition to, the world around them. This way of thinking, he explained, has ultimately led us to hate the perceived "Other," seeing their race, culture, beliefs, or theology as a threat to our own belief system. Furthermore, this way of understanding the world means that we see all forms of life—animals, insects, plants, and ecosystems—as separate, leading us to perpetually misunderstand or exploit them. Our individualistic understanding leads us to worry only about our own survival when, in reality, everything is interconnected and circular. Harming the Other eventually boomerangs. harming us back.

Bateson and Bateson (1972/2000) laid out their ideas on a more dramatic scale by asserting that we are dying from the by-products of our own hate. Accordingly, he proposed that the correct way of thinking involves a dissolution between self and other, which allows for the recognition of both as parts of a larger whole. Bateson expressed that an experience with LSD—or, I will add, with any classical psychedelic, including Ayahuasca—has the potential to correct this faulty understanding of separate parts and, with that, reveal the unity of all. As he put it, "there is a larger mind of which the individual mind is just a subsystem. This larger Mind is comparable to God and is perhaps what some people mean by 'God'" (Bateson & Bateson, 1972/2000, p. 467). According to Flemons (1991), Taoists call this larger Mind *Tao*, a word that is often left untranslated and instead referred to as that which cannot be named or explained. Attempting to explain Tao leaves us tangled up in the limitations of language and the inadequate ways we attempt to make sense of things.

In his book *Completing Distinctions*, Flemons (1991, p. 47) includes a Taoist story by Yen-kuan Ch'i-an that portrays the trickiness of contextualizing such questions:

Student: Where is Tao?
Teacher: Right before us.
Student: Why don't I see it?
Teacher: Because of your egoism you cannot see it.
Student: If I cannot see it because of my egoism, does your reverence see it?
Teacher: As long as there is "I and thou," this complicates the situation and there is no seeing Tao.
Student: When there is neither "I" nor "thou" it is seen?
Teacher: When there is neither "I" nor "thou," who is here to see it?

Can something exist if it is not perceived by a conscious self? Or, as Albert Einstein was once said to ponder, "Do you really believe the moon only exists if you look at it?" (Pais, 1982, p. 5). These questions and more swirled around my mind. Given the synchrony of my introduction to these ideas and my conversation with Cindy, I began to wonder if this confusion might be part of Aya's calling. I started to consider that perhaps it might be my time to embark on a psychedelic experience. Maybe, I thought, this could help me understand Bateson's elusive concept of Mind. Maybe I could catch a glimpse of how the universe works. These curiosities ultimately led me to my first encounter with Ayahuasca in California.

Aya and I: Crossing the Threshold

I sat next to the fire, too anxious to process the words of the shaman about the order of events for the evening. While observing and getting lost in thought, my eyes kept returning to the shaman's pet wolf. Sitting calmly, wearing a leash and several colorful Apache beaded chokers around his neck, this majestic gray and white creature looked off into the distance, glaring intensely at the wooded expanse. I was confused about how a wolf could possibly be sitting on a leash next to a human as a pet, but there were bigger questions on my mind. I was still bewildered by the fact that I was about to ingest a hallucinogenic drug. Though I tried to keep reminding myself that I was there for academic reasons, I chuckled at the notion that anything academic could possibly come from this experience. I was being either incredibly brave or ridiculously foolish; I had yet to find out which.

As I anticipated my first encounter with ayahuasca, I looked through some of Bateson's writings, hoping they would distract me from my own internal panic. I remember looking at his explanation of a phenomenon called Learning III[2] (Bateson & Bateson, 1972/2000), which I think about as the ability to question old, unexamined premises and even change them, possibly freeing yourself up to a new understanding. According to Bateson and Bateson (1972/2000), Learning III is difficult and rare for humans to accomplish; however, it has the potential to happen through experiences such as a psychedelic trip. This was what I kept telling myself as the shaman asked all of us seated in the circle around the fire to approach the altar and receive a cup of the ayahuasca brew. As I prepared for my turn, I reminded myself that ayahuasca would be the doorway through which I would exit the limitations of myself. I was seeking an understanding of the Mind, its ways of learning, and its ways of creating boundaries between ourselves and others. I was seeking to experience what Bateson and Batson (1972/2000) described—that there actually aren't any boundaries at all, and that all of us are parts of one bigger whole. If the illusionary self becomes irrelevant, then I might experience a redefining of my faulty individualistic perspective—the one Bateson believed was imperative to correct for transforming our understanding of the world around us.

Full of trepidation, I took my turn ingesting the foul-smelling, reddish-brown drink. The bitterness hit my tongue almost immediately, and I nearly spit it out. But, worrying about what the other participants would think, I quickly gulped it down and braced myself for what was to come.

The next six hours were some of the scariest of my life. It felt like a thousand hours passed and also, somehow, like time didn't exist at all. The following is a brief excerpt of what I journaled soon after my experience with Aya. It is unedited in order to preserve the felt sense of losing temporal/spatial anchors and self-reference.

> For the first time, I have felt what it's like to go insane. Losing all boundaries, losing all lines: The wise man sees lines and so he draws them, a crazy man sees lines so he draws them. I saw that thin line between the wise and the crazy—and I crossed it. I was in a time capsule, and it was the scariest place I have ever been in. I saw prison cells and prisoners of war. They partly go insane because they lose sense of time and that is crucial for our sanity, or our illusion of sanity. I guess TIME is one of those lines we draw to keep us sane (and crazy) because without time there is no self-corrective circuit, and the system does go on runaway—breaking down[3]. I was in a place where I was not going or coming, this must be the Zen teaching of just being, but I found no enlightenment or peace in that place. As for Learning III[4], it is not a place you want to go to; you lose your sense of self: There is no "my arm," there is no "my leg," there is JUST no "SELF" and I could not stand "myself" (even though there was nothing there to stand). There are no negations: The learning of what is not, is not there. There are no parts and therefore it is impossible to make sense of the whole. The Yin and the Yang were not there; hence opposites don't exist. No up or down, left or right, therefore the pull toward the center is lost. There is no spectrum to move on or levels of abstraction. For the love of G-d, humans are not supposed to process that much disorganized information at once, it will make them go insane. I thought of Huxley and how he wrote about the reducing valve of our mind and how it is there for a reason, to protect us from an overwhelming amount of information. However, he found infinite insight when he crossed that door of the reducing valve, while all I found was complete chaos. Of one thing I'm "sure": There is no truth and no reality, truth is only what you make of it and what you decided to see. Perception of everything is a combination of reality and the self. Korzybski[5] understood all of this when he wrote, "The map is not the territory"—and now I know, the territory should never be seen.

I still remember sitting around the fire thinking about Bateson's teachings. He emphasized that each of us has a map of experience, and on that map are differences. If these differences—which serve to separate, categorize, or compare—get dissolved, then the map ceases to exist, at least in its original form. Under the influencing of Aya, I became keenly aware that the map is a representation of the self, and that identity is created by separating the self from the other—the *this* from the *that*. Therefore, the dissolving of differences that I was experiencing during my Ayahuasca journey were a sign that I was losing my map. For me, this was an incredibly confusing and unsettling prospect. Other than the minimal understanding I gained of dissolution, I didn't feel I accomplished much in my quest to understand Bateson, or myself, more deeply. Accordingly, I determined that my experience was ultimately an irresponsible one. However, as I will explain in the following chapters, preparation, dosage, set, and setting are vital components of any psychedelic experience—something I only came to learn after my initial encounter with the ayahuasca brew.

In my case, I had little to no preparation, and the dosage I consumed was too high for my body. The *set*—my mindset at the time—was marked by confusion and doubt, and the *setting*—the physical and relational container—was far from ideal. I entered the ceremony without understanding the conditions necessary for a safe psychedelic experience, and what unfolded wasn't just a "bad trip," it was something I would later recognize as deeply traumatic. I had a direct encounter with just how powerful these substances are, and just how radically they can alter a person's experience of reality and themselves.

It took years, and many more journeys, for me to make sense of what happened that night. To this day, that initial encounter remains imprinted on me as an unresolved experience that slowly but definitively shaped my path. The memory of that night eventually drew me back to the medicine, this time with a different intention. I wanted to understand what people were referring to when they described experiencing clarity, healing, and even love through Ayahuasca. I wanted to understand what had gone wrong, and to glimpse what might be possible.

I went back to the medicine, again and again. You could say I became something of a repeat customer. But each time, I brought something new to the experience—curiosity, reverence, and, eventually, frameworks for integration. Each journey taught me something new about the medicine, about myself, and about the human condition. These subsequent experiences became foundational to my therapeutic approach. They guided me toward broader philosophical and clinical inquiries (such as Gregory Bateson's systemic understanding of self, other, and interconnectedness) and prompted me to deeply question how personal psychedelic experiences can profoundly influence our capacity to help others.

My psychedelic experiences became essential to my work with clients. They revealed layers of the psyche that no textbook could describe, and illuminated what it truly means to hold space for a person in altered states. They offered a humbling sense of how powerful these substances are, and defined the kind of therapist I wanted to become. This deeply personal initiation clarified for me the essential role that therapists' own psychedelic experiences can play. Beyond offering a personal reference point, they act as a form of embodied ethical practice.

Why Therapists Need Their Own Psychedelic Experiences

> What is a shaman, Abuelo?
> Oh, that is many things, but first and foremost, it is a soul who has first healed himself using our sacred plants.
>
> —*Personal Shaman*

One of the most debated questions in the field of psychedelic therapy is whether therapists need to have direct, personal experience with the medicines their clients are working with. Some argue that it isn't necessary—after all, physicians routinely prescribe medications they've never taken. But psychedelics aren't ordinary medications. They induce subjective, often indescribable states of consciousness that can't be fully grasped through intellectual knowledge or secondhand information.

Without lived experience, therapists may struggle to understand the disorientation, awe, or existential unraveling that clients are navigating in their psychedelic work. These experiences often transcend psychological frameworks. A therapist who hasn't felt the groundlessness of ego death or the emotional process of surrendering to the medicine may unintentionally minimize, pathologize, or misunderstand a client's process. Theoretical understanding can offer structure, but it doesn't offer a true, embodied understanding of what it means to be undone and remade.

This recognition isn't new. As I'll talk more about in a later chapter, research supports the significance of firsthand psychedelic experience for providers. In the early 1970s, researchers at the Spring Grove Hospital administered LSD to over 100 therapists and physicians as part of their training (Pahnke et al., 1969). Many of them reported profound personal and professional growth. Today, the Multidisciplinary Association for Psychedelic Studies (MAPS) includes an optional, but strongly encouraged, MDMA session as part of its therapist training. Although some clinicians decline, it's widely understood that those who engage in their own journeys bring something different, something deeper, to the process. Therefore, therapists guiding clients through these powerful processes should have undergone their own direct experiences with them.

However, advocating for personal psychedelic experiences must also be accompanied by careful ethical consideration. Ideally, these experiences occur within structured, professionally supervised settings, where preparation happens with clear intentionality and rigorous integration practices are followed. Professional accountability, ongoing peer consultation, and reflective self-assessment are essential to ensure that this deeply personal work enhances therapeutic effectiveness without compromising boundaries, client safety, or professional integrity. Rather than using them as a means of legitimizing themselves, therapists should engage in their own psychedelic journeys as a means of achieving genuine presence.

Clients often ask me whether I've taken the medicine, and I always answer honestly: I couldn't imagine guiding someone into that territory if I hadn't been there myself. When I share stories from my own journeys, it builds trust. It becomes a bridge. It allows the space to feel safer, more real. Not every story needs to be told, but my personal experience with altered states changes how I sit in the room. I listen differently. I wait differently. I trust the process more. In psychedelic work, theory and personal experience combine powerfully when applied to clinical practice. To illustrate this, let me introduce Roger, a client whose journey underscored the transformative potential of an embodied, experiential approach to psychedelic therapy.

Roger, a 55-year-old successful and highly educated businessman, was referred to me by a ketamine doctor who wanted him to do therapy before starting ketamine treatment. Roger stated that he had lived his whole life "trying to feel." He hoped the ketamine sessions would help him achieve this, since previous therapies hadn't. Roger shared with me that when he experienced the loss of a loved one, he didn't experience sadness, excitement, joy, passion, or even grief. The only emotion he seemed to have access to was anger, which he believed had impacted his relationships with his wife and children. Roger even questioned whether he might be a psychopath, though several therapists and psychiatrists had reassured him that he wasn't. I agreed. His stories were filled with acts of kindness and generosity. The more I got to know him, the more I sensed a deep empathy beneath the surface—despite his difficulty naming or accessing emotional experiences.

In one session, I asked Roger if he remembered feeling as a child, or if anyone had ever called him too sensitive. He quickly replied that while he didn't remember feeling much, he distinctly remembered his father yelling at him for crying. "Man up and grow up," his dad would bark. His mother offered little comfort, often telling him he was too sensitive and needed to "let things go." Emotional suppression had been a survival strategy in Roger's home, reinforced by generational and cultural norms that equated vulnerability with weakness. He internalized the message that feelings were unsafe, and he learned to block them out. I told him I suspected he was someone who felt too much—not too little—and that it simply hadn't been safe to feel as a child. We agreed to explore how he could internally generate that safety, in preparation for his ketamine work.

Over time, it became clear that Roger's emotional disconnect was about more than seeking safety. He had built a life around his intellect and lived almost entirely in his head—a place where he felt in control. He was a voracious learner, reading one book a week, often in the self-help genre, in hopes of figuring himself out. He had founded multiple successful businesses and regularly attended conferences and trainings. His mind had become his greatest asset—and his greatest barrier.

In one session, I told Roger, "You think too much and know too much." His mind had become overdeveloped at the expense of his feeling self. I added that the answers he was searching for wouldn't be found in any book. With a look of surprise on his face, he responded: "You know, one of my biggest insecurities is that I'm not smart enough . . . that I'm not enough." For the first time, his eyes welled up with tears. I told him that his words reminded me of a psychedelic journey I'd once had—an experience that completely changed my relationship to the mind and its perceived intelligence.

I traveled to Mexico to work with a facilitator who served 5-MeO-DMT, a powerful psychedelic derived from the glands of the Bufo alvarius toad. The substance is inhaled, and the experience lasts around 20 minutes. Many call it "The God Molecule," due to its capacity to elicit a profound sense of unity with the divine. Before my journey, the shaman asked me to name my greatest fear. I answered with the same words Roger had just spoken: "I am not intelligent enough."

After inhaling the smoke, time seemed to stop. I found myself in a luminous, triangular prism, surrounded by radiant light and vibrant colors. When I returned to ordinary consciousness, I felt calm and fully present, as if something essential had been reset within me. The facilitator handed me a deck of cards. I pulled one at random: card VII. He opened a book, *Osho Zen Tarot*, to page VII. The first words I read were, "Mind can never be intelligent—only no-mind is intelligent. Only no-mind is original and radical . . . . Your whole life becomes a flame, and a flame without any smoke. That is what awareness is."

I shared the passage with Roger. He took a photo of it and left my office unusually quiet. The next day, he called and said he had printed and framed the quote and placed it on his desk. He told me he now wanted to explore the idea of no-mind, rather than focusing on feelings. I laughed and gently suggested he didn't have to choose. Feelings, I said, are part of the no-mind.

In our final session before his ketamine treatment, I introduced Roger to the Taoist concept of no-mind—or not-knowing—as "a place where language, perception, and knowing cannot, and perhaps should not, reach" (Flemons, 1991, p. 60). I explained that no-mind isn't something to be understood; it's something to be practiced, often through breathwork and mindfulness. Roger agreed to use the quote, "Mind can never be intelligent," as a mantra during his ketamine session. Though I typically conduct ketamine sessions in my office, Roger's treatment would take place intravenously at the doctor's clinic. We scheduled an integration session for the following day.

During our session, Roger reflected on his journey. Using the mantra, he recalled a concept he'd once read from philosopher Baruch Spinoza—that mind and body aren't separate, but one. In his session, he realized that thinking and feeling were also inseparable. "I cannot think without feeling," he repeated, again and again. This awareness shifted something fundamental for him. I nodded and said, "It sounds like they're part of a larger whole."

Roger also shared that he felt immense love—something he couldn't recall having felt before. I pointed out that he now had access to more feelings than just anger. He left that day with a note in his pocket: "I think; therefore, I feel," which he placed next to the framed quote from Osho. A week later, I received a message: "Hey! I just wanted to say thank you, as I FEEL tears running down my face."

This moment captured more than personal growth: It highlighted the value of embodied, shared experience in psychedelic therapy. My own journey served not as a set of instruction, but as a bridge into his own process. Sometimes, the most transformative insights arise from meeting each other in our humanness—where truth is felt, not taught, and where real healing begins. Over and over, my work reaffirms for me that as therapists facilitating psychedelic work, our own personal experiences with these medicines are essential for offering truly attuned and effective care. These experiences provide more than just insight or stories to share with clients. They invite us into our own inner healing process, allowing us to explore our inner intelligence, confront personal burdens, and access transformation that impacts every aspect of our work and our lives. The deep self-inquiry that psychedelics facilitate can strengthen our capacity for empathy, presence, and attunement, enabling us to meet our clients with deep, embodied understanding.

The issue of having and incorporating our own psychedelic experiences as therapists speaks to a broader gap and limitation in conventional mental health training. Most therapists in training are not required by their training programs to attend their own therapy. This omission serves as a limitation for these developing therapists, as well as for the clients they serve. Through the process of self-exploration, therapists come to understand their internal landscape—their unique map, blind spots, and emotional challenges. Becoming more self-aware through therapy and self-work offers therapists direct insight into how their worldview shapes the therapeutic encounter. It also enables them to monitor and skillfully respond to countertransference as it arises in the therapeutic process. When therapists have personally engaged with psychedelics, they are better equipped to support clients in ethically and emotionally sound ways. These experiences are not just professionally valuable—they can profoundly enrich a therapist's sense of purpose, presence, and perception of the world. In this work, personal transformation isn't optional; it's foundational.

These medicines don't just expand consciousness. They humble us repeatedly, revealing where we cling, avoid, or protect. They continually remind us that our healing is never complete. If we are to authentically guide others into this vulnerable terrain, we must first courageously navigate it ourselves—not as a badge of honor or credential, but as a lived experience that softens and opens us. Ultimately, we can only accompany our clients as far as we ourselves are willing to journey. The deeper we have ventured, the safer it becomes for those who follow.

Notes

1 Shamans—also known as a curanderos, which when translated into English means medicine persons—are individuals who have previously healed themselves from their own life challenges (be they physical, mental, and/or emotional) by using hallucinogenic plants and fungi and whose purpose becomes the healing of others. In some cultures, shamans are also believed to have the ability to communicate with the superhuman plane, to move from one reality to the other, and to bring with them insights and fortunetelling abilities.

2 Bateson proposed a hierarchy of learning, each level more abstract and encompassing than the previous one. Learning 0 refers to what Bateson called the specificity of response in reaction to some sort of sensory input and cannot be corrected. Learnings I through III all involve change as a result of trial-and-error responses to some kind of input. Learning I is a change in the specificity of response. Learning II is a change in the process of Learning I. Learning III is a change in the process of Learning II (Bateson & Bateson, 1972/2000, p. 293).

3 James Clerk Maxwell was a 19th century Scottish mathematician and scientist who emphasized the significance of the relationship between a system and time. He asserted that time is crucial for a system to be self-corrective and maintain steady state, otherwise the system may spiral out of control. (Bateson, 2002, p. 100)

4 Learning III is a very uncommon occurrence in humans that involves a deep restructuring of character, leading to a critical examination and potential transformation of previously unquestioned assumptions. During this process, the self loses its significance and ceases to act as the subjective observer of the learning experience. (Bateson & Bateson, 1972/2000)

5 The Polish-American philosopher who stated, "The map is not the territory." In other words, our understanding of the world is different from the "actual world." (Korzybski, 1931, p. 27)

Chapter 4

Understanding Psychedelics

From Historical Use to Brain Mechanisms

The Long Journey of Psychedelics: Historical and Cultural Context

Humans have always sought ways to transcend ordinary reality—through ritual, meditation, and sacred substances—long before neuroscience provided a biological explanation for these experiences. Archaeological evidence indicates that for thousands of years, homo sapiens have been ingesting psychedelics as a form of spiritual growth and/or healing. The following are just a few examples of such findings:

(1) In the caves on the Tassili plateau of Southeastern Algeria, a fresco depicting a mushroom-holding shaman was discovered that dates back to 5000 BCE.
(2) In 2000 BCE, ergot (a type of fungi) may have been used to make the potion called *kykeon*, which was part of the ancient Greek religious ceremonies known as the Eleusinian Mysteries.
(3) In 1300 BCE, a stone carving was found in northern Peru that depicts a principal deity holding a San Pedro[1] cactus.
(4) In Mexico, statues can be found depicting *Psilocybe mexicana* with a Gd-like figure emerging from it, indicating its religious use (Frame, 2022).

Beyond visual depictions, archaeologists have also identified psychoactive alkaloids in archaeological artifacts and skeletal remains, indicating that psychedelic medicines were ingested ritualistically even thousands of years ago (Guerra-Doce, 2015). In written history, Spanish conquistadors documented a variety of ways in which psychedelic plants were used in indigenous ceremonies. Christopher Columbus, for example, described ceremonies in which tribe members inhaled a powder—now known to come from the seeds of the Anadenanthera peregrina tree—that induced altered states of consciousness.

DOI: 10.4324/9781003541639-7

Across ancient cultures, psychedelics served as one among many ways to achieve altered states of consciousness—among them fasting, temperature extremes, breathing techniques, and meditation (Winkelman, 2021). These states were often central to religious and social practices. In a cross-cultural survey, anthropologist Erika Bourguignon found that among the 488 societies she studied, 437 (around 90%) used altered states of consciousness in rituals (Guerra-Doce, 2015). Such integration underscores how fundamental these experiences were in shaping practices and rituals of collective meaning-making across civilizations.

In contrast, interest in psychedelics didn't begin in the Western world until the late 19th century, when German chemist Arthur Heffter (1897) isolated mescaline from the peyote cactus and documented its psychoactive effects through self-experimentation. Nearly five decades later, Swiss chemist Albert Hofmann synthesized LSD, accidentally discovering its powerful effects. These developments initiated the modern scientific study of psychedelics, which accelerated rapidly in the mid-20th century.

Initially, researchers believed that psychedelic substances produced states that resembled psychosis. They referred to them as *psychotomimetics*, hoping they could offer insight into schizophrenia. But further studies showed key differences between the states. For example, patients diagnosed with schizophrenia were able to recognize the distinction between their own psychotic experiences and LSD-induced states (Passie, 2021).

This realization prompted a shift from psychotomimetic research to psycholytic and psychedelic therapy. Psycholytic therapy involved low to moderate doses—usually of LSD or psilocybin—used in conjunction with psychoanalysis to facilitate symbolic imagery, regression, and transference. It typically involved multiple sessions and focused on personality restructuring and emotional insight.

Psychedelic therapy, in contrast, used high doses to induce mystical or transpersonal experiences. These sessions were fewer, typically one to three, and focused on deep emotional breakthroughs rather than analytic exploration. Humphry Osmond coined the term "psychedelic" from the Greek *psyche* (mind/spirit) and *deloun* (to manifest), suggesting that these substances revealed the contents of the mind (Passie, 2021).

During the 1950s and 1960s, thousands of clinical studies examined psychedelics' therapeutic potential in treating depression, anxiety, addiction, and end-of-life distress. Psychiatrist Stanislav Grof (1979), after facilitating more than 4,500 LSD sessions, noted their extraordinary research potential:

> The capacity of psychedelic drugs to exteriorize otherwise invisible phenomena and make them the subject of scientific investigation gives these substances a unique potential as a research tool for exploration of the

> human mind. It does not seem inappropriate or an exaggeration to compare their potential significance for psychiatry to that of the microscope for medicine or the telescope for astronomy.
>
> (p. 13)

Central to these therapeutic practices—both ancient and modern—is the mystical experience, characterized by profound feelings of unity, interconnectedness, and transcendence. Historically, mystical experiences have played a crucial role in indigenous rituals, religious ceremonies, and community healing, providing insights and transformative potential that closely parallel contemporary therapeutic outcomes. This continuity highlights humanity's enduring quest for meaning, connection, and spiritual insight through altered states.

Despite the promising trajectory of psychedelic research, widespread cultural backlash halted its progress in the late 1960s. Psychedelics became associated with countercultural movements, political dissent, and rebellion, prompting a strict and punishing response from the US government. Between 1968 and 1985, LSD, MDMA, and psilocybin were designated Schedule I substances, effectively banning their clinical and research use (Bonson, 2018).

But after a 25-year hiatus, researchers slowly began to study psychedelics again in the early 2000s. By 2017, the Food and Drug Administration (FDA) had designated MDMA-AT as an intervention for post-traumatic stress disorder (PTSD), and psilocybin therapy as a method for treating treatment-resistant depression. These breakthrough therapies offered a way to accelerate review processes (Multidisciplinary Association for Psychedelic Studies [MAPS], 2017). In 2019, the FDA also approved ketamine (in the form of esketamine) as a treatment for depression (Doblin et al., 2019).

Internationally, Israel has emerged as a pioneer in psychedelic medicine. In 2019, it became the first country to approve the compassionate use of MDMA-AT for PTSD (Psychedelic Newswire, 2020). Following the October 7, 2023, terrorist attacks, which resulted in widespread trauma, Israel took an innovative response. Through MAPS Israel, the HealingOct7 Initiative was launched, offering MDMA-assisted group psychotherapy to those most affected—including survivors of the Nova music festival, residents near the Gaza border, and frontline soldiers (Kustanowitz, 2024).

The initiative offers a four-and-a-half-month program with two MDMA-assisted sessions integrated into a structured group therapy framework (MAPS Israel, 2024). Designed to be scalable and cost-effective, this model provides a potential roadmap for national-scale mental health interventions. However, access largely remains limited to those who can afford private care, highlighting the need for more inclusive policies and funding.

In the United States, however, the regulatory path has proven more complex. In June 2024, the FDA's Psychopharmacologic Drugs Advisory Committee reviewed the New Drug Application for MDMA-AT but did not vote to recommend its approval. Their concerns centered on the integrity of the trial data and the potential safety risks associated with the substance (Kekatos & Nissen, 2024). In August, the FDA issued a Complete Response Letter rejecting the application and requesting additional Phase 3 trials (Lykos Therapeutics, 2024). Lykos has since announced plans to provide further data or launch additional studies. These setbacks underscore the scientific, political, and logistical challenges of integrating psychedelics into conventional mental health care. Nonetheless, progress toward this end is ongoing.

An important contextual factor in the difference between the legal and therapeutic status of ketamine versus that of psilocybin lies in their chemical origins and financial viability. Ketamine, a synthetic anesthetic, allows for precise dosing and patent protection, encouraging pharmaceutical investment. Psilocybin, a natural compound, offers less opportunity for proprietary development, despite its promising effects. This limits the amount of large-scale research funding directed toward its ongoing study.

Although ancient civilizations revered psychedelics as sacred tools for accessing divine wisdom and communal healing, modern science is only beginning to catch up to what's been known for thousands of years. Psychedelics have been used to mediate healing, transformation, and spiritual insight over millennia. That lineage now continues through structured research and clinical care.

How Psychedelics Affect the Brain

The Default Mode Network (DMN): The Brain Conductor

Having historically explored psychedelics as powerful catalysts for spiritual and psychological transformation, I will now offer a glimpse into the insights of contemporary neuroscience, to offer a clearer understanding of how these substances facilitate such profound changes. Robin Carhart-Harris, a neuroscientist who was previously conducting psychedelic research at Imperial College of London and is now at UCSF, has been working to understand the precise mechanisms of action in psychedelic substances. His pioneering research on psychedelic drugs uses brain imaging—specifically, functional magnetic resonance imaging (fMRI)—to examine the effects of psychedelics on brain activity (Logothetis, 2008). Magnetic resonance imaging (MRI) and fMRI are pivotal tools in neuroscience, each serving distinct purposes. While MRI provides high-resolution images of the brain's anatomical structure, enabling the identification of physical abnormalities such as tumors, lesions, or structural changes, the fMRI measures dynamic changes in blood oxygenation levels, reflecting neural activity. This capability allows fMRI to map functional processes in the brain, identifying regions engaged during specific tasks or in response to stimuli (Logothetis, 2008).

In one such study, Carhart-Harris et al. (2012) gave volunteer participants intravenous infusions of either psilocybin or a placebo, then used fMRIs to measure the cerebral blood flow in their brains. Since cerebral blood flow indicates the way oxygen is delivered to the brain, this was used in the study as a measure of participants' brain activity. Although the human brain accounts for only 2% of the body's weight, it consumes around 20% of the oxygen we extract from the air we breathe (Raichle & Snyder, 2007). Therefore, an increase in cerebral blood flow correlates with an increase in brain activity, and vice versa.

In their study, Carhart-Harris et al. (2012) observed that hallucinogens caused decreased activity in certain areas of the brain. While the researchers had previously hypothesized that there must be an overall increase in brain activity due to the dense subjective experiences reported by individuals who had taken these medicines, the data showed the exact opposite. They reported that "the results were remarkable because they showed for the first time [that] characteristic changes in consciousness brought about by a hallucinogen are related to 'decreases' in brain activity" (Carhart-Harris et al., 2014a, p. 663).

Carhart-Harris et al. (2014a) found that the decrease in brain activity was localized in what are known as the hub structures of the brain—namely, the thalamus, the posterior cingulate cortex, and the medial prefrontal cortex—which are also referred to as the default mode network (DMN). In recent years, research has revealed an intimate relationship between the DMN and the so-called self (Carhart-Harris & Friston, 2010; Gattuso et al., 2022). Menon (2023) highlighted the DMN's role in integrating memory, language, and semantic processing to create a coherent sense of self, which serves as the foundation for our internal narrative. Similarly, Bartoli et al. (2024) demonstrated that the DMN's unique neural dynamics are closely tied to internally directed cognition, underscoring its causal role in creative and divergent thinking, as well as mind wandering.

These findings emphasize the DMN's central role in orchestrating the neural mechanisms that underpin the human experience of selfhood. If one were to try locating Freud's concept of the ego within the human brain, it would be found in the DMN. The idea of the self is what allows us to self-reflect. In many ways, it's what gives us a sense of identity—or, as Bateson and Bateson (1972/2000) said, the "sorts of false reifications of the 'self' and separation between the 'self' and 'experience'" (p. 469). The DMN is also responsible for what is called the autobiographical memory (Carhart-Harris et al., 2014a), which is the means by which we construct the story of who we are by taking the things that happened to us and making them part of our narrative. Ultimately, this suggests that a decrease in brain activity in the DMN could be the reason some individuals experience the dissolution of self while on psychedelics.

Notably, when the DMN shows decreased activity under the influence of psychedelics or other factors, there is typically increased activity and connectivity in other areas of the brain (Gattuso et al., 2022). This phenomenon is known as increased global integration or functional connectivity. Psychedelics, therefore, promote greater connectivity between typically segregated neural networks, fostering a more integrated and dynamic brain state. For example, Carhart-Harris et al. (2012) demonstrated that psilocybin decreases DMN activity while increasing communication between the visual cortex and other brain regions, explaining the vivid imagery people often report during psychedelic experiences.

This increased cross-network connectivity enhances the brain's capacity for unconstrained cognition and emotional flexibility, which may underpin the therapeutic benefits of psychedelics for treating conditions such as depression and PTSD (Carhart-Harris & Friston, 2019; Gattuso et al., 2022). The unconstrained cognition and emotional flexibility observed during psychedelic experiences are closely linked to neuroplasticity, which is the brain's ability to reorganize itself by forming new neural connections. Psychedelics enhance neuroplastic mechanisms, which allow the brain to adapt to new experiences, process emotions in novel ways, and break free from rigid cognitive and behavioral patterns.

Tagliazucchi and Carhart-Harris (2014b) found that psychedelics expand the brain's repertoire of dynamical states, allowing for increased entropy and the exploration of novel patterns of activity. Such effects have the potential to disrupt rigid, maladaptive neural pathways, enabling the brain to form new adaptive connections. These findings highlight how the decrease in DMN activity and concurrent increase in global integration are a critical part of what gives psychedelics such transformative potential. Theoretically—albeit controversially—the reduction of activity in the DMN during a psychedelic experience creates a unique neurological state that may be particularly potent for initiating lasting psychological transformation.

Suppressed DMN activity enables the brain to enter a state of heightened neural plasticity and increased connectivity between typically segregated brain regions (Carhart-Harris & Friston, 2019). This state fosters a breakdown of entrenched mental frameworks and allows for the introduction of new cognitive and emotional patterns. Research suggests that therapeutic interventions or guided introspection during this period of DMN deactivation can lay the foundation for lasting change, as the brain is more receptive to adopting novel perspectives and behaviors. This dynamic interplay between neuroplasticity and reduced DMN activity is a core mechanism underlying the long-term therapeutic benefits of psychedelics in treating conditions like depression, PTSD, and anxiety (Melani et al., 2025).

Experts in the field of psychedelic therapy believe that psychedelics have the potential to benefit individuals whose storylines are filled with self-criticism or who engage in negative self-talk (Carhart-Harris et al., 2014a). Clients come into therapy wanting to redefine themselves. They want to redefine who they believe themselves to be, their lives, and their relationships. Psychedelics provide individuals the opportunity to temporarily rewire their brains and leave behind toxic or self-destructive patterns of thinking.

For example, a person who has been diagnosed with depression will often cycle through a variety of particular negatively biased thoughts, such as, I have no hope that things will get better; Nothing ever goes right for me; My life will always be a disappointment. A person in addiction constantly thinks about when and how they will have their next cigarette or drink. Similarly, a person diagnosed with OCD is often absorbed by pathological patterns of thoughts and behaviors. Psychedelics bring those choreographed dances to a halt, giving the mind the opportunity to create new ones. The brain can finally operate with greater flexibility in a freer, less constrained manner (Carhart-Harris et al., 2014a).

To help illustrate the clinical implications of these neurological insights, I want to present the story of a former client, whose transformative ketamine-assisted therapy sessions offer an example of the profound psychological shifts a person can experience through a change in DMN activity. Noelia[2], a 34-year-old woman, couldn't shake the feelings of disappointment and anger she harbored toward her husband, Ryan. Though he was a loving and supportive partner who provided a stable life, Noelia felt let down by his inability to achieve the wealth and status she equated with success. She was more than comfortable in material terms, yet she equated being rich with being important, so she lived in fear that she might one day return to the invisibility and unimportance she had felt as a child.

Noelia had immigrated to Miami from Cuba as a child with her parents, fleeing Castro's regime with little more than the clothes on their backs. Her father, once a man of stature and influence in Havana, had been forced to completely rebuild his life, and his family's, in a new and unfamiliar land. To support the family, he threw himself into fundraising, often courting wealthy benefactors whose generosity helped secure their future. His relentless and all-consuming pursuit of these powerful figures left Noelia feeling neglected and unseen. Over time, she internalized the belief that money was the key to being valued and visible. These feelings quietly followed her into adulthood and shaped her expectations of Ryan.

Noelia's disappointment became a source of tension in their marriage. She voiced her frustration through cutting remarks, accusing Ryan of being "less of a man" for his inability to provide the kind of financial success she believed would bring her status and security. Her words wounded Ryan deeply, though he rarely pushed back. Meanwhile, Noelia's anger festered, driving an emotional wedge between them that threatened the foundation of their relationship.

It was during a low-dose ketamine-assisted therapy session that Noelia began to unravel the roots of her anger and see her marriage in a new light. In this altered state, her usual defensiveness softened, allowing her to confront her beliefs and behaviors with clarity and compassion. As her journey unfolded, Noelia found herself reexamining the dynamic with Ryan. She saw his contained reactions to her harsh words in a new way—not as evidence of weakness but as signs of his remarkable emotional strength. Ryan endured her criticisms not because he was weak but because he cared deeply for her and their partnership. This realization filled Noelia with awe and respect for the quiet resilience her husband had shown, even in the face of her most hurtful comments.

Noelia also came to understand how much of her dissatisfaction with Ryan was rooted in her unmet childhood need to feel seen. Her father's absence imprinted a sense of invisibility on her, and she had transferred this into the relationship with her husband. Yet, in her ketamine-assisted session, Noelia realized that Ryan saw her in a way her father never had. He recognized and loved her completely—not because of her outward success or social standing, but because of who she was. This realization touched something deep within Noelia, meeting the need for visibility that had driven so much of her anger and shame. As Noelia continued to process her insights, her attachment to wealth as a measure of worth began to dissolve. She saw that Ryan's steadfast love, and the strength of their partnership, were far more fulfilling and secure than the fleeting validation she had been chasing.

After her session, Noelia approached Ryan with renewed empathy, respect, and gratitude. She apologized for the pain her words had caused and expressed a deep appreciation for his strength and love. For the first time in years, they were able to talk openly about their struggles and begin rebuilding trust and intimacy. Noelia's anger subsided and was replaced by a profound sense of connection and belonging. Now that she felt seen, wealth and status no longer held the same grip on her. Her marriage, once teetering on the edge of collapse, became safer, creating the possibility for more meaningful change. Through her journey, Noelia not only improved her relationship but also gained a deeper understanding of herself. The insights she uncovered during her ketamine therapy allowed her to practice releasing the patterns from her past and embrace the strength and love in her present, creating the possibility of a more fulfilling future.

This shift in Noelia's perspective illustrates the brain's remarkable ability to reorganize itself, when given the opportunity to get free from rigid thinking patterns. During her ketamine journey, the DMN—the part of the brain often associated with self-referential thinking and ingrained beliefs—was temporarily quieted, allowing her to explore new ways of understanding herself and her relationship. Noelia's experience illustrates how the quieting of the DMN can shift ingrained patterns and open the door to new insights.

One useful way to understand the role of the DMN is to imagine it as the conductor of an orchestra. The conductor's job is to direct and organize the players in performing a specific melody. Without a conductor present or directing, the musicians are free to play all kinds of new melodies—no matter how disorganized or improvisational they might be. In this state of creative disarray—what researchers call a prototypical high-entropy state of consciousness (Carhart-Harris et al., 2014b)—the brain becomes more flexible and inventive. This is believed to be one reason why psychedelics seem to enhance creativity, emotional insight, and outside-the-box problem solving.

In an interview, podcaster Joe Rogan conducted with Michael Pollan, the two psychedelic enthusiasts discussed the subject of ego dissolution and its ability to disrupt rigid or maladaptive thought patterns (JRE Clips, 2018). Pollan offered a metaphor that can help clients conceptualize how psychedelics temporarily alter DMN activity, allowing for increased cognitive flexibility and the emergence of new perspectives. He referred to a conversation he once had with Dutch scientist Mendal Kaelen, who explained how psychedelics impact the brain like this:

> Think of your mind as a hill covered in snow, and your thoughts are sleds going down that hill. After a while, after a lot of thoughts have gone down that hill, there will be these grooves. and they will get deeper and deeper; and at a certain point, you can't go down that hill without slipping into those grooves. That is who we are at this age, and what psychedelics do is flatten the snow, lots of fresh powder, and you can then take the sled wherever you want to go.
>
> (JRE Clips, 2018, 0:48)

Thoughts slide down these hills in an automatic way, making it difficult to avoid the grooves and change habits or ways of relating with the world. The fresh powder allows the sled to go anywhere on the mountain, and even create new grooves. In other words, the brain on psychedelics allows for streams of thought that are unconstrained, facilitating a vast amount of creativity. With the assistance of these medicines, the many presuppositions and limiting identities the self has created over time are lifted, allowing us to sense the world the way we did when we were infants. This creates the potential to experience everything in a newer, simpler way that isn't conditioned or constrained by longstanding patterns of thinking and being. As German philosopher Arthur Schopenhauer (1969) put it, "every child is in a way a genius; and every genius in a way is a child" (p. 451). He believed that true intelligence is reached when one can remain a pure knowing subject with a clear vision of the world and without barriers. This is something psychedelics can facilitate.

Mystical Experiences

In addition to facilitating cognitive flexibility and emotional shifts, reduced DMN activity may also have something to do with the mystical experience commonly associated with psychedelic experiences. Across cultures and historical periods, people have reported profound experiences characterized by a deep sense of unity, interconnectedness, and transcendence (Griffiths et al., 2006). Contemporary neuroscience suggests that when psychedelics decrease activity in regions responsible for maintaining our ordinary sense of self, the boundaries that typically separate self from other dissolve, facilitating these universally recognized mystical states (Carhart-Harris et al., 2012). Such experiences have enduring therapeutic benefits, including relief from anxieties around mortality, isolation, and meaninglessness (Griffiths et al., 2016).

During such a state, individuals report a deep and often ineffable sense of oneness with all things—whether that be a connection to the larger Mind, Tao, God, the Universe, or another concept of a higher power. These experiences are frequently described as among the most meaningful of a person's life, with lasting benefits that include emotional healing, renewed purpose, and, most notably, a reduction in existential fear.

This phenomenon is explored more deeply in later chapters. For now, it's important to understand that the impact of a mystical experience often extends far beyond the session itself. My clients frequently report profound psychological relief, an expanded capacity for meaning-making, and an enhanced ability to live more openly and fully in the present moment. Long after their psychedelic journeys, they continue to report feeling less fear and greater acceptance.

One of the most widely reported effects of a mystical experience is a shift in how individuals relate to the more common existential anxieties. This aligns closely with the work of renowned existential psychologist Irvin Yalom, who believed that most of human anxiety stems from what he called the four ultimate concerns or sources of existential pain:

1. The inevitability of death.
2. The responsibility of freedom.

3. Our fundamental aloneness.
4. The absence of inherent meaning in life (Yalom, 1989, p. 4).

Yalom (1989) explained that although the conscious mind often shields us from these concerns, they continue to influence our inner world—manifesting as anxiety, depression, or other forms of psychological distress. His therapeutic work was aimed at helping clients transform their relationship to these four concerns, and to the reality of death, in particular, so they could live with greater clarity, freedom, and vitality.

While Yalom approached this through talk therapy, psychiatrist Stanislav Grof (2006)—a pioneer in psychedelic-assisted psychotherapy—asserted that mystical experiences induced by substances like LSD could offer a more direct path to existential relief. Over the course of more than 4,500 sessions, Grof observed that when clients entered non-ordinary states of consciousness and connected with what he called the universal mind, they often reported a profound shift in how they saw life and death.

Grof (2006) found that clients would often emerge from these sessions with a renewed sense of meaning, a deeper appreciation for everyday experiences (like walking in nature or sharing a meal), and a dramatically decreased fear of death. He emphasized that in mystical states, the boundary between life and death often dissolves, and clients encounter something that feels infinite, cyclical, or divine. Death becomes a transformation instead of an endpoint, making it possible to live more freely and less afraid.

As powerful as these revelations may be, they are not a modern invention. The use of psychedelics as a way to access mystical and healing states has existed for millennia. Long before clinical trials and fMRI scans, humans across cultures used plant medicines in sacred rituals to connect with the divine, resolve inner turmoil, and understand their place in the cosmos.

With this integrated historical and neuroscientific foundation established, we can now examine each psychedelic substance in greater depth, highlighting their distinct therapeutic potential and historical significance.

Notes

1 This cactus contains psychoactive alkaloids, with mescaline being the principal psychedelic-producing substance (Doesburg-van Kleffens et al., 2023).
2 All patient names and identifiable information have been changed to protect patient privacy.

Chapter 5

Understanding and Choosing Psychedelic Medicines

The landscape of psychedelic therapy is as vast and varied as the medicines themselves. Each compound offers a doorway into the psyche, with its own tone, rhythm, and depth of inquiry. For therapists working in this field, understanding the differences is a matter of presence, discernment, and care. The more we understand how these medicines work and what they tend to reveal, the more skillfully we can match the medicine to the needs of each unique client.

This chapter offers a clinical and relational overview of five central psychedelics in contemporary therapeutic practice: ketamine, psilocybin, MDMA, LSD, and ayahuasca. These are the medicines most commonly used and studied in legal settings today. I will explore each of them through the lens of history, neuroscience, psychological impact, and practical application. My choice to include them in this chapter reflects both the current trajectory of research and their relevance in my own clinical experience.

While other psychedelic medicines—such as ibogaine, DMT, and mescaline—have important therapeutic potential, they are outside the scope of this text due to safety concerns, legal restrictions, or limited integration into mainstream or underground clinical work. For example, ibogaine shows promise in the treatment of addiction and PTSD, particularly among veterans, but its medical risks and the intensive monitoring required for safe use place it in a more specialized category (Brown & Alper, 2018).

The goal of this chapter is not to offer a technical manual on dosing or contraindications; rather, it is to give the reader a sense of the distinct psychological effects, therapeutic potential, and clinical considerations associated with each medicine. As renowned psychiatrist Dr. Scot Shannon said at a virtual psychedelic conference I attended in 2019, these substances can be thought of as different types of submarines. While all of them are capable of exploring the depths of the mind, each takes the traveler on a different route, at a different speed, and with a different set of lights. Some are gentler and heart-centered. Others are expansive and cosmic. Some allow for emotional processing, while others offer an existential perspective.

DOI: 10.4324/9781003541639-8

What matters most is not which medicine is "best," but rather which is most aligned with the client's needs, goals, readiness, and context. Psychedelic therapy is not a one-size-fits-all approach. This chapter is designed to support therapists in deepening their understanding of each substance's unique properties while beginning to develop the intuitive and clinical judgment required to choose wisely. As a reference for the reader, Table 5.1 offers a quick overview of the core pharmacology and clinical characteristics of each of the five substances covered in this chapter.

Ketamine

Chemistry of Ketamine

Ketamine, a versatile and clinically important compound, is a chiral cyclohexanone derivative with the chemical formula $C_{13}H_{16}ClNO$. It belongs to the class of arylcyclohexylamines, sharing structural similarities with phencyclidine (PCP) and other NMDA receptor antagonists (PubChem, 2025; Kryst et al., 2020). Ketamine was first synthesized in 1962 by researcher Calvin Stevens, who was seeking alternatives to PCP—a highly effective but dangerous anesthetic (Domino, 2010). Although ketamine was found to be one-fourth as potent as PCP, it produced significantly fewer side effects, making it safer to administer (Domino et al., 1965; Kolp et al., 2014).

Beyond its use as an anesthetic, ketamine was later found to have therapeutic potential in treating addiction and mood disorders when used in

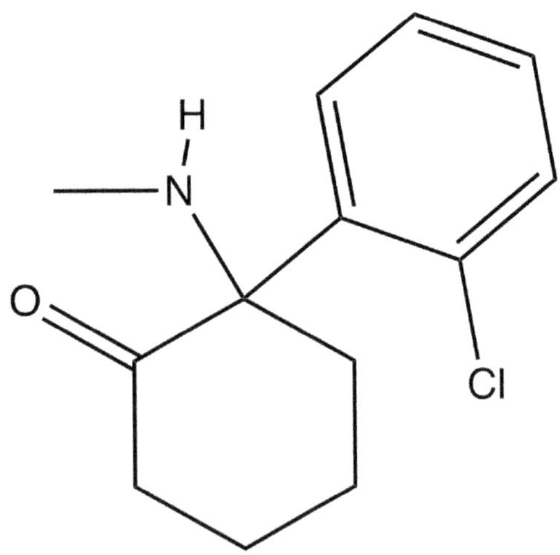

Figure 5.1 Chemical structure of ketamine. Created with ChemDraw by the author.

Table 5.1 Core Pharmacology and Clinical Characteristics of Five Psychedelics

	Ketamine	*Psilocybin*	*MDMA*	*LSD*	*Ayahuasca*
Chemical name	2-(2-Chlorophenyl)-2-(methylamino) cyclohexanone	4-Phosphoryloxy-N, N-dimethyltryptamine	3,4-Methylenedioxymethamphetamine	1-Lysergic acid diethylamide	N,N-dimethyltryptamine (DMT) and harmala alkaloid
Common street names	K Special K Kit kat	Psilocybin mushroom Magic mushroom Shrooms	Molly Ecstasy Love drug	Acid L Lucy	Huasca Caapi Grandma plant
Drug classification	Dissociative	Classic psychedelic	Empathogen	Classic psychedelic	Classic psychedelic
Drug type	Synthetic	Synthetic Psilocybin mushroom	Synthetic	Synthetic	Plant mixture
Clinical trial dose and duration	Intravenous line: 5 mg/kg Intramuscular: 1–2 mg/kg Lozenge: 50–300 mg Duration: 2–4 hours	Low: 10–19 mg Medium: 20–29 mg High: > 30 mg Duration: 3–6 hours	Initial dose: 75–125 mg Supplement dose: 2 hrs. later, 50% of the original dose is given Duration: 4–6 hours	Low: 5, 10, and 20 µg Medium: 200 µg Duration: 8–12 hours	0.36 mg/kg Duration: 4–6 hours
Main mechanism of action	N-Methyl-D-aspartate NMDA receptor antagonist	High affinity agonist at serotonin 2A (5-HT2A) receptors	Binds to and reverses transporter proteins. Increases release of serotonin, norepinephrine, and dopamine	High affinity agonist at serotonin 2a (5-ht2a) receptors	Harmala alkaloids inhibit MAO in the gut allowing DMT to reach brain. Potent Partial agonist at serotonin 2a (5-ht2a) receptors

conjunction with psychotherapy (Dore et al., 2019). Unlike traditional sedatives, ketamine induces a dissociative state marked by feelings of disconnection from the body and environment. Individuals often describe sensations of floating, disembodiment, or even a sense of ego dissolution—feeling as though they are in outer space or without physical form.

Early studies by scientists Guenter Corssen and Edward Domino (1966) revealed that ketamine, rather than inducing sedation, produced a trance-like state resembling catalepsy. This dissociative state is attributed to ketamine's function as an NMDA receptor antagonist, which limits the transfer of electrical signals between neurons in the brain and spinal column. In simpler terms, ketamine blocks incoming sensory signals, disrupting normal processing and amplifying internal experiences (Kolp et al., 2014).

Ketamine is structurally classified as an arylcyclohexylamine and exists as a racemic mixture of two enantiomers: S-ketamine and R-ketamine (Kryst et al., 2020). Over the past five years, research has highlighted the distinct pharmacological properties of these enantiomers. S-ketamine, marketed as Spravato, was approved by the FDA in 2019 for treatment-resistant depression and again in 2025 for major depressive disorder (Johnson & Johnson, 2025; U.S. Food and Drug Administration, 2019). S-ketamine is a more potent NMDA receptor antagonist than R-ketamine and is known for its rapid antidepressant effects. However, emerging research suggests that R-ketamine may provide longer-lasting relief with fewer dissociative side effects, making it a promising candidate for future study.

Importantly, ketamine's therapeutic effects are not limited to NMDA antagonism. Recent studies show that ketamine also activates AMPA receptors, which are responsible for facilitating signal transmission between brain cells (Duman et al., 2019; Zanos & Gould, 2018). This activation contributes to the release of brain-derived neurotrophic factor and triggers the mTOR pathway, a cellular mechanism that supports synaptogenesis—the formation and strengthening of synaptic connections (Duman et al., 2019; Zanos & Gould, 2018). These neurobiological processes are believed to underlie ketamine's rapid and robust antidepressant effects.

Over time, ketamine has been recognized for its wide range of clinical uses, including anesthesia, pain relief, and the prevention of brain damage following epileptic seizures, strokes, head trauma, or heart attacks (Domino, 2010). Most recently, ketamine has gained prominence as a novel treatment for depression (Domino, 2010). Its effectiveness depends partly on its method of administration. Listed from highest to lowest bioavailability, ketamine can be delivered intravenously (100%), intramuscularly (93%), intranasally (8–45%), or orally (17–29%). The intravenous and intramuscular methods are more costly than the intranasal and oral, which tend to be more commonly used in antidepressant treatment protocols (Wesley et al., 2016).

Ketamine's antidepressant potential represents a significant breakthrough in mental health care. By disrupting entrenched neural pathways and fostering new synaptic connections, ketamine provides a powerful means of reshaping mood and thought patterns. The following section explores the growing body of research that supports these clinical applications.

History of Ketamine

In 1965, the first human study on ketamine was conducted by Edward Domino to assess its safety and efficacy as an anesthetic (Domino et al., 1965). The trial took place at a state prison and included 20 male volunteers who received a dose of intravenous ketamine, followed by a second dose at least one week later. During the sessions, researchers tested the volunteers' pain response by applying pressure to their arms or chests with a hemostat. Although the drug proved effective in inducing anesthesia and analgesia, the participants described their experiences as unusual and, at times, frightening. They reported experiences such as a sense of death or the sensation of floating, as if in outer space. Notably, these effects were short-lived, with all volunteers returning to baseline shortly after the drug wore off. Based on these dissociative effects, the researchers concluded that ketamine represented a new category of anesthetic. Accordingly, they introduced the term *dissociative anesthetic* to describe it.

In the early 1970s, the US FDA approved ketamine for use as an anesthetic (Grof, 2016a). Shortly thereafter, the United States military adopted its use for treating wounded soldiers on the battlefield during the Vietnam War, where its reliability and rapid onset made it invaluable for trauma care (Grof, 2016a, 2016b). Since then, ketamine has remained a widely used anesthetic, and its applications have expanded to include pain management, neuroprotection, and, more recently, treatment for depression and addiction.

In recognition of its medical importance, ketamine was added to the World Health Organization's (WHO) Model List of Essential Medicines in 1985 (World Health Organization, 2017). Its inclusion was based on its safety, efficacy, and accessibility—particularly in low-resource settings, where advanced medical infrastructure may be lacking. Unlike many other anesthetics, ketamine does not suppress respiratory function and can be administered without oxygen or ventilators, making it especially useful in field hospital settings, emergency surgeries, and humanitarian crises.

Over the years, ketamine's essential status has been reaffirmed by the WHO, even as some countries have pushed for tighter regulations due to concerns over recreational misuse. In 2015, the WHO issued a strong recommendation against placing ketamine under international control, citing that such restrictions would likely lead to severe global shortages and, therefore, disproportionately affect low- and middle-income countries whose access to anesthesia is already limited (World Health Organization, 2015).

Ketamine Research

In 1971, psychiatrist Salvador Roquet was the first clinician to publish results for the use of Ketamine in psychotherapy (Krippner, 2016; Roquet et al., 1971). Roquet began using several mind-altering substances—specifically LSD, ketamine, psilocybin, and morning glory seeds—in conjunction with psychotherapy to speed up the emotional healing process of his patients. He believed that allowing his patients to regress to prenatal memories and combining disintegration and death[1]—followed by a rebirth—provided patients with the ability to heal deep wounds and traumas (Krippner, 2016).

Roquet guided weekly group therapy sessions with his patients, during which he administered a cocktail of psychedelics (Krippner, 2016). The group then processed the experience together by dancing, crying, and turning to each other for support. During the experience, Roquet moved around the room as an additional form of support for his patients and grouped together people with similar challenges. Roquet claimed that ketamine was especially useful for patients struggling with depression and those who needed to face or resolve conflicting aspects of their personality. He also used ketamine to help his patients alleviate anxiety brought on by difficult journeys with other psychedelics (Dawson et al., 2014). Unfortunately, Roquet did not track or report the specific dosages or substances he used, the type of psychotherapy he applied, or how many patients he treated with this method. Therefore, most of the information available is from colleagues and patients who either took part in or witnessed Roquet's sessions (Krippner, 2016).

Roquet eventually introduced ketamine to Stanislov Grof, a renowned psychiatrist in the United States who was well-known for administering more LSD-assisted therapy sessions (numbered in the thousands) than any other professional in the field. Grof was largely interested in the study of consciousness and believed that psychedelics were an important part of that research. He considered psychedelic medicines to be "nonspecific amplifiers" of the mental processes, which could often lead to useful and original insight (Pollan, 2019). In other words, psychedelics can reveal authentic expressions of the psyche that are ordinarily not available for observation and study (Grof et al., 2008). Grof (2016a) self-experimented with ketamine and reported the following: "I was introduced to the strangest psychoactive substance I have ever experienced in the 50 years of my conscious research. The effect of those compounds are so extraordinary that they stand out even in the group of psychedelics" (p. 73).

Grof (1980) believed that ketamine had the ability to give individuals profound insight into their consciousness, their psyche, and the world around them. Through this substance, he asserted, people can explore their own inner workings and embark on fantastic voyages through other realities, such as extraterrestrial civilizations and parallel universes, the astrophysical worlds, the animal and botanical world, foreign countries, and other historical time periods. Grof shared that in his personal use of ketamine, he experienced profound discoveries and insights. One time, he experienced himself as petroleum, filling enormous cavities in the earth. This generated a deep feeling of evil and facilitated a new ecological awareness of what it would take for life on our planet to survive. On several occasions, he journeyed to foreign countries and connected with the archetypal worlds associated with their cultures, giving him deeper insight into the psyche of their people. Grof (2016a) later explored ketamine's use as an addition to his work with LSD, in hopes that it could help patients more effectively integrate previous LSD sessions.

One person who can be credited with much of the scientific information about ketamine that we have today is John Lilly, a physician and psychoanalyst who self-administered psychedelic substances, specifically ketamine, as a way to fearlessly explore human consciousness. Lilly documented his ketamine use and found a subjective relationship between the level of each dosage and the quality of the journey (Kolp et al., 2014). This was later confirmed by controlled clinical trials that corroborated his findings (Collier, 1972; Khorramzadeh & Lofty, 1973; Kolp et al., 2014). Lilly reported the following experiences and observations about his intramuscular injections: At 25 mg, the ketamine did not produce any visual images; at 30 mg, it produced images only when his eyes were closed; at above 50 mg but below 75 mg, the visual images became stronger; at above 75 mg and below 150 mg, the visual images significantly increased, and dissociation between the mind and body began; at above 150 mg, the mind completely disassociated from the body, and feelings of dissolution of ego were common; above 300 mg, ketamine produced unconsciousness (Metzner, 2016). The study results provided valuable information for mental health professionals wanting to work with ketamine and administer the right dosage to their patients.

Ketamine induces four different non-ordinary states of consciousness that depend on dosage (going from lower to higher milligrams), set (the individual's mindset), and setting (the physical environment where the study took place) (Kolp et al., 2014). The first state is an empathogenic state, which refers to a state of empathy or heart-opening. The second state is an out-of-body experience, which includes a complete sense of separation from one's body—a dissolution of ego. The third state is a near-death experience, which is a departure from one's body, or the loss of identity. The fourth state is an ego-dissolving transcendental experience, which is defined as an ecstatic state in which the boundaries between self and external reality dissolve, facilitating a sense of unity with nature and the universe. Participants in ketamine research have identified near-death experiences and ego-dissolving transcendental experiences as the most meaningful, leading to significant changes such as the resolution of addictions to various substances, the overcoming of considerable life problems, and even spontaneous healing from chronic psychosomatic illnesses (Kolp et al., 2014).

In Iran, psychiatrists Khorramzadeh and Lofty (1973) conducted a study with 100 individuals (61 males and 39 females, ranging in age from 16 to 66) at an inpatient psychiatric university hospital. All of the patients had been diagnosed with various psychiatric illnesses, such as anxiety, OCD, hysteria, depression, conversion reaction, and hypochondriasis. The patients were all given a series of ketamine in three-dose increments between 0.2 mg/kg of their body weight and 1 mg/kg of their body weight. Seventy-four patients experienced intense visionary experiences, and 51 of the 74 patients recalled and worked through painful childhood events.

Khorramzadeh and Lofty's (1973) study became a significant contribution to the body of research on ketamine due to its post-study observations and results. Interviews and observations during the patients' journeys revealed reactions and experiences that were therapeutically beneficial. One participant reported a sense of frustration over never standing up for himself against people he believed to be ill-intentioned: "I always desired to make a nasty remark but dared not." Another participant, who had previously experienced what she described as sensations of physical anxiety, reported feeling the heaviness lift: "The injection took away the heavy discomfort on my chest" (Khorramzadeh & Lofty, 1973, p. 2). These experiences left participants with a valuable understanding.

Khorramzadeh and Lofty's work highlights an important direction for future clinical exploration: identifying which types of internal experiences—whether emotional release, memory retrieval, or symbolic breakthroughs—correlate with longer-term therapeutic outcomes. As psychedelic therapies evolve, it will be essential for psychedelic researchers and clinicians to refine how we track and interpret subjective experiences. The researchers noted minimal complications due to the ketamine; only two patients experienced vomiting, and three experienced nausea.

Six months after the ketamine injections, only nine of the 100 patients reported that they were doing poorly or were not experiencing any symptom relief; the other 91 reported that they were doing quite well (Khorramzadeh & Lofty, 1973). One year after the injections were administered, the researchers were still observing 88 patients, 86 of whom reported significant symptom relief from their respective psychiatric illnesses. Based on these results, Khorramzadeh and Lofty (1973) concluded that ketamine is a safe and effective treatment for various psychiatric illnesses. There were, however, several important limitations to the study. Specifically, there was no control group, and the researchers did not provide a clear explanation of any other treatment form that took place, such as psychotherapy, which is a common component of any psychedelic therapeutic research.

Evgeny Krupitsky, a Russian psychiatrist and neurologist, conducted a 10-year clinical study using ketamine as a treatment for addiction to alcohol and heroin. Krupitsky and Grinenko (1997) hypothesized that administering ketamine in conjunction with psychotherapy would be a beneficial approach to the treatment of addiction. Ketamine treatment was especially powerful in Russia, where there was no psychedelic revolution in the 1960s like the one that took place in the United States. At the time of the study, psychedelic use—both medical and recreational—was virtually nonexistent in Russia. Therefore, ketamine appeared particularly unusual and powerful to those interested in studying it. Krupitsky's study included 211 male participants; 111 were randomly assigned to a ketamine psychedelic therapy group, and the other 100 were assigned to a control group, which included a conventional treatment approach.

The treatment in this study was divided into three stages. In the first stage, preparation, participants attended psychotherapy sessions designed to establish trust and orient them to the process. This phase included a detailed explanation of what they could expect during the ketamine experience. The second stage involved the ketamine administration session itself, in which the psychedelic compound was administered under clinical supervision. Finally, participants went through an integration stage, during which they reflected on their experiences and processed the material that had surfaced, often through guided therapeutic conversations aimed at fostering insight and emotional coherence.

The preparation stage began with a set of psychotherapy sessions that explored the participants' relationship to alcohol and the negative effects of alcohol abuse versus the positive effects of abstaining from alcohol consumption (Krupitsky & Grinenko, 1997). During the preparation stage, the participants were briefed on what they could expect from an altered state of consciousness under the influence of ketamine. They also received information about how that special state could resolve their dependence on alcohol.

The second stage was the ketamine administration session itself, which lasted approximately 45 minutes (Krupitsky & Grinenko, 1997). During this stage, doctors administered an intravenous injection of ketamine (2–3 mg/kg) to the participants in the experimental group, in the presence of a psychotherapist. During the peak of the ketamine experience, the researchers emphasized the positive values of a sober lifestyle. They then gave the participants an opportunity to smell alcohol, the idea being that if the participants were to come close to drinking again, the smell of alcohol would be quickly associated with the insight they gained during their ketamine journey.

In the third stage, the psychotherapist facilitated a group therapy session with the participants who had taken part in the ketamine journey the previous day (Krupitsky & Grinenko, 1997). The discussion in this session was organized around the participants' psychedelic experiences, the problems they experienced in the past, and their hopes for the future. In hopes of making the information more memorable and impactful, as well as diminishing the possibility of future alcohol cravings, the researchers encouraged participants to expand upon and highlight the insights they received during the ketamine treatment.

Krupitsky and Grinenko's (1997) study produced significant findings. After one year, 73 of the 111 patients were abstinent from alcohol, compared to only 24 of the 100 participants in the control group. The researchers found that their patients had become less anxious and depressed, were more responsible and emotionally mature, had increased ego strength, and experienced positive changes in self-concept. These findings helped them conclude that ketamine therapy was a safe and effective form of treatment. Moving forward, this structured three-phase model—preparation, dosing, and integration—offers a valuable framework for therapists seeking to build clinical protocols that are both scalable and deeply therapeutic. I hope to see more research exploring how this model can be adapted across diverse populations and therapeutic contexts.

Around the time that Krupitsky's findings were published, the National Institute of Mental Health (NIMH) began awarding grants for studies on the potential efficacy of low doses of ketamine for individuals struggling with treatment-resistant depression, and to find out whether the psychedelic effect of the drug could be excluded. Although the NIMH's goal of excluding a psychedelic effect failed, ketamine proved to be a promising and fast-acting form of treatment for depression. The term "ketamine afterglow" is commonly used among experts to describe the way patients appear soon after treatment. The term was first coined by Pahnke et al. (1970a) to describe the post-hallucinogenic state they observed in patients after several days or weeks of ketamine use. They described the phenomenon this way: "Mood is elevated and energetic; there is a relative freedom from concerns of the past and from guilt and anxiety, and the disposition and capacity to enter into close interpersonal relationships it enhances" (p. 1860). Those same studies have demonstrated that ketamine can be used effectively for the treatment of mental health disorders such as depression. By contrast, drugs such as selective serotonin reuptake inhibitors (SSRIs) and serotonin and norepinephrine reuptake inhibitors (SNRIs) have shown limited results for decades (Wesley et al., 2016).

The results of three meta-analyses showed that ketamine had a rapid antidepressant and anti-suicidal effect in most patients diagnosed with major depressive disorder and bipolar disorder (Caddy et al., 2014; Fond et al., 2014; McGirr et al., 2015). As Krupitsky did in his study, McGirr et al. (2015) included individuals diagnosed with major depression and bipolar disorder. They conducted eight studies with a total of 183 patients. Among them, 34 were diagnosed with bipolar disorder and 149 were diagnosed with major depression. The study sought to assess the efficacy of ketamine for the treatment of depressive episodes, and the findings suggested that it was, in fact, an effective intervention.

McGirr et al. (2015) evaluated participants at post-treatment increments of 24 hours, three days, and seven days post-treatment. They concluded that ketamine is effective in the rapid treatment of unipolar and bipolar depression, suggesting that additional research should be conducted to explore the best dosing schedules, administration form (e.g., intravenous or oral), and potential efficacy of glutamatergic agents. In their studies, Caddy et al. (2014) and Fond et al. (2014) combined ketamine treatment with electroconvulsive therapy (ECT). Both found that ketamine infusions resulted in a rapid antidepressant effect when administered alone or in combination with ECT up to three days after treatment.

One common limitation in each of the three studies was that for most participants—except for a small percentage who sustained the benefits of treatment in the months following the study—the response to the ketamine treatment was short-lived, and improvements diminished within a few days to a few weeks of the treatment (Caddy et al., 2014; Fond et al., 2014; McGirr et al., 2015). This important finding can help practitioners working with ketamine to set expectations for their patients regarding the short-term nature of its effects. It can also help encourage an emphasis on the creation of long-term goals in the treatment planning stage.

In Brazil, Lara et al. (2013) aimed to extend ketamine's anti-depressive properties by putting their patients on a microdosing regimen, which consisted of an extremely low dose of sublingual ketamine for a specified time period. They conducted their study in a clinical setting with patients who were diagnosed with major depression (single episode or recurring) or bipolar disorder and were currently experiencing a depressive episode. Although the study included a small sample of 26 individuals in outpatient treatment, the results were significant. Each patient was put on a regimen of 10 mg of sublingual ketamine every two to three days. The researchers studied patients for anywhere from 30 days to 66 months[2], depending on each patient. Twenty of the patients (77%) reported rapid, clear, and sustained effects, such as improved mood level and stability, improved cognition, and improved sleep throughout the study. Additionally, there were no significant side effects reported other than mild lightheadedness shortly after the ingestion of the ketamine.

Overall, ketamine research has established that this substance is a powerful, fast-acting antidepressant and effective addiction treatment, with effects that can be felt in the short-term and, for some, sustained over time. The individuals who show the most significant effects are those for whom traditional pharmaceuticals have failed—people carrying immense, treatment-resistant suffering. For them and for others navigating depressive symptoms, ketamine offers immediate relief and a new path forward.

Currently, ketamine remains the only legally available psychedelic treatment in the United States and is increasingly being used by mental health practitioners nationwide. But the story is still unfolding. Emerging research continues to explore ketamine's broader potential—not only for trauma and end-of-life anxiety but also for existential and spiritual distress. As the field matures, many are now asking *what* ketamine heals, and *how* it can be integrated into long-term frameworks that address the full spectrum of the human experience—body, mind, and soul.

Clinical Considerations

Ketamine remains the most accessible psychedelic currently available to licensed mental health professionals in the United States and many other countries. It is commonly used in the treatment of severe depression, suicidality, PTSD, and anxiety, particularly in cases where traditional therapies have failed. Ketamine may also be beneficial for clients who are psychologically overwhelmed and need a short-term reset before beginning deeper therapeutic work.

This medicine is often appropriate for clients who are not ready for long or emotionally intense psychedelic journeys. The relatively short duration of its effect, usually less than 90 minutes, makes it an ideal entry point for cautious clients or those with demanding schedules. Ketamine can be delivered in a variety of ways: intravenous, intramuscular, intranasal spray, or sublingual lozenge, each offering different levels of accessibility and intensity.

At the same time, ketamine's dissociative effects can present challenges. Some clients may find the experience confusing or disorienting, especially if it is not well-framed or supported. Without strong preparation and intentional integration, its rapid effects may offer only temporary relief. Therapists need to reinforce meaning-making and establish a supportive container before and after the dosing experience. Integration practices such as guided journaling, body-based processing, or post-session dialogue can help clients digest insights and connect them to their daily lives.

It is also important to stay aware of who ketamine may not be suitable for. Individuals with a personal or family history of psychosis, unmanaged trauma, or unstable dissociation may be at higher risk and require a more cautious approach. Tracking subtle cues, like rapid emotional shifts or confusion around relational boundaries, can help determine whether a client is ready.

Used with intention, humility, and presence, ketamine can serve as a powerful bridge. For some, it provides immediate relief and the first steps toward change. For others, it opens the door to deeper work, allowing them to approach longer sessions or more emotionally demanding psychedelics with greater trust and stability. Either way, the medicine is only part of the story. The depth of the therapeutic process and the relationship that holds it remain central to its impact.

Psilocybin

Chemistry of Psilocybin

Psilocybin is a naturally occurring psychedelic compound found in many species of mushrooms across the globe. It was first isolated in 1957 by Swiss chemist Albert Hofmann, who is best known for discovering LSD. Psilocybin is classified as a serotonergic psychedelic, meaning it works primarily by activating serotonin 2A receptors (5-HT2AR) in the brain (Vollenweider et al., 1998). These receptors are involved in perception, mood, and cognition, and their stimulation is believed to be responsible for the

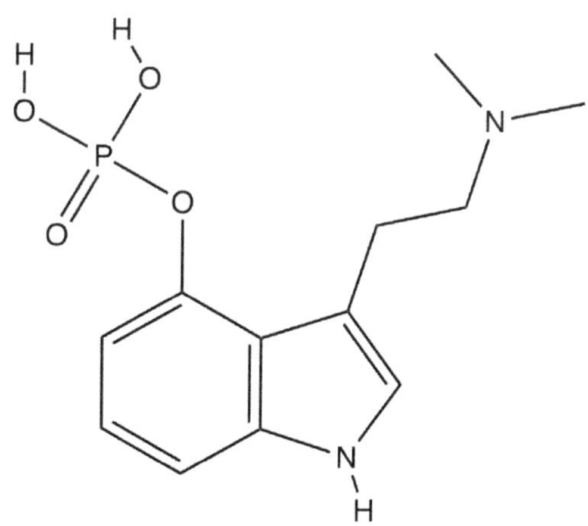

Figure 5.2 Chemical structure of psilocybin. Created with ChemDraw by the author.

hallucinogenic and consciousness-altering effects of psilocybin. Interestingly, this same receptor activity can mirror some of the symptoms observed in psychotic states, including changes in sensory processing and working memory.

One of the key effects of psilocybin is the disruption of normal filtering between the thalamus and cortex, the brain regions responsible for regulating sensory information (Passie et al., 2002). With these filters loosened, a broader range of internal and external stimuli reaches conscious awareness, leading to the profound perceptual shifts reported during psychedelic experiences. Once psilocybin is ingested, approximately half of it is absorbed into the body and quickly metabolized by the liver into psilocin, the active compound responsible for the psychoactive effects (Passie et al., 2002). Psilocin then spreads throughout the body and begins to influence the brain's chemistry and perception.

Understanding dosage is crucial when working with psilocybin. Unlike with other medications, dosing is not strongly correlated with body weight (Garcia-Romeu et al., 2021). A moderate psychedelic experience typically begins with around 20 mg of psilocybin, which is equivalent to roughly 3 g of dried mushrooms. At this dose, individuals often retain awareness of their surroundings but may experience visual distortions, shifts in thought patterns, and a heightened emotional state. A higher dose—around 30 mg or 5 g—can intensify these effects significantly and may lead to a temporary dissolution of the ego or loss of connection with ordinary reality.

Unlike many other substances, psilocybin does not cause physical dependence, even with repeated use (Passie et al., 2002). This makes it particularly promising in the treatment of addiction. Though tolerance can quickly develop over periods of repeated use, psilocybin itself is non-addictive (Carhart-Harris et al., 2016; Griffiths et al., 2016), and early studies have shown promising results in helping individuals struggling with substance use disorders (de Veen et al., 2017).

History of Psilocybin

Psilocybin-containing mushrooms have been used for centuries as tools for healing and spiritual exploration. Across various indigenous cultures, they served as remedies for physical and emotional ailments, as well as gateways to mystical states that offered a deeper understanding of the self and the universe. The Mazatec people of Mexico, for example, have long used *Psilocybe mexicana* in shamanic ceremonies to facilitate healing and divination. Similar ceremonial practices have been found across Mesoamerican cultures, including the Aztecs, who referred to psilocybin mushrooms as *teonanácatl*—translated as "flesh of the gods" (Carod-Artal, 2015; Fagetti & Mercadillo, 2022).

In the Western world, the cultural acceptance and integration of psilocybin took a significant turn in the 1960s, when a group of Harvard psychologists—Drs. Timothy Leary, Ralph Metzner, and Richard Alpert (later known as Ram Dass)—began exploring its effects on human consciousness. Through the Harvard Psilocybin Project, these pioneering researchers administered the substance to student volunteers and documented the results. In one study of 167 participants, they collected data through post-experience questionnaires, audio recordings, written reflections, and direct observation. Seventy-three percent of the participants described the experience as pleasurable, and 95% reported that it had a lasting, life-changing impact (Leary & Penner, 2014). However, the project's credibility suffered due to the team's failure to adhere to standard research protocols, eventually leading to their dismissal from Harvard (Pollan, 2019).

Despite the controversy, their work helped spark broader interest in psychedelics, including psilocybin, within both scientific and spiritual communities. Following its isolation and synthesis by Albert Hofmann in 1958, psilocybin began to gain traction as a potential treatment for mood disorders and existential distress, particularly among terminally ill patients. But as recreational use became more widespread and psilocybin became associated with the counterculture movement, political backlash followed. In the 1970s, it was classified as a Schedule I substance, halting clinical research for decades (Woźniak et al., 2023).

Even with these legal barriers, interest in psilocybin never disappeared. Underground therapists and spiritual practitioners continued to explore its healing potential outside of formal research settings. In recent years, with the revival of psychedelic science, psilocybin has regained its footing in both research and public discourse. Studies now point to its ability to produce immediate and sustained improvements in depression, anxiety, PTSD, and other psychiatric conditions. As clinical trials expand and regulations begin to shift, psilocybin is emerging once again as a powerful therapeutic ally (Strumila et al., 2021).

Psilocybin Research

Contemporary research on psilocybin has demonstrated its potential for treating a range of psychiatric conditions, including depression, anxiety, OCD, and substance use disorders. Clinical trials have shown that a single supported therapeutic dose of psilocybin can produce significant and lasting reductions in depressive symptoms, with some studies reporting sustained improvements for up to six months post-treatment (Back et al., 2024). The mechanism by which psilocybin exerts its therapeutic effects is believed to involve the modulation of neural plasticity and functional connectivity. Neuroimaging studies indicate that psilocybin reduces activity in the default mode network (DMN), a brain network associated with self-referential thinking and rumination, which is often hyperactive in individuals with depression. This disruption allows for increased cognitive flexibility and the emergence of novel perspectives, facilitating profound psychological insight and emotional breakthroughs (Woźniak et al., 2023).

Recently, psilocybin has even been investigated for its potential role in mitigating occupational burnout, particularly among frontline healthcare workers. A study involving Emergency Medical Service Workers found that a single therapeutic dose of psilocybin mushrooms led to significant improvements in burnout measures, with these benefits persisting for at least two months (Ferreira et al., 2024). Participants in the study attributed their improved well-being to the emotional breakthroughs and psychological insights they experienced during their psychedelic sessions.

Psilocybin has earned the designation of "breakthrough therapy" for treatment-resistant depression by the US FDA. This designation facilitates expedited research and regulatory review, paving the way for potential approval as a prescription drug in the coming years (FDA, 2023).

Researchers continue to conduct clinical trials to explore psilocybin's efficacy across various psychiatric and neurological disorders. Despite ongoing regulatory challenges affecting the accessibility of psilocybin and the standardization of treatment protocols, the accumulating evidence suggests that psilocybin may soon emerge as a mainstream therapeutic tool with applications far beyond its traditional and historical use (Strumila et al., 2021). At the time of this writing, there are over 150 active clinical trials involving psilocybin being conducted in the United States, at institutions including Johns Hopkins and the University of California.

Although contemporary research has significantly advanced the scientific understanding of psilocybin's therapeutic potential, the investigation of this substance is not a recent phenomenon. The exploration of psychedelics in clinical and academic settings dates back to the mid-20th century, when early researchers sought to understand psilocybin's effects on consciousness, mental health, and behavior. These early studies were often fraught with methodological limitations, ethical concerns, and political controversy. But despite these challenges, they laid the groundwork for modern psychedelic science, and they continue to influence contemporary research. The following section examines some of the most notable early psilocybin studies, their findings, and the subsequent critiques that shaped the trajectory of psychedelic research.

Between 1961 and 1963, Timothy Leary led an experiment with 32 male individuals at a maximum-security prison (Leary & Penner, 2014). He predicted that through a combination of psilocybin and psychotherapy, inmates would gain insights that might lead them to understand themselves differently, change their behavior, and ultimately lower the probability of recidivism. The inmates in the study participated in the following interventions:

- three orientation sessions
- a guided psilocybin session
- three more post-integration sessions
- a second psilocybin session
- additional post-integration sessions

The pre- and post-testing measures demonstrated marked changes in hostility, cynicism, and depression. Overall, the results of the study indicated that the inmates experienced an increase in optimism, tolerance, and sociability. Additionally, the researchers reported that 10 months after the inmates' release, the recidivism rate for those who received psilocybin was only 25%, compared to a rate of 80% among those in the control group (Leary & Penner, 2014; Pollan, 2019).

Like those of the Harvard Psilocybin Project, the results of the inmate study were quickly discredited. Leary's colleagues and psychedelic researchers, such as Harvard department chair David McClelland, critiqued his methodological shortcomings in recording and analyzing the data, going so far as to say that his work was "the sort of research that made scientists wince" (Pollan, 2019, p. 191).

Leary's most scientifically credible study was a collaboration with one of his students at Harvard, Walter Pahnke. At the time, Pahnke was a Ph.D. student in Harvard's Divinity School who was working on a thesis[3] about the potential for psychedelic drugs and, more specifically, psilocybin, to facilitate mystical experiences. Pahnke believed that such mystical experiences would generate positive changes in individuals' attitudes and behaviors, thereby substantially improving their quality of life (Leary & Penner, 2014).

Pahnke conducted a double-blind study with 20 White, Protestant male divinity students from Harvard, using Boston University's Marsh Chapel as the research setting. The volunteers were divided into five groups. Each group was composed of psilocybin and placebo participants, as well as two research assistants who provided emotional support to the participants[4] (Leary & Penner, 2014). Ten of the participants received psilocybin, and the other 10 received a Niacin placebo, which causes a flushing reaction in the body. After experiencing the effects of either the psilocybin or the placebo, participants filled out a post-questionnaire designed to help the researchers determine whether the psilocybin group "had truly experienced a classical mystical experience" (Leary & Penner, 2014, p. 187).

Eight of the 10 participants who took the psilocybin pill reported experiencing a mystical consciousness, compared to only one participant in the control group (Pollan, 2019). The eight individuals who experienced a mystical journey reported greater emotional sensitivity, a deeper purpose of life, and a complete reduction in anxieties about death and guilt. Despite its intriguing results, the study drew criticism from religious leaders, who were skeptical of what the team defined as a mystical experience—something they deemed tough to define. Religious leaders were also alarmed by the idea that divine inspiration came as the result of drug stimulation and associated changes in brain chemistry (Leary & Penner, 2014).

Thirty-seven years later, researcher Rick Doblin (1998), who founded MAPS, reconstructed Leary's original studies and conducted follow-up interviews with some of the original participants. One of the experiments Doblin (1998) questioned was Leary's Concord Prison Experiment. In an effort to re-analyze the original data, Doblin accessed the criminal justice system's records of Leary's participants and interviewed those who were willing to participate again. Doblin found that Leary's claim of a 23% recidivism rate was based on a misleading use of the data and, therefore, inaccurate. Leary captured the recidivism rate of participants in the experimental group after they had been out of jail for 10 months and compared it to a base-rate group, who had been out of prison for an average of 30 months. Leary did not specify this fact in his findings. When Doblin compared identical 10-month post-release periods, the recidivism rate for the control group was 34.3% compared to 32% for the experimental group. This 2.3% reduction does not constitute a statistically significant difference.

Doblin (1991) also conducted a follow-up study of Pahnke's famous Good Friday Experiment with 16 of the participants from the original 1960s study. This time, the results were consistent with Pahnke's original findings. The participants still claimed to have vivid memories of their experience and shared how impactful it was for them, even 25 years later. They unanimously described their Good Friday psilocybin experience as one of the most impactful moments of their spiritual life, and many reported an enhanced appreciation of life and of nature. For example, Doblin (1991) recorded the following account from one of the participants:

> Something extraordinary had taken place which had never taken place before. All of sudden I felt sort of drawn out into infinity and all of sudden I had lost touch with my mind. I felt I was caught up in a vastness of creation . . . the main thing about it was a sense of timeless. I got the impression, sensation . . . of what people are in their essence, that somehow, they continue to live.
>
> (p. 16)

It is important to add that eight of the 10 participants spoke about moments of intense psychic struggle, during which they feared they were going crazy, experiencing death, or becoming too weak for the ordeal they were going through. Unfortunately, these types of challenging moments were underreported in Pahnke's original thesis. According to accounts from Doblin's study, one of the participants became overwhelmed and needed to be sedated. This participant was deeply moved by the sermon that emphasized the obligation of all Christians to tell people that there was a man on the cross. The participant attempted to go outside and preach, but was tranquilized with a Thorazine[5] injection and remained calm for the rest of the experiment (Doblin, 1991). Overall, the study supported Pahnke's original findings and hypothesis that psychedelic drugs can help facilitate a mystical experience when used by religiously inclined people in a religious setting. However, not all studies need to be done in a religious setting.

Another use of psilocybin is to help cancer patients minimize the increased feelings of anxiety and depression brought on by their diagnosis. Psilocybin has been shown to be a powerful treatment in decreasing both depression and anxiety, allowing users to return to their pre-diagnosis daily routines (Griffiths et al., 2016). Anxiety and depression, or a combination of both, tend to reduce the quality of life of individuals with cancer, often causing them to decrease their treatment adherence, endure prolonged hospitalizations, and experience an increase in thoughts of suicide.

Stephen Ross, a professor from New York University, and Roland Griffiths, the director of the Center for Psychedelic and Conscious Research at Johns Hopkins University, conducted two of the largest studies on psilocybin use among cancer patients (Griffiths et al., 2016; Ross et al., 2016). Both studies included a sample of 80 patients with life-threatening cancers to demonstrate how effective psilocybin is at treating the debilitating symptoms of anxiety and depression for some individuals after being diagnosed with cancer. Prior to taking part in the study, a large percentage of the participating cancer patients (30–40%) reported cancer-related psychological distress, such as anxiety and depression, due to their diagnosis (Mitchell et al., 2011). These symptoms were associated with reduced quality of life, decreased treatment adherence, and prolonged hospitalization (Arrieta et al., 2013).

Ross et al. (2016) conducted a blind, controlled, crossover study with 29 participants. The researchers gave the experimental group 0.3 mg of psilocybin and the control group a Niacin placebo. Seven weeks after the first dose, they administered a second dose of psilocybin to the experimental group. The researchers found that a single dose of psilocybin, in combination with psychotherapy, produced a rapid and robust reduction in anxiety and depression for patients with life-threatening cancer. They followed up with their participants eight months after the second dose and found that 80% of those who received the psilocybin were continuing to experience the benefits.

In their study, Griffiths et al. (2016) administered a single, high dose of psilocybin in combination with psychotherapy to 51 participants who were diagnosed with both life-threatening cancer and symptoms of anxiety and/or depression. The participants were divided into two groups, with the experimental group receiving a high dose of psilocybin (22 mg or 30 mg/70 kg) and the control group receiving a low dose of psilocybin (so low that it operated as a placebo). Five weeks later, the control group received the high dose of psilocybin, while the experimental group received the placebo-level dose of psilocybin. A statistically significant 83% of the participants reported a significant decrease in anxiety and depression as long as six months after the study. Additionally, 80% of participants reported an increase in their well-being and life satisfaction, even those with terminal diagnoses. Single supported therapeutic doses of psilocybin have been shown to drastically reduce symptoms of mental health conditions (Strumila et al., 2021).

In both studies, the researchers reported that none of the participants experienced serious negative side effects associated with the administration of psilocybin. The most common side effects reported during the session were headaches, nausea, transient anxiety, and transient psychotic-like symptoms.[6] For example, one participant was observed having paranoid ideation, and another was observed having thought disorders (Griffiths et al., 2016; Ross et al., 2016). All side effects fully resolved by the end of the session (Griffiths et al., 2016; Ross et al., 2016), with the exception of a moderate headache reported by two of the participants the day after the session (Griffiths et al., 2016).

The findings of Griffiths et al.'s (2016) study further support Ross et al.'s results (2016), suggesting that the administration of a high dose of psilocybin in a therapeutic setting offers significant benefits for individuals diagnosed with a life-threatening cancer diagnosis and struggling with depression and anxiety. The researchers conducted a five-week follow-up using two clinician-rated measures (GRID-HAMD and HAM-A) and found that 78% of participants showed symptom remission for depression and 83% for anxiety. At the time of their 6-month follow-up, the participants' rates of symptom remission were 65% for depression and 57% for anxiety (Griffiths et al., 2016). Among the participants in both studies, those who reported profound mystical experiences showed improved attitudes toward their existential fears of death. Participants reported that their fear of death had diminished after the study. Psilocybin experiences were often reported to be spiritual, which is consistent with the results of previous studies conducted with healthy volunteers (Doblin, 1991; Griffiths et al., 2006, 2008, 2011, 2016; Pahnke, 1963).

Carhart-Harris et al. (2016) expanded on the use of psilocybin as a treatment for depression by studying a sample of 19 participants (5 females and

14 males) with treatment-resistant depression. The participants in the study had all been diagnosed with severe, unipolar, treatment-resistant major depression. The researchers administered two oral doses of psilocybin (10 mg and 25 mg) to the participants seven days apart. They provided psychological support before, during, and after each of the psilocybin treatments (one given pre-treatment, and two given during post-treatment integration sessions).

After receiving each dose of psilocybin, the participants filled out an extensive Altered State of Consciousness questionnaire (Carhart-Harris et al., 2016). They also completed the Quick Inventory of Depressive Symptomology (QIDS-SR16) at the following time intervals: week 1, week 2, week 3, week 5, three months, and six months. Despite the study's limitations (e.g., small sample size made up of mostly males, and no control conditions), the results were promising. All 19 participants in the experimental group showed a significant decrease in depressive symptoms and suicidality on each of the follow-up inventories. At the six-month follow-up, only 3 of the 19 participants reported a relapse in depressive symptoms.

Back et al. (2024) conducted a landmark investigation into the therapeutic potential of psilocybin for frontline healthcare workers experiencing psychological distress induced by the COVID-19 pandemic. The study, which was a double-blind, randomized clinical trial conducted between February 2022 and December 2022, was aimed at evaluating psilocybin's efficacy in treating physicians, advanced practice practitioners, and nurses who developed moderate to severe depression as a result of their experiences during the pandemic. Unlike prior studies that focused on treatment-resistant depression or end-of-life anxiety, this study specifically targeted a cohort of individuals with no documented history of psychiatric conditions before the pandemic, offering a unique perspective on psilocybin's role in addressing acute, occupation-related mental health crises.

The trial enrolled 30 clinicians who had worked on the frontline for at least one month during the pandemic and who met criteria for moderate to severe depression, based on the Montgomery-Åsberg Depression Rating Scale (MADRS) (Back et al., 2024). To qualify for inclusion in the study, participants were required to have experienced persistent symptoms for at least six months, despite therapeutic interventions such as antidepressants or counseling. To control for confounding variables, individuals with pre-pandemic mental health diagnoses, substance use disorders, or family histories of schizophrenia or bipolar disorder were excluded. Participants were randomly assigned to one of two groups: the psilocybin group, which received a 25 mg dose of psilocybin, and the control group, which received 100 mg of niacin as an active placebo. The intervention followed a structured protocol consisting of two preparatory sessions, one medication session, and three integration visits. The preparation sessions allowed facilitators to guide participants in setting intentions, addressing pandemic-related trauma, and preparing for the psychedelic experience. The medication session was conducted in a controlled environment with two trained facilitators per participant, utilizing music and sensory deprivation techniques to enhance introspection. The integration sessions focused on helping participants process their experiences and apply insights to their professional and personal lives.

The primary outcome measure was the change in MADRS scores, from baseline to day 28 (Back et al., 2024). The results demonstrated a statistically significant reduction in depression symptoms among participants in the psilocybin group, whose MADRS scores decreased by an average of 21.33. The scores for those in the control group reduced by 9.33 points. The difference between these scores points to the strong antidepressant effect of psilocybin. Participants in the psilocybin group also showed greater reductions in burnout symptoms—as measured by the Stanford Professional Fulfillment Index (SPFI)—as well as PTSD symptoms—as measured by the PTSD Checklist for DSM-5 (PCL-5). Although the differences between treatment groups on these secondary measures did not reach statistical significance, they suggest a meaningful trend that warrants further investigation with larger sample sizes.

Back et al.'s (2024) study builds upon prior research demonstrating psilocybin's ability to modulate DMN activity, which is associated with ruminative thought patterns common in depression. Psilocybin's affinity for 5-HT2A receptors is believed to facilitate neuroplasticity, potentially allowing individuals to process and integrate traumatic experiences more effectively. The structured integration sessions in this study were pivotal in helping participants derive long-term benefits from their experiences, reinforcing the importance of psychotherapy alongside pharmacological intervention. Participants' qualitative feedback supported these findings, with many participants describing profound emotional breakthroughs and enhanced cognitive flexibility. Several participants reported that they were able to let go of pandemic-related guilt, reconnect with the reasons they entered their profession, and adopt a healthier perspective on their work-life balance. One participant reported, "I was shown my tendency to be a superhero. . . .[During my trip I received] messaging that 'It's not about you'—that was done with grace, love, and accountability" (Back et al., 2024, p. 8). Another participant shared, "I'm reaching out and leaning on others . . . and trusting that the people around me can support me. I don't have to carry it all by myself" (Back et al., 2024, p. 8). Describing the fundamental shift in perception they experienced through their psilocybin journey, another participant shared, "I'm learning to just embrace dystopia . . . you have to adapt" (Back et al., 2024, p. 8).

The implications of this study extend beyond individual treatment outcomes, raising important questions about the role of psychedelic-assisted therapy in addressing occupational burnout and moral injury among healthcare professionals. The COVID-19 pandemic exacerbated preexisting issues within healthcare systems, leaving many clinicians grappling with systemic failures, unrealistic workloads, and emotional exhaustion. Back et al.'s (2024) study suggests that psilocybin-assisted therapy could serve as a novel intervention for alleviating work-related psychological distress in medical professionals. If further studies corroborate these findings, psilocybin could become an essential tool for supporting clinicians' mental health, potentially reducing burnout-related attrition from the medical field.

The studies I've reviewed here point to psilocybin's potential as a rapid-acting, highly effective antidepressant, with additional benefits for healthcare professionals experiencing burnout and symptoms of PTSD. As interest in psychedelic medicine continues to expand, future research should focus on longitudinal outcomes, optimal treatment protocols, and broader systemic integration of psychedelic-assisted therapy into clinical practice. Given the severity of clinician burnout and the ongoing mental health crisis within healthcare professions, psilocybin may soon emerge as a transformative intervention for preserving the well-being of those dedicated to caring for others.

Terrance K. McKenna (1992), an American ethnobotanist mostly known for his advocacy of psychedelic plant use and mysticism, developed the stoned-ape theory, which aligns with Carhart-Harris's theory of neuroplasticity and draws a connection between psilocybin and human evolution. In *Food of the Gods*, McKenna stated that psilocybin can cause neuroplasticity in the brain, resulting in an increase of neurons and neuron connections. He asserted that the use of psilocybin is ultimately what led humans to be the first primate species to create a complex form of language and way of thinking. His main argument is that in a span of under three million years, humans are the only primates to show enormous changes in brain size and behavior. These changes have resulted in a cognitive evolution for mankind. According to McKenna, food scarcity led primates to eat small mushrooms containing psilocybin, which enabled them to self-explore and reach higher forms of consciousness.

Although he is more of a self-taught guru than an academic researcher, Paul Stamets is one of the leading experts on psilocybin and a central figure in the advancement of understanding about psilocybin's therapeutic benefits. Stamets, an American mycologist, has written and spoken extensively about the importance of mushrooms for the world and its population. Stamets is also credited with discovering four new species of mushroom, including *Psilocybe cyanofibrillosa* and *Psilocybe azurescens* (Stamets, 2020).

Stamets believes that everything is interconnected, and that fungi are the reason this is possible. According to Stamets (2005), the survival of our ecosystem depends on mycelial networks—the vast, interconnected network of fungal threads that live underground. He asserted that mushrooms have a special kind of intelligence that offer valuable information about humanity, the human psyche, and—most importantly—the web of nature (Pollan, 2019). As he puts it:

> I see the mycelium as the Earth's natural Internet, a consciousness with which we might be able to communicate. Through cross-species interfacing, we may one day exchange information with these sentient cellular networks. Because these externalized neurological nets sense any impression upon them, from footsteps to falling tree branches, they could relay enormous amounts of data regarding the movements of all organisms through the landscape.
>
> (Stamets, 2005, p. 31)

Stamets credits his devotion to mushrooms, his shift in worldview, and the freedom he gained from a lifelong stutter to his first psilocybin experience at age 19. He believes humanity's survival depends on recognizing that we are not separate from our environment or from each other, and that what we call individuality is merely a construct of the mind. Mushrooms, Stamets asserts, can teach us about the deep interconnectedness of all life and the molecular matrix we share (Pollan, 2019). Healing, then, unfolds not only within the individual but within the larger system that contains them.

Psilocybin invites a reorganization of the psyche that feels both ancient and entirely new. It loosens rigid mental patterns, awakens insight, and restores a sense of connection, offering profound therapeutic potential for those struggling with depression, anxiety, trauma, and existential distress. But its impact reaches beyond symptom relief. Psilocybin becomes a mirror, revealing what needs to be healed and what has always been whole. It invites us to remember the truth of who we are.

Clinical Considerations

Psilocybin is one of the most researched and therapeutically promising psychedelic compounds. Legal access is expanding through state-regulated programs in places like Oregon and Colorado, as well as international retreats. It is particularly well-suited for individuals struggling with depression, existential anxiety, obsessive thought patterns, or those facing major life transitions, end-of-life concerns, or spiritual disconnection. Its ability to loosen rigid mental frameworks and promote insight makes it valuable for clients who feel emotionally or cognitively stuck.

Psilocybin sessions usually last between four and six hours. The experience tends to be more immersive and emotionally intense than ketamine, often with profound symbolic and mystical elements. For this reason, it may not be ideal for clients with high levels of psychological fragility, unresolved trauma, or a personal or family history of psychosis. Careful screening and thorough preparation are essential.

Because psilocybin does not guide—it reveals—it can bring to the surface complex emotional material such as grief, fear, longing, or wonder. These moments can offer deep healing, but only when held with spaciousness and trust. Therapists should prepare clients for this possibility and remain grounded and attuned throughout the process.

Integration is crucial. Clients benefit from having tools to make sense of what was uncovered, whether through journaling, art, nature, breathwork, or continued therapeutic dialogue. A strong relational container helps transform insights into lasting change.

Psilocybin invites both therapist and client into the unknown. When held with presence and care, it becomes a mirror—revealing not only what needs to be healed, but also what has always been whole.

MDMA

Chemistry of MDMA

In 1912, the pharmaceutical company Merck first synthesized the psychoactive compound

3,4-Methylenedioxymethamphetamine (MDMA). Chemically classified as a phenethylamine, MDMA stimulates the release of key neurotransmitters in the brain—primarily serotonin, but also dopamine and norepinephrine. It not only promotes the release of these chemicals but also blocks their reuptake, prolonging their effects in the brain and producing a powerful mood-elevating and empathogenic response (Shulgin, 1986).

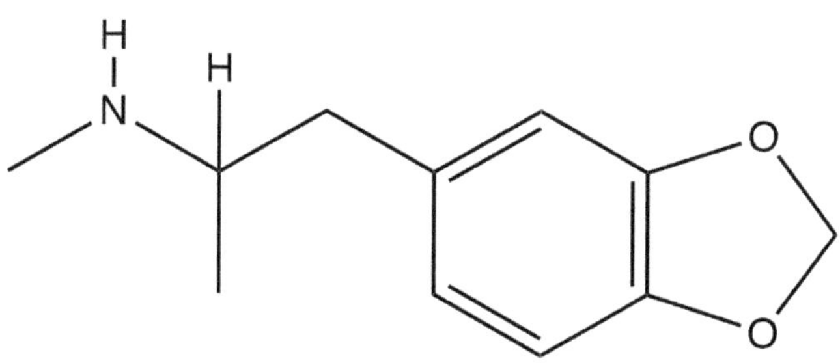

Figure 5.3 Chemical structure of MDMA. Created with ChemDraw by the author.

MDMA is often categorized as an entactogen or empathogen, a class of substances known to increase emotional openness, reduce fear, and enhance feelings of connection and empathy (Harris et al., 2002; Kolbrich et al., 2008; Nichols, 1986). These qualities are precisely what make MDMA uniquely suited for therapeutic use, particularly in the treatment of trauma.

In clinical trials, fixed doses of MDMA are generally used to account for the wide variability in how individuals metabolize the substance (Kolbrich et al., 2008). Typical therapeutic doses range from 75 to 225 mg, with onset beginning around 30–60 minutes after ingestion. The effects usually peak between 75 and 120 minutes and last for about 3–6 hours.

Although MDMA is generally well-tolerated in healthy individuals (Gillespie, 2020; Mitchell et al., 2021; Mithoefer et al., 2019), studies conducted with animals have raised some concerns. In rodent studies involving high and repeated doses—typically more than 50 administrations at greater than 3 mg/kg—there was evidence of serotonin depletion and potential neuronal damage (Baumann et al., 2007; Pantoni et al., 2022). Although these doses far exceed those used in therapeutic settings, they underscore the importance of safe, controlled use and further research into MDMA's long-term effects.

The most commonly reported side effects include muscle tension, fatigue, irritability, trouble concentrating, and occasional headaches. These symptoms typically emerge one to three days after administration and resolve within a week or two (Harris et al., 2002; Morgan, 2000; Sumnall & Cole, 2005). In cases of very high lifetime use—defined in some studies as 200 or more tablets—there have been reports of persistent depression and elevated anxiety (Gamma et al., 2000; Parrott et al., 2000).

History of MDMA

In 1912, MDMA was developed through efforts to derive substances that might help with blood clotting (Benzenhöfer & Passie, 2010). It remained largely obscure for decades, with no known therapeutic or recreational applications. In the 1970s, Sasha Shulgin—a brilliant and unconventional chemist with a Drug Enforcement Administration (DEA) license to work with Schedule I substances—resynthesized MDMA while exploring the psychoactive properties of phenethylamines. After trying the compound himself and experiencing a notable sense of openness and emotional warmth, Shulgin shared it with a small circle of friends and therapists. He found the drug's capacity to reduce fear, promote empathy, and foster interpersonal connection to be remarkable. As he described it, MDMA had the unique ability to "allow you to see yourself without fear" (Shulgin & Shulgin, 1991, p. 735).

In 1978, Shulgin and his colleague David Nichols published the first scientific paper on the pharmacological effects of MDMA in humans (Shulgin & Nichols, 1978). The paper highlighted the drug's ability to shift states of consciousness and enhance emotional and sensual awareness. Around this time, therapists—especially in the San Francisco Bay Area—began using MDMA in clinical practice, often referring to it as "Adam" rather than "ecstasy" to convey its potential to return clients to a state of emotional innocence or unguardedness (Benzenhöfer & Passie, 2010).

Throughout the early 1980s, a growing number of psychotherapists began legally using MDMA in sessions, particularly in couples counseling and trauma therapy. Anecdotal reports from clinicians described clients making profound emotional breakthroughs, healing from long-held wounds, and experiencing unprecedented levels of self-acceptance (Sessa, 2017). However, as recreational use of MDMA surged under the street name "ecstasy," public and governmental concerns mounted.

In 1985, the US DEA classified MDMA as a Schedule I drug, despite opposition from many therapists and researchers who testified to its therapeutic benefits (Doblin, 2002). This designation placed MDMA alongside substances deemed to have no accepted medical use and a high potential for abuse, effectively ending its legal therapeutic use and halting most scientific research.

In response, Rick Doblin, who founded MAPS in 1986 with the goal of reinstating MDMA as a legal medicine through FDA-approved research. Doblin and his colleagues argued that the DEA's decision had ignored promising clinical outcomes, and that scientific inquiry—not politics—should determine the drug's future in medicine (Doblin, 2002).

Over the following decades, MAPS spearheaded a rigorous research agenda, leading to a growing body of evidence supporting the safety and efficacy of MDMA-AT, particularly for the treatment of PTSD. In 2017, the FDA granted MDMA-AT "breakthrough therapy" status, acknowledging its potential to substantially improve outcomes over existing treatments (MAPS, 2017). This pivotal moment marked the beginning of MDMA's reemergence as a legitimate and respected therapeutic tool. From a forgotten laboratory compound to a beacon of hope for trauma survivors, the history of MDMA reflects both the limitations of prohibition and the resilience of those committed to healing through connection, courage, and scientific integrity.

MDMA Research

Nearly a decade after Shulgin's observations, psychiatrists Greer and Tolbert (1986) conducted one of the first uncontrolled studies of MDMA for the purposes of helping a group of volunteers achieve their individual desired goals. Even though the study had too many limitations to be categorized as clinically significant (e.g., no control group or controlled setting), its results encouraged further research into the beneficial effects of MDMA.

The study consisted of 29 people who were given MDMA in a therapeutic setting, some individually and others as a group (Greer & Tolbert, 1986). The sessions were conducted mostly in the participants' homes. Either Greer or Tolbert—sometimes both—would administer an initial MDMA dose between 75 and 150 mg, then a second dose of 50 mg two hours later. The researchers were present during the entire study, offering support and responding to participants' requests or needs. All 29 participants reported positive changes in their feelings and/or attitudes. Twenty-two of them reported cognitive benefits, including expanded mental perspective, resolution of issues, and new insight into personal problems or patterns. Participants reported feeling "fresher," "more alive," and "euphoric" and spoke about "loving feelings," greater self-confidence or self-acceptance, and being able to lower their "defenses" (Greer & Tolbert, 1986, p. 320).

All of the participants in Greer and Tolbert's (1986) study reported undesirable effects during or after the session, such as jaw tension, fatigue, insomnia, and nausea, and one participant reported experiencing blurry vision. The longest side effects persisted for one week after the study, except in two participants who experienced increased appetite for a few weeks, which led to 15 pounds of weight gain. Another participant experienced increased anxiety, which limited his ability to cope with work, friends, and family. In both cases, participants still found the MDMA session to be a "good thing" overall (Greer & Tolbert, 1986, p. 321). Greer and Tolbert concluded that MDMA had positively impacted all 29 volunteers and were encouraged by how the drug could facilitate individuals' learning about themselves and improve their interpersonal relationships.

As previously mentioned, Rick Doblin made it his mission to further MDMA research by starting MAPS. He founded MAPS after the DEA criminalized MDMA as a Schedule I drug. At the time, MDMA had gained popularity as a street drug better known as ecstasy. Young adults across the country sought out the substance, and rates of abuse increased. Doblin passionately believed that MDMA and other psychedelics had the potential to heal and, therefore, dedicated much of his life to using the vehicle of MAPS as a way to promote the legalization and medicinal use of psychedelics.

Since 1993, Doblin has successfully garnered government approval for many clinical trials (Elton, 2019). He has also raised approximately $80 million in private and government funding. Most of Doblin's research has centered on MDMA-assisted therapy (MDMA-AT), specifically for individuals diagnosed with PTSD. Doblin's focus on PTSD comes from his hope that appealing to the needs of military veterans would provide MAPS with the best chance of getting support from both Republicans and Democrats. Despite this strategic thinking, Doblin sincerely believed that MDMA-AT would be a promising intervention for veterans suffering from PTSD, particularly since this population often has limited access to effective treatment interventions (Mithoefer et al., 2019). In one interview, Doblin stated the following:

> PTSD is a disorder of fear; MDMA reduces fear. Also, people who have trauma have learned to be suspicious, and they often don't have trust for people because they've been betrayed or attacked or in some way traumatized. By stimulating the release of oxytocin, MDMA promotes what we call a therapeutic alliance. We know from psychotherapy outcome research that the therapeutic alliance is the most important factor in whether patients get better.
>
> (Elton, 2019, para. 9)

If an individual can lower their protective fear mechanisms, they can more easily open up and trust their therapist, which is a vital component of successful psychotherapy. Furthermore, MDMA has been found to increase compassion and understanding, two qualities that are imperative for effectively exploring previous trauma in a therapeutic setting, especially for individuals diagnosed with PTSD (Mitchell et al., 2021). Since MAPS' inception, researchers around the globe have conducted approximately 78 human trials, many of which have been led and funded by MAPS (MAPS, 2021). Currently, researchers at MAPS are conducting a Phase 3 study[7] on MDMA-AT, which is the final step before approval as a prescription drug.

A group of researchers, including Doblin, analyzed six Phase 2 randomized, double-blind, controlled clinical trials conducted at five different study sites between 2004 and 2017 (Mithoefer et al., 2019). All five studies were funded by MAPS and conducted with the same study objectives and design. Collectively, the Phase 2 studies consisted of 105 volunteers diagnosed with PTSD who previously failed to respond to other pharmacotherapies (mainly sertraline and paroxetine) and/or trauma-focused psychotherapy (e.g., cognitive processing therapy and prolonged exposure therapy). Researchers administered an active dose of MDMA (75–125 mg) or a placebo/control dose (0–40 mg) to the volunteers. The sessions consisted of two to three 8-hour MDMA sessions (spread one month apart), each supported by a male/female co-therapy team. Additionally, each volunteer had three sessions before the first MDMA session (preparation sessions) as well as three to four therapy sessions after each MDMA session (integration sessions).

The findings from the analysis of these trials revealed that the MDMA treatment was safe and effective for individuals with PTSD (Mithoefer et al., 2019). Participants' responses to the PTSD Scale (CAPS-IV), which they completed, revealed that the volunteers who received the MDMA experienced a significantly greater reduction in PTSD symptoms than the volunteers in the control group (54.2% vs. 22.6%). Volunteers in the active dose group[8] experienced further improvement of their symptoms after an average of three MDMA sessions.

Based on the encouraging findings from the Phase 2 trials, researchers at MAPS are currently conducting Phase 3 trials. Their initial findings, published in the MDMA Investigators Brochure (13th edition; Mitchell et al., 2021), show that 67% of participants in the MDMA-AT group no longer met criteria for PTSD—based on their CAPS-IV scores—after having three MDMA sessions, compared to 32% of participants in the placebo therapy group.

So far, findings from the Phase 3 trials indicate that 90 volunteers participated in three MDMA-administered sessions, along with preparation and integration sessions before and after the administration of MDMA (Mitchell et al., 2021). Preliminary results indicate that MDMA-AT represents a potential breakthrough treatment, which merits an expedited review by the FDA. The researchers report that two to three single-dose sessions with MDMA, spaced one month apart, is enough to result in significant therapeutic outcomes. Furthermore, participants in the trials who exhibited dissociative subtypes of PTSD—a population that is usually harder to successfully treat—experienced a greater reduction in symptoms than those with other subtypes (Elton, 2019). Under Doblin's direction, MAPS has directed funding toward exploratory research and proposed protocols for other populations, including individuals on the autism spectrum, those facing anxiety related to terminal illness, and those with eating disorders (Danforth et al., 2018; MAPS, 2021).

One recent study explored the effects of MDMA on 12 adults on the autism spectrum who were diagnosed with severe social anxiety (Danforth et al., 2018). Participants received either MDMA (75 mg or 125 mg) or an inactive placebo (0 mg) during two, eight-hour sessions, spaced one month apart, in a controlled clinical setting. The participants also took part in three therapy sessions before and after each MDMA session (preparation and integration sessions) and completed the Leibowitz Social Anxiety Scale (LSAS) at baseline, day 1, two weeks, and four weeks. The researchers evaluated the participants six months after the experimental sessions concluded. Those in the MDMA group dropped between two and four levels in the LSAS's severity category, while participants in the placebo group dropped zero to three levels. As hoped, the feasibility and safety of MDMA-AT for autistic adults were successfully established, despite the small sample size. The promising results suggest a need for further research with MDMA-AT in adults on the autism spectrum.

Two therapists, Almond and Allan (2019), have proposed using MDMA-AT in conjunction with emotionally focused therapy (EFT) for romantic couples impacted by the harmful effects of trauma and PTSD. They suggest that there are several potential benefits to incorporating MDMA therapy when at least one of the individuals in a relationship has had a traumatic experience and reports having symptoms of PTSD. They claim that although PTSD is viewed as an individual disorder, clinical and anecdotal evidence reveal the detrimental impact the disorder has on interpersonal relationships, specifically romantic ones.

Among its many benefits, MDMA helps users more readily access information contained in their thoughts, feelings, and memories. Individuals who take MDMA are able to reassess many aspects of their lives and relationships from a broader perspective of love and security, rather than fear. Almond and Allan (2019) suggest that incorporating MDMA in couple therapy sessions could be a catalyst for helping traumatized clients explore and regulate difficult emotions, reduce defensiveness, and share more openly with their significant other. They believe that incorporating MDMA can further one of the primary goals of EFT, which is to create a more secure bond between partners, generating a sense of safety that can help trauma survivors cope and heal more successfully.

The unique psychoactive properties of MDMA make it a potent agent for enhancing social connection, empathy, and emotional openness. Research has consistently demonstrated that MDMA facilitates bonding and warmth, fulfilling the fundamental human need for social connection. Lyubomirsky (2022) presented a conceptual model describing how MDMA influences proximal psychological mechanisms—such as lowered fear and increased sociability—that may have long-term effects on relationship quality and overall well-being. By modulating neurochemical pathways and reducing the fear response associated with emotional vulnerability, MDMA may enable individuals to foster deeper social bonds, reducing loneliness and improving relational satisfaction.

In the realm of relationship science, MDMA has been proposed as a means of exploring mechanisms of partner responsiveness and communication. The potential for MDMA to heighten empathy, reduce defensiveness, and enhance intimacy has led researchers to investigate how it might be used to enhance couple therapy. The neurobiological and psychological effects associated with the use of MDMA can promote attachment security, facilitate non-avoidance of difficult conversations, and encourage emotional safety (Wagner, 2021). By increasing serotonin, oxytocin, and dopamine, while simultaneously reducing activity in the amygdala, MDMA can help couples approach painful topics with greater openness, fostering honest discussions without triggering defensive reactions. This pharmacological action has significant implications for the treatment of relationship distress, particularly in cases where emotional withdrawal, trauma, or communication breakdowns have hindered resolution.

Shannon and Geller (2024) emphasized that MDMA has the potential to be useful for a range of psychiatric and relational difficulties. Since MDMA-AT integrates the substance's effects within a structured psychotherapeutic framework, it can powerfully facilitate emotional processing, trauma resolution, and personal insight. The so-called "psychedelic framework" within MDMA-AT consists of three core components: the container (therapeutic setting and rapport), the catalyst (MDMA's pharmacological action), and the carrier (curated music and guided introspection). This model ensures that MDMA's neurochemical properties—such as increased oxytocin release and enhanced fear extinction—are leveraged to optimize psychological healing. Emerging research suggests that MDMA-AT may be a helpful intervention for individuals suffering from anxiety, depression, addiction, and personality disorders. This merging of psychopharmacology with psychotherapy constitutes a paradigm shift in mental health care.

Despite its promising therapeutic potential, MDMA is not a substance meant for frequent use, as its effects are most profound when administered strategically within a clinical context. Unlike conventional psychotropic medications that require daily dosing, Phase II and III clinical trials indicate that as few as one to three MDMA-AT sessions can yield a significant and lasting reduction in symptoms. This time-limited but profound impact differentiates MDMA from standard psychiatric treatments, reinforcing its potential as an intervention that catalyzes deep psychological change with minimal pharmacological exposure. However, there are still numerous challenges when it comes to standardizing treatment protocols, addressing regulatory concerns, and mitigating risks such as transient physiological side effects, functional unblinding in clinical trials, and variability in individual responses.

As researchers continue to study MDMA's role in psychiatric and relational treatment, they will need to thoughtfully consider the elements of safety and efficacy associated with this substance. Future studies must refine their application across diverse populations, evaluate long-term outcomes, and address ethical considerations associated with their use. If integrated responsibly, MDMA-AT may offer an unprecedented healing modality, bridging the gap between neurobiology, psychotherapy, and human connection.

Inouye et al. (2023) investigated the potential of MDMA-AT for individuals diagnosed with borderline personality disorder (BPD), a population often considered treatment resistant due to the complex and pervasive nature of their symptoms. Individuals diagnosed with this personality disorder typically exhibit emotional dysregulation, interpersonal instability, and impulsivity, and they often have a co-occurring diagnosis of PTSD. Despite the high prevalence of PTSD among individuals with BPD, research into alternative treatment modalities remains scarce. Inouye et al. explored whether MDMA-AT, a promising intervention for treatment-resistant PTSD, could also offer therapeutic benefits for individuals with BPD.

MDMA-AT has demonstrated significant efficacy in reducing PTSD symptoms, with Phase III clinical trials showing that 71% of full-dose participants no longer met PTSD criteria (Inouye et al., 2023). Although PTSD and BPD are distinct diagnoses, they share a substantial etiological overlap, particularly in terms of trauma-related symptomatology. Given that individuals with BPD frequently experience early-life emotional neglect, attachment trauma, and chronic invalidation, Inouye et al. sought to examine the conceptual, mechanistic, and therapeutic intersections between MDMA-AT and dialectical behavioral therapy (DBT), the current gold standard for BPD treatment.

To achieve this, Inouye et al. (2023) conducted qualitative interviews with four clinicians: two specializing in DBT for BPD, and two experienced in administering MDMA-AT. By comparing their insights, the study aimed to identify potential areas of complementarity as well as limitations that might preclude the safe and effective application of MDMA-AT for BPD patients.

The clinicians specialized in both DBT and MDMA-AT agreed that BPD is rooted in emotional dysregulation, difficulties with self-identity, and interpersonal instability, often stemming from attachment disruptions and early-life trauma (Inouye et al., 2023). The DBT practitioners emphasized that their approach focuses on equipping patients with skills for distress tolerance, emotional regulation, and interpersonal effectiveness. In contrast, the clinicians experienced with MDMA-AT noted that the psychedelic experience allows for deep, accelerated processing of traumatic material by reducing fear responses, increasing self-compassion, and enhancing emotional openness.

One of the key concerns the study participants raised was whether individuals with BPD would be able to tolerate the emotionally intense and potentially destabilizing effects of MDMA without first undergoing DBT-based stabilization (Inouye et al., 2023). The DBT clinicians expressed skepticism that patients without prior training in emotional regulation could safely engage with MDMA-induced insights without risking an increase in some of their symptoms, such as impulsivity or suicidality. However, the MDMA-AT clinicians suggested that, under appropriate conditions, MDMA could facilitate profound breakthroughs in self-perception and interpersonal relationships. In this way, MDMA treatment would address some of the core BPD features in ways that traditional psychotherapies often don't.

Inouye et al.'s (2023) study also highlighted the role of MDMA in fostering a sense of coherence and self-integration, which is particularly relevant for individuals with BPD who experience identity fragmentation. Many MDMA-AT participants report experiencing a sense of peace and clarity about their emotions and relationships that was previously inaccessible. This phenomenon, which some researchers describe as *restorative coherence*, could hold promise for individuals with BPD who struggle with chronic feelings of emptiness and dissociation.

Although Inouye et al.'s (2023) study suggests that MDMA-AT could potentially complement existing BPD treatments, the researchers note several limitations and ethical concerns. First, BPD is associated with a high prevalence of self-harming behaviors and suicidality, which could pose significant safety concerns in the context of MDMA-AT. Unlike in the treatment of PTSD, where trauma processing is often the primary focus, treating BPD requires ongoing interventions for self-regulation. For this reason, it is unclear whether MDMA-AT could be safely administered without a prior foundation in DBT or similar modalities. Second, the potential for MDMA to induce transient but intense emotional states raises questions about the risk of re-traumatization or destabilization. Third, existing MDMA clinical trials have systematically excluded individuals with BPD because of these concerns, rendering the existing data on its efficacy and safety for this population speculative.

Despite these challenges, the study concludes that a carefully structured integration of MDMA-AT and DBT might hold potential for future clinical applications (Inouye et al., 2023). One proposed model involves a staged approach, in which individuals first undergo DBT to build emotional regulation skills and then use MDMA-AT for deeper trauma processing. This would ensure that patients have the necessary coping mechanisms in place, while allowing them to access MDMA's unique therapeutic benefits. Ultimately, the study calls for further empirical research into the feasibility of MDMA-AT for BPD, particularly in the context of its overlap with complex PTSD. Given the high burden of suffering and limited efficacy of current treatments, exploring innovative approaches remains an ethical imperative.

Stauffer et al. (2022) examined the inclusion of transgender and gender diverse (TGD) individuals in MDMA-AT trials for PTSD. Recognizing that TGD individuals experience disproportionately high rates of trauma and PTSD, the study highlights the historical exclusion of this population from clinical trials and the urgent need for gender-affirming, trauma-informed research methodologies. Given the promising results of MDMA-AT in Phase II and III clinical trials for PTSD, the study explored how this treatment can be adapted to address the unique mental health needs of TGD individuals while ensuring equitable access and ethical research practices.

Stauffer et al. (2022) conducted three virtual focus group discussions with a total of 17 TGD participants, each of whom had prior experience with trauma-related mental health care. These focus groups were facilitated by TGD-identified clinicians trained in trauma-informed care and psychedelic-assisted psychotherapy. The study employed a qualitative, thematic analysis approach to identify the barriers that TGD individuals face in trauma treatment, assess their openness to experimental PTSD interventions, and gather feedback on how to structure MDMA-AT protocols to meet their specific needs.

The findings underscore several critical issues within the mental health care system for TGD individuals (Stauffer et al., 2022). Many participants reported experiencing systemic discrimination and invalidation from mental health providers who were often lacking in cultural humility or basic knowledge of TGD identities. This contributed to widespread distrust of the medical system, with participants frequently feeling compelled to educate their therapists on gender identity rather than receiving adequate treatment. Additionally, the study identified significant barriers to accessing gender-affirming, trauma-informed mental health care, with many participants describing a lack of providers competent in both areas. Several participants also highlighted the intersection of economic marginalization and healthcare access, noting that high-quality trauma therapy was often prohibitively expensive, and insurance coverage for affirming mental health care remained inadequate.

Despite these challenges, many participants expressed strong interest in MDMA-AT, provided that research protocols were adapted to address their specific concerns (Stauffer et al., 2022). Several themes emerged regarding how existing MDMA-AT protocols could be modified for TGD inclusivity. First, participants emphasized the need for gender-inclusive data collection, suggesting that clinical trials routinely collect and report on gender identity beyond the male–female binary. Second, they advocated for an explicitly gender-affirming treatment framework in which the clinical staff was trained in TGD cultural competency and the treatment setting avoided making cisnormative assumptions. Third, participants stressed the importance of diverse co-therapy dyads, arguing that the traditional male–female therapist pairing required in MDMA-AT trials was restrictive and could reinforce binary gender norms that alienate TGD participants.

Participants also highlighted the importance of ensuring that patients remain physically and psychologically safe while experiencing the altered states of consciousness induced by MDMA (Stauffer et al., 2022). Many TGD individuals have experienced medical trauma, making it imperative that their treatment settings feel safe and inclusive. They recommended that therapy rooms avoid overly clinical aesthetics, which could trigger past medical trauma, and that treatment environments incorporate visual cues signaling inclusivity, such as pride flags or gender-neutral signage. Some participants suggested that group-based MDMA therapy models could be particularly beneficial for TGD individuals, fostering community and reducing isolation in a population that often lacks affirming social support networks.

Beyond protocol modifications, the study underscores the ethical imperative of including TGD voices in early-stage research planning (Stauffer et al., 2022). Historically, psychedelic research has been dominated by cisgender, White participants, leading to treatment models that may not generalize to structurally marginalized populations. By integrating TGD perspectives into study design, researchers can ensure that MDMA-AT is both accessible and effective for those who stand to benefit most. Furthermore, the study highlights the need to address the broader social determinants of health affecting TGD individuals. Although MDMA-AT may offer powerful individual benefits, it cannot address broader systemic barriers like discrimination or economic inequality. These concerns, shared by both researchers and participants, underscore the need for a holistic approach that bridges healing and social justice. Therefore, the researchers call for a holistic approach that combines psychedelic therapy with broader structural interventions to support TGD mental health.

As the FDA moves toward the approval of psychedelic-assisted therapies, making their clinical implementation more common, it is essential that researchers include TGD individuals and consider how they will make these treatments accessible to them. Future studies should focus on refining gender-affirming adaptations of MDMA-AT, assessing its efficacy in diverse TGD populations, and developing ethical guidelines to safeguard the well-being of participants. This research represents a crucial step in bridging the gap between psychedelic medicine and the mental health needs of TGD individuals, ultimately fostering a more inclusive and equitable paradigm for PTSD treatment.

Although most research on MDMA has, so far, focused on how it can catalyze healing for PTSD—with especially promising outcomes—new conversations are revealing other promising implications for this treatment, especially for clients who have not responded to traditional methods. It was once expected that MDMA could become an FDA-approved treatment as early as 2023, following decades of research and advocacy by figures such as Rick Doblin and MAPS. However, in a significant setback for the field of psychedelic-assisted therapy, the FDA's advisory committee recently voted against recommending approval of MDMA-AT for PTSD, citing concerns over study methodologies, potential biases, and the long-term safety profile of the treatment. This decision has introduced uncertainty regarding the future of MDMA accessibility within the framework of regulated psychiatric care.

Doblin had long sought to accomplish what Timothy Leary started at Harvard in the 1960s, using a rigorously scientific and politically strategic approach aimed at securing mainstream acceptance of psychedelic medicine. As he put it, "It was crucial for me to be here to bury the ghost of Timothy Leary" (Elton, 2019, para. 5). The FDA's recent rejection challenges that ambition. Although MAPS and other proponents of MDMA-assisted therapy may pursue further clinical trials and appeals, this moment represents a pivotal crossroads that could delay or reshape the trajectory of MDMA's integration into psychiatric care.

The future of MDMA as a therapeutic tool—whether through revised protocols, expanded studies, or state-level legalization efforts—remains uncertain. But the larger vision it represents—a model of healing rooted in compassion, connection, and trauma resolution—continues to resonate with clinicians, researchers, and patients alike. This moment highlights the enduring tension between the urgency of innovation and the slow pace of institutional change. For those on the frontlines of mental health, it is a reminder that transformation takes persistence, trust in the process, and the unwavering belief that healing is possible.

Clinical Considerations

MDMA is uniquely suited for clients working through trauma, especially those who struggle with fear, emotional withdrawal, or a lack of connection. Its ability to reduce the fear response and increase feelings of empathy and safety makes it particularly powerful in the treatment of PTSD and in therapeutic work involving interpersonal wounds. Unlike other psychedelics, MDMA tends to increase clarity rather than dissolve the ego, allowing clients to revisit difficult memories while remaining grounded in a state of emotional openness.

MDMA sessions typically last 6–8 hours and can be physically and emotionally intense. While the medicine creates a sense of safety, it may also surface repressed material that clients are not fully prepared to process. This makes careful preparation and a strong therapeutic alliance essential. Clients need to know that whatever emerges will be held with steadiness and without judgment.

This medicine is not suitable for everyone. Individuals with untreated trauma, cardiovascular issues, or histories of mania may be at higher risk. It is also not appropriate for clients with poor impulse control or high emotional volatility unless they have completed foundational work in emotional regulation. Screening should include both medical and psychological histories, as well as an honest exploration of the client's relational patterns and support systems.

Therapists must also be attuned to the emotional vulnerabilities that can arise during and after MDMA work. While the medicine often leaves clients with a deep sense of connection, the emotional openness it fosters may lead to disorientation, longing, or even grief in the days that follow. Clients may feel raw or exposed, especially if their insights are not integrated into daily life. Post-session support, therefore, must include practices that reconnect clients to their bodies, clarify insights, and reinforce the safety of the therapeutic relationship.

MDMA has a unique capacity to soften defenses and catalyze relational healing. In couples work, it can help partners break through cycles of blame and reconnect through vulnerability. In trauma work, it can allow clients to revisit painful material with compassion rather than fear. But this medicine is not a shortcut. Its success depends on the presence and skill of the therapist, the strength of the therapeutic container, and the client's willingness to engage in integration over time.

When held with care, MDMA becomes a mirror—revealing not only what needs to be healed, but also what is already intact. It offers a path toward healing that is rooted not in transcendence, but in the courage to stay present with what is. For many clients, that is the most transformative journey of all.

LSD

Chemistry of LSD

In 1938, diethylamide of d-lysergic acid (LSD) was first synthesized by Albert Hofmann, a chemist working for the chemical-pharmaceutical laboratory Sandoz, where he was studying various ergot alkaloids (Grof et al., 2008). Ergot is a type of fungus that grows mainly on rye, and lysergic acid

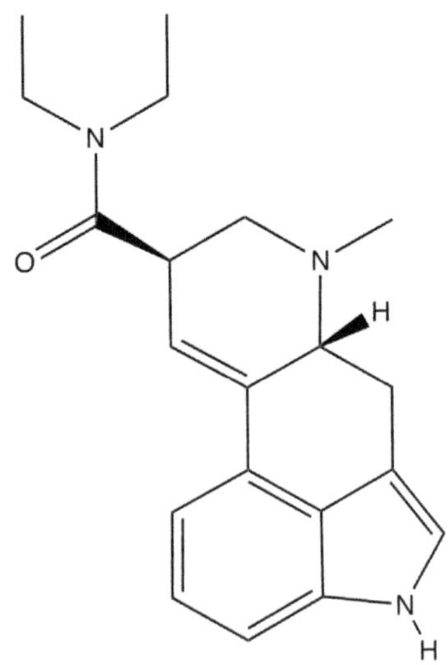

Figure 5.4 Chemical structure of LSD. Created with ChemDraw by the author.

is what remains when the nucleus is isolated. At the time, ergot was recognized as an important treatment for a variety of maladies, due to its multifaceted ability to induce uterine contractions, stop gynecological bleeding, and relieve migraine headaches. Hofmann had determined to find an ergot derivative that would have optimal therapeutic properties with the fewest possible side effects. It was through this endeavor that Hofmann synthesized LSD from ergot for the first time; however, the medical community didn't take any interest in his discovery or recognize this substance as a medical treatment. In 1942, Hofmann became newly curious about the substance he had created several years prior and decided to experiment with it again. He asserts that divine intervention led him to revisit LSD, and while he was working on the sample, he accidentally intoxicated himself during the purification process. In his book, *LSD, My Problem Child,* he shared the following about his experience:

> Last Friday, April 16, 1943, I was forced to interrupt my work in the laboratory in the middle of the afternoon and proceed home, being affected by a remarkable restlessness, combined with a slight dizziness. At home I lay down and sank into a not unpleasant intoxicated-like condition, characterized by an extremely stimulated imagination. In a dreamlike state, with eyes closed (I found the daylight to be unpleasantly glaring), I perceived an uninterrupted stream of fantastic pictures, extraordinary shapes with intense, kaleidoscopic play of colors. After some two hours this condition faded away.
>
> (Hofmann, 1980, p. 23)

Hofmann (1980) was so puzzled and curious about his experience that 3 days later, he decided to experiment with the substance by self-administering what he believed to be a minuscule amount of 250 μg of LSD. Today, that dosage is considered moderately high. His experience has become known by psychedelic enthusiasts *as bicycle day,* because Hofmann began to feel the effects of the LSD while riding his bike home from work. He recalled his first experience as one of the most terrifying and wonderous of his life. For the first few hours after he ingested the LSD, Hofmann worried that it might cause him to become insane and ultimately kill him. His assistant urgently summoned a doctor, but by the time the doctor arrived, the climax of the experience had already passed, and Hofmann was beginning to enjoy the perception of colors and shapes that appeared behind his closed eyes. Soon after, he went to sleep, and when he woke the next morning, he described that "a sensation of wellbeing and renewed life flowed through me," "as if the world was newly created" (Hofmann, 1980, p. 33). The self-administered episode was the first-ever planned human experiment with LSD, which led to the discovery of LSD's profound psychoactive effects. However, what Hofmann didn't realize at the time was that his experiment would be among thousands, if not millions, of clinical and non-clinical human experiments with LSD.

Since LSD is absorbed completely through the gastrointestinal tract, it is most often administered sublingually (Hofmann, 1980). Like other classic psychedelics, LSD binds to the 5-HT receptors and acts as an agonist to other serotonin and dopamine receptor sites (Burt et al., 2021). Dosing of LSD most commonly ranges from 25 µg to 300 µg, though participants in some studies receive doses as high as 800 µg; interestingly, an amount as small as ½–2 µg/kg body weight has been shown to be an active dose. The effect sets in from 30 to 90 minutes after ingestion and lasts between 10 and 12 hours. Individuals can quickly build tolerance to LSD, and research has shown that if it is administered repeatedly, its effects are no longer felt in as few as three days in a row (Halberstadt, 2015).

For some time, the results of studies receiving widespread attention, such as one conducted in 1967 by Cohen et al., indicated that LSD could cause fetal deformities or damage chromosomes and genetic material; however, a few years after Cohen et al.'s study, that claim was disproven (Fort & Metzner, 1969). Gable (2004) estimates that the lethal oral dose of LSD for humans is 14,000 µg (or 14 mg), which is 100–200 times greater than a typical recreational dose of 100–200 µg. Unlike what is widely believed about LSD, its toxicity has been found to be extraordinarily low when tested on animals.

History of LSD

In 1947, Walter Stoll, the son of Albert Hofmann's superior at the psychiatric clinic in Zurich, published the first study to examine the effects of LSD on 16 individuals without psychiatric diagnoses and six patients diagnosed with schizophrenia. Little was recorded about this experiment, but Hofmann (1980) noted that the volunteers were administered between 20 and 130 µg of LSD, and the experiences were observed to be predominantly euphoric. Like Hofmann, Stoll also self-experimented with LSD, aiming to gain firsthand insight into the psychological states of his patients. This kind of empathetic endeavor—researchers using psychedelics to experience altered mental states themselves—was common in the early era of LSD research. Many clinicians saw the potential for LSD to temporarily reproduce the perceptual and emotional distortions associated with schizophrenia. The extraordinary potency of LSD—and the fact that even a tiny amount could produce such effects—led some scientists to speculate that similar neurochemical disruptions might underlie psychotic disorders. They theorized that by studying LSD's impact, they might uncover an internal auto-intoxication of the brain caused by pathological shifts in body chemistry (Grof et al., 2008).

Supporting this hypothesis, Sandoz Laboratories began distributing LSD under the trade name Delysid for investigational use, accompanied by the following dosage and usage instructions:

Indications and dosage

1. Analytical psychotherapy, to elicit release of repressed material and provide mental relaxation, particularly in anxiety states and obsessional neuroses. The initial dose is 25 μg (1/4 of an ampoule or 1 tablet). This dose is increased at each treatment by 25 μg until the optimum dose (usually between 50 and 200 μg) is found. The individual treatments are best given at intervals of one week.
2. Experimental studies on the nature of psychoses: By taking Delysid himself, the psychiatrist is able to gain an insight into the world of ideas and sensations of mental patients. Delysid can also be used to induce model psychoses of short duration in normal subjects, thus facilitating studies on the pathogenesis of mental disease. In normal subjects, doses of 25–75 μg are generally sufficient to produce a hallucinatory psychosis (on average 1 μg/kg body weight). In certain forms of psychosis and in chronic alcoholism, higher doses are necessary (2–4 μg/kg body weight). (Hofmann & Ott, 1980, p. 27)

The term *normal subjects*, commonly used in the mid-20th century, referred to individuals without diagnosed psychiatric conditions. Though considered standard language at the time, it has since been critiqued for oversimplifying the spectrum of mental health.

The model psychosis theory, though historically important, has also received significant criticism in recent decades for its reductive view of mental illness and for assuming a direct parallel between chemically induced states and chronic psychiatric disorders. Still, this framework initially drove many early investigations and sparked a flurry of research activity. By 1963, more than 1,000 papers had been published on the effects of LSD in humans (Bonson, 2018), reflecting both the scientific excitement and the widespread availability of Delysid, which Sandoz provided free of charge to researchers and clinicians around the world.

LSD Research

In the early 1950s, psychiatrist Albert Kurland and his colleagues provided LSD-assisted psychotherapy to patients with schizophrenia at the Spring Grove State Hospital (Cholden, Kurland, & Savage, 1955). Kurland, a psychiatrist at the hospital, had been conducting numerous studies on anti-psychotics. He hoped that LSD might prove to be a beneficial treatment for schizophrenia. Kurland and his team conducted a study in which

20 patients diagnosed with schizophrenia were administered 100 μg of LSD daily in a single intramuscular injection for what was supposed to be 14 days of psychedelic-assisted therapy sessions.

However, by the second day, the team discovered LSD's rapid tolerance effect: The same dose no longer had a noticeable impact (Cholden et al. 1955). To address this, they increased the dosage by 100 μg each day—administering 100 μg on day 1, 200 μg on day 2, and so on, up to 500 μg. Despite these escalating doses, patients continued to show diminished responses after day two. The team concluded that a six-day drug-free interval was required to restore LSD's initial potency.

The researchers had hoped LSD might function like a chemotherapeutic psychiatric drug, but the outcomes were disappointing. One account (Cholden et al., 1955) described a catatonic patient who, 35 minutes after LSD administration, began sobbing and then laughing uncontrollably. Later that day, she was seen smiling, laughing, and even playing basketball—something she had previously refused. By the next morning, however, she returned to her mute, catatonic state. Subsequent doses produced diminishing effects—some laughter at first, then total unresponsiveness by day three.

Kurland, like many of his peers, recognized that LSD's potential for treating schizophrenia was both overstated and fundamentally flawed. Theories linking LSD toxicity to the biochemical makeup of schizophrenia were unsupported by the data (Hofmann, 1980), and studies began to show worse outcomes for patients exposed to LSD (Tomsovic & Edwards, 1970). Many clinicians concluded that LSD was doing more harm than good.

Nevertheless, Kurland's interest in LSD continued. In 1964, he received a grant from the NIMH to explore LSD's use in treating alcohol addiction (Kurland et al., 1967). His team continued their work at Spring Grove Hospital and soon published promising results. Sixty-nine patients received psychedelic-assisted therapy, and nearly all showed improved scores on the Minnesota Multiphasic Personality Inventory (MMPI)—with the exception of the hypomania scale. Six months later, 23 patients (33.3%) remained abstinent from alcohol compared to only 12% of those undergoing conventional treatment at the same facility. A major limitation of this study was the absence of a control group. According to Kurland et al. (1967), the staff believed so strongly in LSD's efficacy that they felt it would be unethical to deny treatment to qualifying patients.

Kurland later refined the study design to include a low-dose control group (Kurland et al., 1971). In the follow-up study, 135 participants were randomly assigned to receive either a high dose of LSD (450 μg) or a low dose (50 μg). The lower dose was intended to induce mild perceptual effects without a full psychedelic experience. All participants underwent psychological assessments—such as the MMPI—prior to the intervention and one week after their session. Additional follow-ups were conducted at 6, 12, and 18 months.

Both groups initially improved on their MMPI scores, but by the six-month mark, 53% of the high-dose group remained abstinent compared to only 33% in the low-dose group (Kurland et al., 1971). Although several other clinical trials examined LSD's potential for treating alcoholism, most did not replicate the robust differences Kurland observed between the treatment and placebo groups.

A more recent meta-analysis by Fuentes et al. (2020) reviewed eight studies assessing LSD's therapeutic use in psychiatry. Most showed that participants in both the LSD and control groups had similar outcomes in alcohol abstinence—likely due to the shared psychotherapy and support both groups received. However, four of the eight studies reported that the LSD group experienced greater improvements in quality of life and general health, pointing to the potential for meaningful secondary benefits even when abstinence rates were comparable.

One area where LSD proved particularly useful was in self-experimentation by mental health professionals, who sought to better understand the experiences of psychotic patients. These clinicians believed that by personally experiencing altered states, they could develop greater empathy and more effective therapeutic interventions. In addition to his research on LSD-assisted therapy for schizophrenia, Walter Stoll explored LSD's effects on himself (Hofmann & Ott, 1980). In a 1969 self-experiment, Stoll found the experience provided valuable professional insights and deepened his understanding of patient experiences. He believed LSD allowed physicians to gain firsthand insight into the altered states of consciousness experienced by their patients, enabling more accurate interpretations and treatment approaches.

Between 1969 and 1976, Yensen and Dryer instituted a program at Spring Grove Hospital that offered one to three LSD training sessions to 203 health care professionals. The goal was to enhance clinical insight and therapeutic capacity by offering a direct experience of:

- The unconscious or primary process.
- The challenges faced by youth involved in drug abuse.
- Improved study design for psychedelic research.
- Greater empathy and psychological insight.

Yensen and Dryer modeled their program after earlier LSD studies. The participating professionals were interviewed by psychiatrists, attended preparatory sessions, and—following their LSD session—participated in integration sessions. In follow-up reports, participants described significant benefits, including increased insight into philosophical and spiritual matters, relief from emotional and physical distress, enhanced well-being, and overall functional improvement (Kurland et al., 1967).

It is important to note, however, that while this program was historically influential, allegations of misconduct were later raised against Yensen regarding severe boundary violations in clinical settings. These ethical concerns do not negate the reported outcomes of the study but must be considered when evaluating its legacy and implications for current practice.

Around the same time, Eric Kast and Sidney Cohen conducted pioneering studies using LSD with patients diagnosed with terminal illnesses, especially cancer. They observed encouraging effects, such as superior pain relief, reduced depression, improved sleep, and a lessened fear of death (Cohen, 1965; Kast, 1966; Kast & Collins, 1964).

Pahnke et al. (1969) also focused on using LSD in end-of-life care, believing it could help people confront and process existential fears. He proposed that rather than numbing consciousness—as many painkillers do—LSD could open the door to deeper emotional experiences and facilitate more authentic interpersonal connections. At the Maryland Psychiatric Research Center (formerly Spring Grove Hospital), Pahnke et al. (1969) conducted a pilot study with 22 patients experiencing severe anxiety, depression, or panic related to terminal illness. Each received 200–500 μg of LSD in a single session. Despite the study's limitations—no control group and a small sample—the results were promising. Six patients showed dramatic improvement, eight showed moderate improvement, and eight were unchanged. None experienced harm, and those who reported the most profound benefits also described having had a mystical psychedelic experience.

Drawing on the work of William James and W. T. Stace, Pahnke (1963) outlined nine core features of a mystical psychedelic experience:

- A sense of unity or oneness.
- Transcendence of time and space.
- A sense of sacredness.
- A perception of objective truth or reality.
- Deeply felt positive emotions (e.g., joy, peace, and love).
- Feelings of awe and reverence.
- Insightful psychological or philosophical understanding.
- Ineffability (difficulty describing the experience).
- Paradoxical awareness (coexistence of opposites).

The six patients who experienced dramatic improvement in the 1969 study reported at least six of these features. They experienced reduced anxiety, depression, and fear and even increased pain tolerance, requiring less medication. Many also reported enhanced peace, serenity, and a diminished fear of death.

In a Harvard lecture, Pahnke (1969) emphasized that mystical experiences often bring a lasting sense of security and acceptance of mortality:

> Our experiments have indicated that deep within every human being there are vast usually untapped resources of love, joy, and peace. One aspect of the mystical psychedelic experience is a release of these positive feelings . . . . The data shows that these feelings are released most fully when there is a complete surrender to the ego-loss experience of positive ego transcendence . . . life and death can be looked at from a new perspective.
>
> (Pahnke, 1969, p. 15)

Pahnke et al. (1970) conducted a follow-up study with six metastatic cancer patients. Each received a single LSD session (200–300 μg), following a preparatory rapport-building session with a therapist. After the LSD session, patients attended integration therapy and were assessed using the Rating Sheet for the Emotional Condition of Patients (RSECP). Although the original plan had included more comprehensive instruments (e.g., MMPI), these were deemed too demanding for physically weakened participants.

Therapists rated each patient on levels of depression, psychological isolation, anxiety, fear of death, and focus on physical pain (Pahnke et al., 1970). All six patients required less pain medication post-session and showed improvement on all emotional indicators. Although Pahnke was not surprised by these psychological benefits, he was puzzled by the reduction in physical pain, as LSD is not classified as an anesthetic. William Richards, a co-researcher, later offered three possible explanations:

1. Increased individual pain tolerance.
2. A broadened field of awareness diverted focus from pain.
3. A stronger "here and now" orientation disrupted temporal components of suffering. (Richards et al., 1972, p. 53).

During this period of research, Pahnke was himself diagnosed with cancer and passed away in 1971. Following his death, the Maryland Psychiatric Research Center asked Stanislav Grof to continue the work alongside William Richards. Like Pahnke, Grof believed that mystical peak experiences had profound healing potential, both for individuals and society at large.

In his first study, Stanislav Grof administered LSD to 31 cancer patients (8 men and 23 women) who were experiencing physical pain, depression, or anxiety (Richards et al., 1972). Before their sessions, participants engaged in interviews designed to build rapport and explore key life challenges—including unresolved family issues, difficulty accepting their diagnoses, and fears surrounding death. Family members were often included to reduce the psychological isolation that commonly accompanies terminal illness.

The day after the LSD session, and throughout the following week, participants attended integration sessions to help them apply their insights in daily life (Richards et al., 1972). A global index was used to estimate therapeutic success, combining results from the Rating Sheet of Emotional Condition of Patients with data on narcotics consumption. A dramatic improvement was defined as an increase of four or more points, a moderate improvement as two to four points, and a minimal change as fewer than two. Of the 31 patients, 9 demonstrated dramatic improvement, 13 showed moderate improvement, and 9 exhibited minimal change.

As in Pahnke's earlier studies (Pahnke et al., 1969, 1970), those who showed the most dramatic improvements were the patients who had experienced a mystical psychedelic experience. These individuals exhibited the greatest reductions in fear of death.

After her LSD session, one patient shared the following:

> I've made my peace with God. Each man has to make his or her own . . . . They can do whatever they want with my body. Life has been beautiful, even though painful and hard. It's been beautiful . . . . I've made my peace with death. I've been there. I wasn't afraid. I thought I had accepted it before; now I really accept it.
>
> (Richards et al., 1972, p. 137)

Rather than being viewed as the ultimate end, death was reframed as a transition into a different state of existence. For many, this shift in perspective brought much-needed peace to longstanding existential distress.

While clinical research on LSD's therapeutic potential was progressing, the substance was simultaneously gaining popularity as a recreational drug throughout the Western world—especially in the United States. Media outlets and publications had already exposed the general public to accounts of psychedelic experiences, but it was the controversial activities of Timothy Leary and Richard Alpert at Harvard University that pushed LSD into national headlines. In his memoir *High Priest*, Leary reflected on his first LSD experience: "Since that time five years ago I have been acutely aware of the fact that everything I perceived, everything within and around me is a creation of my own consciousness" (Leary, 1969, p. 256).

Leary promoted LSD not only as a tool for self-discovery and spiritual exploration, but also as the most potent aphrodisiac known—claims that captivated a younger audience. The numerous experiments with LSD that were designed to capture this cultural momentum were often conducted irresponsibly, with little regard for set, setting, or safety. Leary's infamous slogan, "Turn on, tune in, and drop out," encouraged young people to abandon social conventions, reject formal education and employment, and devote themselves to inner transformation (Hofmann, 1983).

As Leary's notoriety grew, so did the public backlash against him. He became a pariah within academic circles and a target of political ire. Ronald Reagan even described him as "the most dangerous man in America" (Iannelli, 2020, p. 7). Sensational media reports of individuals spiraling into panic, experiencing psychosis, or engaging in criminal behavior after unsupervised LSD use further fueled public fear. Although LSD remained legal at the time, the misuse of the drug alarmed Sandoz Laboratories, the company that had synthesized and distributed it. Albert Hofmann later shared that a Sandoz executive told him, "I would rather you had not discovered LSD," expressing concern that its powerful effects might ultimately do more harm than good (Hofmann, 1983, p. 38).

In 1970, 42 years after Hofmann first synthesized LSD, Congress classified the substance as a Schedule I drug (Bonson, 2018). Following this designation, LSD research came to an almost complete halt in the United States. But in recent years, a quiet renaissance has begun. Recent studies have taken a new approach. No longer focusing on modeling psychosis, current LSD researchers are exploring how the substance can support cognitive flexibility, resilience, end-of-life treatment, and depression.

In one of the first studies reviving interest in LSD, a team of researchers in Solothurn, Switzerland, evaluated the use of LSD-assisted psychotherapy for individuals with terminal illness (Gasser et al., 2014a). The double-blind, active placebo-controlled pilot trial included 12 patients with life-threatening conditions, all of whom were experiencing anxiety about their prognosis. The researchers hypothesized that LSD could alleviate emotional distress.

The study design included two preparatory psychotherapy sessions focused on establishing trust and exploring participants' mindset (or "set") (Gasser et al., 2014a). Patients then received two LSD-assisted psychotherapy sessions spaced two to three weeks apart. The sessions took place in warmly furnished treatment rooms designed to foster comfort and safety. Participants were randomly assigned to either an LSD group (200 μg) or an active placebo group (20 μg). Following each psychedelic session, the participants engaged in three integration sessions to discuss their experience and reflect on their insights. The researchers conducted follow-up assessments at 2 and 12 months after the sessions, using the State-Trait Anxiety Inventory. The LSD group showed notable reductions in state anxiety, and there was a strong trend toward reduced trait anxiety as well.

Gasser et al. (2014a) proposed that these trait-level improvements may be linked to LSD's neurobiological effects, which could accelerate the therapeutic process. Based on these promising results, the researchers concluded that further investigation into LSD-assisted psychotherapy was warranted, especially for individuals with life-threatening conditions who may benefit from enhanced emotional well-being and existential peace.

Another study by Kanen et al. (2023) examined the effects of LSD on reinforcement learning in humans—a key cognitive process involved in adaptive decision-making and psychiatric disorders. Given that LSD is a non-selective serotonin 2A (5-HT2A) receptor agonist, the researchers aimed to explore its influence on learning rates, cognitive flexibility, and probabilistic decision-making. This aligns with broader theoretical frameworks suggesting that psychedelics exert their therapeutic effects by enhancing neuroplasticity and reshaping maladaptive associations.

Kanen et al. (2023) employed a within-subject, placebo-controlled design involving 19 healthy participants who received intravenous LSD (75 μg) or a saline placebo in separate sessions. Participants completed a probabilistic reversal learning task designed to assess their ability to adapt to shifting reward contingencies. The primary objective was to determine whether LSD affected mechanisms such as learning rates, valuation of stimuli, and exploratory behavior.

The results of the study indicated that LSD significantly increased learning rates, especially in response to rewards, suggesting a state of heightened neural plasticity (Kanen et al., 2023). Computational modeling revealed that LSD accelerated the updating of learned values and made participants more responsive to new information. It also increased exploratory behavior, evidenced by reduced stimulus stickiness—a tendency to repeat the same choice, regardless of previous outcomes. These findings align with prior research showing that 5-HT2A receptor activation enhances cognitive flexibility by decreasing habitual behavior and promoting adaptive exploration.

Interestingly, LSD's impact was more pronounced in reward learning than punishment learning (Kanen et al., 2023). This asymmetry hints at potential applications for LSD to treat conditions characterized by rigid, negative thinking, such as depression. The study also found that participants under the influence of LSD exhibited stronger connections between early learning and subsequent perseveration, meaning that behaviors learned early persisted more strongly, even after the rules changed. This could imply that LSD helps reinforce adaptive behaviors while promoting the revision of maladaptive ones.

These findings support the growing consensus that psychedelics can enhance cognitive flexibility and help revise entrenched thought patterns (Kanen et al., 2023). By accelerating learning and encouraging exploration, LSD may offer therapeutic benefits for disorders such as OCD, addiction, and depression. However, the findings also underscore potential risks. For example, heightened plasticity could reinforce maladaptive behaviors if the surrounding context is not supportive.

Kanen et al. (2023) provided a compelling account of how LSD influences learning and decision-making, framing reinforcement learning as a key neurocognitive process through which psychedelics operate. The study highlights the need for further research to understand the conditions under which heightened plasticity yields therapeutic gains versus unintended consequences. Future studies should assess the stability of LSD-induced learning changes, investigate individual variability in response, and explore how these mechanisms apply to clinical populations.

The LSDDEP2 study, conducted by ----Daldegan-Bueno et al. (2024), is a Phase 2b randomized, double-dummy, triple-blind, active placebo-controlled, parallel-group trial investigating the efficacy and safety of LSD microdosing for major depressive disorder (MDD). Given the pervasive nature of MDD and the many limitations associated with existing treatments, the researchers designed the study to evaluate whether LSD microdosing—a practice gaining popularity in lay communities—offers a viable alternative to treating MDD. Building on the open-label LSDDEP1 pilot study, which demonstrated feasibility and tolerability, LSDDEP2 aims to rigorously assess changes in depressive symptoms (as measured by the Montgomery-Åsberg Depression Rating Scale) along with effects on anxiety, rumination, stress, anhedonia, quality of life, and various biomarkers of neuroplasticity and neurophysiology.

To ensure strong internal validity, the study includes 90 participants who meet DSM-5 criteria for MDD, randomly assigned to receive either LSD microdoses (titrated between 4–20 μg) or an active placebo (caffeine or methylphenidate) over an eight-week period (----Daldegan-Bueno et al., 2024). The participants self-administer two doses of LSD each week in a naturalistic setting, along with one in-clinic session for physiological and subjective assessments. The triple-blind design ensures that the participants, investigators, and outcome assessors remain unaware of the assigned intervention. A mobile platform—Mobile Directly Observed Therapy (MDOT)—is incorporated in the study to ensure adherence to the protocol and prevent the unintentional stacking of doses. Beyond measuring primary symptoms, the trial also incorporates secondary and exploratory metrics, including personality inventories, EEG recordings, blood biomarkers, sleep and activity tracking, and interviews. These measures aim to shed light on LSD's mechanisms of action, such as its potential to influence brain connectivity and plasticity.

The study also addressed concerns around safety and tolerability (----Daldegan-Bueno et al., 2024). Although prior microdosing studies with healthy volunteers reported minimal side effects, LSDDEP2 monitors adverse events, cardiovascular markers, and laboratory results in a clinical population. A personalized titration protocol allows participants to adjust doses within a safe range, improving tolerability. A notable feature is the study's naturalistic design, in which participants engage in self-selected, psychologically beneficial activities during their microdosing regimen. This reflects growing theories that psychedelics enhance experience-dependent neuroplasticity, in which context shapes outcome.

If LSD microdosing proves effective and safe, its applications could extend beyond MDD to address other diagnoses including anxiety, PTSD, and cognitive decline (----Daldegan-Bueno et al., 2024). However, the study's rigorous design and use of an active placebo are essential to helping disentangle LSD's pharmacological effects from expectancy biases—an issue that has clouded prior research.

Ultimately, LSDDEP2 represents a critical step toward establishing an evidence base for psychedelic microdosing in clinical psychiatry. Whether or not the results show efficacy, the study will contribute key insights into the biological and psychological effects of low-dose LSD, shaping future research and practice.

Not all of the research on LSD is positive. A study by Korman (2024) explored resilience in the face of job loss following prior *naturalistic* use of MDMA (i.e., use outside of a therapeutic or research setting). Using data from the National Survey on Drug Use and Health (2008–2019), the study assessed whether unemployed individuals with a history of LSD use experienced less psychological distress than non-users. Contrary to expectations, the participants in the study who had previously used LSD users were more likely to report severe distress following job loss, challenging the narrative that psychedelics enhance resilience.

The study's limitations include its reliance on self-reported, cross-sectional data, which makes it impossible to infer causality (Korman, 2024). The timing of participants' LSD use, relative to their job loss is unclear. It's possible that at least some of the individuals had their last experience with LSD years before losing their job. It's also unclear how relevant this study's findings are to the therapeutic use of LSD. Naturalistic use lacks the structure of psychedelic-assisted therapy, which includes preparation, guidance, and integration. Without these safeguards, the benefits may be diminished or absent. Therefore, this study doesn't deny the effectiveness of LSD-assisted therapy, only the notion that unsupervised use promotes resilience. Still, it raises important questions and underscores the need for more rigorous research. Future studies should employ controlled designs to evaluate how the context and framework of LSD-assisted therapy shape the relationship between the psychedelic subject and the psychological outcomes.

Despite ongoing political and cultural baggage, momentum around LSD research is growing. Scientists and clinicians are actively reviving studies to investigate its therapeutic potential. As proponents of LSD assert, even one session can help individuals identify core conflicts, illuminate the structure of their symptoms, and differentiate between relevant and irrelevant problems (Grof et al., 2008). According to Grof, the experiences individuals can have with the assistance of LSD often reveal the psychological roots of their suffering and, therefore, have the potential to help them integrate their past and present life challenges.

Like other psychedelics, LSD is more than a pharmacological agent; it's a key to unlocking the psyche's deeper architecture. It is capable of dissolving rigid mental patterns, enhancing emotional insight, and fostering radical shifts in perception. From its controversial history to its reemergence in clinical and spiritual settings, LSD continues to reveal itself as a complex and powerful tool. Its potential lies not only in alleviating suffering, but also in expanding consciousness, reshaping identity, and reimagining what is possible in mental health and human development. To explore LSD is to engage with the mystery of mind, and to discover the healing that can emerge when that mystery is embraced rather than feared.

Clinical Considerations

LSD is a powerful psychedelic that brings with it both profound potential and significant demands. Its long duration, often 8–12 hours, makes it one of the most intense medicines to hold in a therapeutic context. For this reason, it is best suited for clients who have a stable sense of self, good emotional regulation, and a strong commitment to inner work. LSD is not a gentle medicine. It often invites clients into symbolic, archetypal, or existential terrain that can feel disorienting without proper support.

This substance can be particularly helpful for individuals facing meaning crises, end-of-life concerns, or entrenched mental patterns that have not shifted through conventional therapy. It has shown promise in the treatment of depression, addiction, and spiritual disconnection. Its effects tend to be more expansive than directive, opening access to the imaginal and transpersonal realms. This makes it an ideal medicine for clients who are comfortable with nonlinear experiences and open to working with metaphor, memory, and mystery.

Because LSD magnifies internal states and can produce powerful projections, the therapeutic relationship must be grounded and resilient. The therapist's presence and attunement serve as anchors throughout the journey. Clients may feel exposed, euphoric, terrified, or all of these at once. Clear framing, pacing, and preparation are essential. Therapists should work with clients in advance to identify psychological anchors and post-session care, as the intensity of the experience often lingers long after the session ends.

LSD is not appropriate for individuals with a history of psychosis, bipolar disorder, or dissociative tendencies. Screening must be thorough, and integration must be taken seriously. Clients benefit from reflecting through modalities such as dreamwork, expressive writing, spiritual dialogue, or symbolic art. Without a strong integration process, the experience may feel fractured or overwhelming.

Although LSD is not yet legally accessible in most therapeutic settings, research is steadily growing. If approved, it will require therapists who can hold long sessions and work at deep psychological and existential levels. Used responsibly, LSD can reveal hidden sources of suffering and untapped inner resources. It is not a quick fix, but it can be a profound invitation—to expand, to reflect, and to remember what has been forgotten. When approached with care, it opens a wide and powerful doorway into healing.

Ayahuasca

Chemistry of Ayahuasca

Ayahuasca (nicknamed Aya) is a South American psychoactive beverage that contains the naturally occurring psychedelic compound N,N-dimethyltryptamine (DMT) (Riba et al., 2001). It is made by brewing together a combination of two plants—most commonly *Banisteriopsis caapi*, which is rich in beta-carboline harmala alkaloids (a monoamine oxidase inhibitor, or MAOI), and the leaves of *Psychotria viridis*, which contain DMT. DMT is a potent psychedelic agent that binds primarily to serotonin 5-HT2A receptors in the brain, producing altered states of consciousness, emotional release, and complex visual imagery (Callaway et al., 1999).

The main role of the MAOI component in ayahuasca is to inhibit monoamine oxidase (MAO), an enzyme in the gut and liver that would otherwise rapidly break down DMT before it could become psychoactive. Without the *caapi* vine (MAOI), the DMT in *Psychotria viridis* would be inactivated

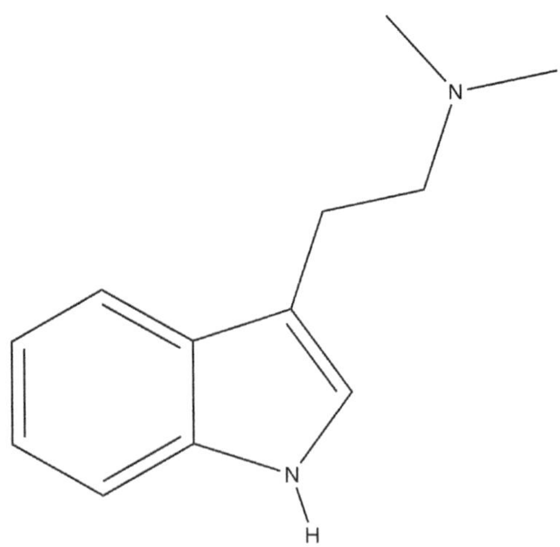

Figure 5.5 Chemical structure of DMT. Created with ChemDraw by the author.

before it could enter the bloodstream (Hamill et al., 2019). It is this sophisticated pharmacological pairing of two distinct plants that allows ayahuasca to be orally active—a fact that has been well-known by Amazonian healers for thousands of years and that modern medicine has recently begun to recognize (Callaway et al., 1999).

Throughout South America, ayahuasca has been used in both religious and medicinal contexts (Barbosa et al., 2012; Riba et al., 2001). In Quechua, the word "ayahuasca" is often translated as "vine of the soul" or "vine of the dead" (Dos Santos & Hallak, 2021; Hamill et al., 2019), reflecting the Indigenous belief that the brew is animated by a spiritual force. In many Indigenous and mestizo communities, the medicine is used as a means of physical and emotional healing, as well as a sacred tool for accessing the spirit world. It is common for those who partake in ayahuasca ceremonies to describe experiencing visions, deep emotional catharsis, communication with spiritual entities or ancestors, and transformative insight into personal and transpersonal realms.

In clinical settings, ayahuasca is typically administered in encapsulated, freeze-dried form, with doses ranging from 0.5 mg to 1.0 mg of DMT per kilogram of body weight—approximately 0.5 mg in a low dose, 0.75 mg in a medium dose, and 1.0 mg in a high dose (Riba et al., 2001, 2002a, 2002b, 2003). In traditional ceremonial settings, ayahuasca is brewed as a tea and consumed in liquid form, typically in doses ranging from 50 to 100 ml (Frecska et al., 2004; Santos et al., 2007), with DMT concentrations averaging about 0.73 mg/ml (Callaway et al., 1996). The onset of ayahuasca's effects typically begins 30–60 minutes after ingestion, reaching peak intensity between 60 and 120 minutes, and generally returning to baseline after four to six hours (Barbosa et al., 2012; Riba et al., 2002a, 2002b).

A hallmark of the ayahuasca experience is its purgative effect—often referred to as *la purga*—which may involve vomiting, diarrhea, or intense sweating. Although sometimes viewed as side effects, these processes are widely understood by traditional practitioners and many participants as part of the medicine's healing mechanism, cleansing not only the body but also the emotional and energetic fields (Callaway et al., 1999). In this context, the purge is not seen as toxic, but tonic.

Though ayahuasca is considered physically safe when taken in appropriate ceremonial or clinical contexts, it comes with some risks. Interactions with certain medications—particularly SSRIs—or underlying psychiatric conditions may pose significant dangers, which is why careful screening and preparation are essential (Dos Santos et al., 2021).

History of Ayahuasca

The small Christian sect known as União do Vegetal (UDV), meaning "the Union of the Plants" (Thomas et al., 2013), was founded in the 1950s by

José Gabriel da Costa in his hometown in Brazil. Da Costa first encountered ayahuasca in Bolivia, where he drank the brew with a group of Indigenous people and underwent a profound spiritual experience. Moved by this revelation, he returned to Brazil determined to share the plant's message. Over the following decades, he gathered a devoted following and helped spread UDV across many cities in Brazil and, eventually, around the world (Grob et al., 1996).

Long before its emergence in Western religious and therapeutic circles, ayahuasca was used for centuries—if not millennia—by Indigenous peoples throughout the Amazon basin. In these traditional settings, the brew is regarded not simply as a chemical compound, but as a sacred plant teacher with a spirit of its own. Ceremonies are typically led by shamans or curanderos who undergo extensive training over many years, learning to navigate the visionary realms, sing healing icaros (medicine songs), and interpret the symbolic content that emerges during journeys. These ceremonial practices are often used for diagnosing illness, resolving spiritual imbalances, communicating with ancestors, or seeking guidance during important life transitions.

The preparation of ayahuasca is itself a ritual, involving intentionality, prayer, and a deep relationship with the plants. Each community may have different customs, lineages, and protocols; what remains consistent is the profound reverence given to the brew and the recognition of its power to connect the physical, emotional, and spiritual dimensions of life.

Until 2006, ayahuasca remained classified as a Schedule I substance in the United States. That changed when the US Supreme Court ruled in favor of the União do Vegetal (UDV), granting them the legal right to use the brew as a religious sacrament. The ruling—based on the First Amendment's protection of religious freedom—marked a turning point in the legal and cultural recognition of psychedelics in spiritual contexts. It opened a narrow but significant legal precedent for the sacramental use of psychedelic substances, even while broader prohibition remained in place.

Since that decision, hundreds of ayahuasca ceremonies have legally taken place across the United States, contributing to a surge of interest in the brew's healing potential. In recent years, researchers have studied ayahuasca as a treatment for a variety of mental health conditions, including depression, anxiety, and substance use disorders. It has also gained attention for its potential to facilitate spiritual exploration and catalyze insights into the nature of consciousness, imagination, and self-awareness (Dos Santos & Hallak, 2021).

Ayahuasca Research

In 1993, a pioneering study known as the Hoasca Project brought together several influential figures in the field of psychedelics: Dennis J. McKenna, a research pharmacologist; his brother Terence K. McKenna, a well-known psychedelic advocate; psychiatrist Charles Grob; and a team of interdisciplinary researchers. The team traveled to the Brazilian Amazon with the goal of investigating the psychological and physiological effects of ayahuasca. This was the first modern study of its kind, and its primary objective was to assess both potential therapeutic benefits and adverse effects of long-term ayahuasca use.

The researchers worked with 15 longstanding members of the UDV, each of whom had been part of the organization for at least 10 years and consumed ayahuasca, on average, twice a month as part of ceremonial sacrament. The volunteers were all men who agreed to undergo a battery of assessments, including psychiatric diagnostic interviews, personality tests, and neuropsychological evaluations. They also completed structured interviews to explore how ayahuasca had impacted their personal, familial, and professional lives. To provide a point of comparison, the researchers also recruited a control group: 15 age-matched males who were friends or siblings of the UDV participants. These individuals had no prior history of ayahuasca use and likely shared similar diets, socioeconomic status, and cultural backgrounds.

During their interviews, all 15 UDV members reported transformative life changes since joining the religion and engaging in regular ayahuasca use. They described a fundamental reorganization of their values, relationships, and sense of purpose, attributing this shift directly to their work with the brew. Many credited ayahuasca with helping them overcome past struggles and improve their overall functioning in family, work, and community life.

The assessment data reflected significant differences between the two groups. The UDV members scored higher on measures of optimism, emotional regulation, and confidence in the face of uncertainty. Most notably, none of the UDV participants met criteria for a current psychiatric disorder. In contrast, two members of the control group had diagnosable conditions: one with alcohol misuse and one with illness anxiety disorder (formerly called hypochondriasis).

The retrospective data were even more striking. Prior to joining UDV, 5 of the 15 participants had met criteria for alcohol use disorder—often accompanied by aggressive behavior during binges. Eleven had been addicted to tobacco, two had experienced major depressive episodes, and three had struggled with anxiety disorders. After years of participation in ayahuasca ceremonies, all of them reported that their symptoms had resolved or were no longer present.

Although the Hoasca Project had limitations—including its small sample size, male-only participant pool, and remote research setting—it offered compelling evidence that regular, ritualized ayahuasca use may play a role in emotional healing, substance use recovery, and psychological transformation. The findings helped spark further international interest in the therapeutic potential of ayahuasca and laid the groundwork for more rigorous clinical studies.

Jordi Riba, a Spanish pharmacologist, conducted the first placebo-controlled study on ayahuasca in a small group of healthy volunteers (Riba et al., 2001). All six participants were male, had previous experience with ayahuasca, and were confirmed physically and psychologically healthy through rigorous screening.[9] Riba's aim was to better understand ayahuasca's psychological effects and to demonstrate that it could be administered safely in a controlled setting.

The study took place at a research facility in Spain, where participants received three increasing doses of encapsulated, freeze-dried ayahuasca—specifically, 0.5 mg, 0.75 mg, and 1.0 mg DMT per kg of body weight (Riba et al., 2001). Riba's team assessed the safety of dose escalation and monitored hallucinogenic intensity using visual analog scales (VAS), which participants completed before ingestion and every 30 minutes afterward for a total of four hours. The participants also filled out self-report questionnaires before and after each session.

All three doses produced noticeable psychoactive effects in nearly all participants (Riba et al., 2001). One subject mistook the lowest dose (0.5 mg/kg) for a placebo, but even at that level, statistically significant changes were observed across multiple VAS items. At medium and high doses (0.75 mg and 1.0 mg/kg), participants reported both heightened psychotropic effects and, for some, an initial sense of anxiety or fear. However, this unease tended to subside as the session progressed. Five out of six volunteers described feeling a deep sense of well-being after the peak effects wore off.

The study concluded that ayahuasca could be safely administered to healthy individuals and that its effects were largely perceived as pleasant and psychologically beneficial (Riba et al., 2001). One participant opted out after the medium dose due to intense anxiety. The researchers attributed his reaction to limited previous exposure to psychedelics, particularly ayahuasca.

Riba went on to lead several additional clinical trials, which further investigated the effects of ayahuasca on the brain and body. His research incorporated neuroimaging using electroencephalography (EEG), cardiovascular assessments, and immunological analyses (--Dos Santos et al., 2011; Riba et al., 2002a, 2002b, 2003, 2004). These studies advanced scientific understanding of ayahuasca's therapeutic potential, consistently demonstrating that it produces measurable physiological and neurological changes.

Whereas Riba focused on the biological and pharmacological dimensions of ayahuasca, Barbosa et al. (2005) turned their attention to the subjective and psychological experiences of first-time users in religious contexts.

Their research took place within the UDV and Santo Daime, two Brazilian religious traditions that use ayahuasca ceremonially to support spiritual development. The team recruited 28 volunteers who were about to participate in their first ayahuasca ceremony and evaluated them through interviews and psychological assessments—before the ceremony, as well as one to two weeks after the experience.

None of the participants reported adverse effects (Barbosa et al., 2005). On the contrary, most described entering a state of inner peace and emotional clarity. Many expressed that the experience had fostered meaningful self-insight and contributed to their spiritual growth. The most striking result was a notable reduction in minor psychiatric symptoms. Participants described feeling calmer, more assertive, and more emotionally open, along with having more energy and a higher sense of general well-being.

Barbosa et al. (2005) proposed that there were two primary mechanisms behind those observed improvements. First, the intense spiritual and existential insights elicited by the brew may prompt individuals to reassess their lives, leading to meaningful changes in how they relate to themselves and others. Second, the emotionally charged and symbolically rich ceremonial context offers a striking departure from the routine of everyday life, potentially interrupting rigid psychological patterns and opening space for transformation.

Other researchers have echoed these observations, pointing to similar outcomes in various studies of psychedelics in ceremonial and therapeutic contexts (Griffiths et al., 2006, 2018; Grob et al., 1996; Santos et al., 2007). These findings continue to support the idea that, when used with intention and in a structured setting, ayahuasca can be a powerful tool for psychological healing and spiritual transformation.

Expanding on previous research, Barbosa et al. (2009) selected 23 members who had recently joined the church to participate in a longer-term, case-controlled study that would assess their psychological traits and states before and after their use of ayahuasca in a religious setting, over a span of six months. The researchers conducted assessments one to four days before the ritual, two weeks after the ritual, four weeks after the ritual, and again six months after the ritual. The findings showed a significant reduction in minor psychiatric symptoms such as depression, anxiety, and obsession[10] at the 2-week mark. Additionally, participants reported fewer physical pain complaints.

However, the data collected at the six-month follow-up revealed a key insight: Only those individuals who continued to regularly partake in ayahuasca ceremonies sustained their improvements (Barbosa et al., 2009). A positive correlation emerged between frequency of use and improvements in emotional, psychological, and physical symptoms. In contrast, participants who did not continue regular use no longer showed significant improvements beyond four weeks post-ritual. These findings suggest that although the benefits of ayahuasca may fade over time, continued ceremonial use contributes to lasting positive outcomes.

Nonetheless, Barbosa et al. (2009) also emphasized that even a single ayahuasca experience, when paired with psychotherapy, can offer meaningful psychological benefits. The heightened suggestibility brought on by ayahuasca may help individuals confront difficult personal issues, and the accompanying spiritual experience can elicit profound shifts in perspective.

In 2001, Grob returned to Brazil to study the use of ayahuasca among adolescent members of the UDV (Da Silveira et al., 2005). The objective was to assess the mental health status of these adolescents and compare it to that of peers with no ayahuasca experience. Participants were matched by age, sex, and education level. Grob's team included 80 adolescents, split evenly into two groups: 40 who had consumed ayahuasca at least 24 times in the past two years, and 40 control participants who had never used ayahuasca. The researchers interviewed all of the participants and assessed them for psychiatric conditions. They found that the ayahuasca group experienced fewer symptoms of anxiety, body dysmorphia, and attention deficit disorder than their peers. However, the difference between the two groups was less stark than in Grob's (1996) previous study on adults. Though the researchers did not address the possible reasons for this, the age of ayahuasca users is a factor worth exploring in future research.

More recent research has focused on ayahuasca-assisted therapy for addiction and its related symptoms, including anxiety and depression. Researchers are examining the neurochemical, psychological, and transcendent effects of ayahuasca that may support healing among individuals in this population (Liester & Prickett, 2012). A growing body of qualitative research and large-scale surveys supports the potential of ayahuasca in conjunction with therapy for treating substance use disorders (Giovannetti et al., 2020; Perkins et al., 2022; Talin & Sanabria, 2017; Thomas et al., 2013).

In Canada, a MAPS-funded study followed 12 participants who attended a four-day addiction recovery retreat involving ayahuasca-assisted group therapy (Thomas et al., 2013). For five months, researchers collected data using questionnaires to measure participants' relapse rates, level of mindfulness, anxiety and depression symptoms, and quality of life. All 12 participants showed statistically significant improvements across all measures. They reported increased empowerment, hopefulness, and connectedness to self and others. The researchers concluded that ayahuasca-assisted group therapy may play a key role in reducing substance use and called for further research.

In 2016, Giovannetti et al. (2020) conducted a similar study at a residential ayahuasca treatment center in Peru. The study included 31 men from diverse backgrounds and incorporated the Beck Anxiety Inventory, the Beck Depression Inventory, and an addiction severity questionnaire. The average treatment lasted six and a half months and involved 14 ayahuasca sessions and 19 individual therapy sessions. Among the 31 participants, 38% began with moderate to severe depression and 61% with moderate to severe anxiety. By discharge, 81% had minimal anxiety levels and 87% had minimal depression. Participants also reported improvements in quality of life, spirituality, and reductions in addiction severity.

A large international cross-sectional survey involving 8,269 participants reinforced these findings (Perkins et al., 2022). Ayahuasca use was associated with significantly higher odds of rarely or never using alcohol or drugs, particularly among those with a history of substance use disorder. Spiritual experiences during ceremonies were strongly associated with reductions in substance use. Participants reported that ayahuasca helped them recognize and reframe the negative thought patterns driving their addictions, leading to decreased anxiety and depression.

To broaden the use of ayahuasca beyond addiction treatment and adopt a more relational approach, Roseman et al. (2021) conducted a study in Israel with Palestinian and Israeli participants—two groups entrenched in a long-standing ethnopolitical conflict. The researchers explored ayahuasca's potential in promoting peacebuilding by shifting participants' negative perceptions of one another. They conducted 31 in-depth interviews: 13 participants identified as Arab-Palestinians and 18 as Jewish Israelis. Notably, the ayahuasca ceremonies were not designed with peacebuilding as their primary aim; most participants cited psychospiritual growth as their reason for attending.

Using a grounded theory approach,[11] Roseman et al. (2021) identified three primary relational themes. The first theme was unity-based connections. These experiences emphasized shared human similarities and a sense of oneness. Participants described moments of deep togetherness that transcended social and political divisions. One Arab-Palestinian woman shared the following: "We stop viewing each other as 'You're Israeli,' or 'You are Palestinian.' We stop viewing each other as male or female. We don't view Muslim, Christian, it all melts, like melts down, and dissolves through the journey" (Roseman et al., 2021, p. 7).

The second theme was recognition and difference-based connection (Roseman et al., 2021). Participants became aware of their political and cultural differences when they emerged during the ceremony through things like language, prayer, and music. Although these moments initially provoked discomfort, working through it led to healing. A Jewish-Israeli participant described this experience:

> Suddenly you hear the language you most hated . . . and suddenly it is sending you into love and light . . . . Whatever the song, whatever the words, you melt—that's our peace, to sit and listen to a song in Arabic, that's peace.
>
> (Roseman et al., 2021, p. 8)

The third theme was conflict-related revelations (Roseman et al., 2021). Many participants experienced visions involving intergenerational trauma and collective grief. A Jewish-Israeli man who had served in an elite combat unit described a vision of Palestinian suffering, which led to profound empathy and emotional reckoning. He recounted seeing how his past actions had contributed to generational trauma and felt the collective pain of "the Other." Participants often cried together, describing the experience as transformative for healing relations between the two groups. The researchers concluded that psychedelics could facilitate interpersonal reconciliation, collective empathy, and potentially, larger sociopolitical shifts.

In a separate study, Apud (2023) conducted a systematic review and meta-analysis examining the relationship between ayahuasca consumption and personality traits, synthesizing findings from multiple cross-sectional studies. The research drew from studies utilizing Cloninger's Temperament and Character Inventory and the Big Five model to evaluate long-term ayahuasca users. One of the most striking findings was a significant reduction in Harm Avoidance, a trait linked to anxiety, fear of uncertainty, and social inhibition. Regular ayahuasca users demonstrated greater emotional resilience and openness, suggesting that the substance may recalibrate the stress response system and promote neural plasticity (Carhart-Harris et al., 2018). Participants also exhibited lower scores in fatigability, suggesting better adaptability and stress management (Apud, 2023).

In addition to reduced anxiety-related traits, Apud (2023) found increased social and spiritual personality dimensions. Long-term ayahuasca users scored higher in reward dependence, attachment, and helpfulness—traits linked to prosocial behavior and emotional warmth. The most profound changes were observed in the self-transcendence dimension, including spiritual acceptance (g = 1.02) and self-transcendence (g = 0.91). These traits are associated with experiences of interconnectedness, existential awareness, and unity with a higher consciousness. These personality shifts appear to be influenced by not only the pharmacology of DMT—the primary psychoactive compound in ayahuasca—but also the communal and ritualistic settings in which it is typically consumed. Many participants belonged to spiritual communities such as UDV and Santo Daime, where spiritual development and social bonds are central.

However, Apud (2023) notes several limitations to the review that should be considered. The studies reviewed were cross-sectional, meaning they captured personality differences at a single point in time. This raises questions about causality: Do individuals with certain personality traits gravitate toward ayahuasca use, or does the substance itself reshape personality? Longitudinal studies are needed to answer this question. Additionally, most data came from Brazil, Spain, and the United States, limiting generalizability across cultures. It remains unclear whether the same personality effects would be observed in secular or non-communal ayahuasca contexts.

Apud's (2023) findings contribute to the growing literature on psychedelics and personality transformation. Long-term ayahuasca users demonstrate lower anxiety, enhanced social connectedness, and heightened spiritual awareness. These findings have implications for mental health, therapeutic interventions, and consciousness exploration. As research expands, understanding how ayahuasca influences personality through both biological and sociocultural mechanisms will be essential for advancing psychedelic science.

A review by da Silva et al. (2021) explored the anti-inflammatory properties of ayahuasca and its potential therapeutic applications in neurological and psychiatric disorders. Ayahuasca, a traditional Amazonian brew containing β-carbolines and tryptamines, exerts its effects by inhibiting MAO and activating serotonin receptors (5-HT1A, 5-HT2A, and 5-HT2C). Recent research highlights its anti-neuroinflammatory action, attributed to DMT and 5-methoxy-DMT, which modulate immune homeostasis and inflammation via sigma-1 receptors. Given that neuroinflammation is a major factor in conditions such as depression, anxiety, cognitive decline, and neurodegenerative diseases like Alzheimer's and Parkinson's, ayahuasca's immunomodulatory effects may provide a novel pharmacotherapeutic approach.

Preclinical and clinical studies indicate that ayahuasca reduces pro-inflammatory cytokines, promotes neuroplasticity, and enhances neurotrophic factors such as brain-derived neurotrophic factor, suggesting potential benefits for mood disorders and cognitive impairments. Although current data supports ayahuasca's safety profile and antidepressant properties, further research is needed to fully understand its mechanisms and establish its clinical efficacy.

Schlag et al. (2022) critically examined public concerns regarding psychedelic substances such as psilocybin, DMT, ayahuasca, mescaline, and LSD. Historically misrepresented and stigmatized, these substances are now undergoing a renaissance in therapeutic research. Schlag et al. distinguished between scientifically validated risks and fears rooted in anecdotal or historical misinformation, noting that media sensationalism and restrictive legislation from the mid-20th century created a distorted view of psychedelics as dangerous and harmful.

One of the most persistent myths is that psychedelics are physiologically toxic (Schlag et al., 2022). However, the study shows that classic psychedelics possess low toxicity, minimal overdose risk, and rare associations with long-term physiological harm. Psychological risks such as challenging experiences—often referred to as bad trips—are real but generally short-lived and greatly mitigated in clinical settings. More serious outcomes such as persistent psychosis or HPPD are exceedingly rare, especially when clinical trials rigorously screen participants for predispositions to psychiatric disorders.

Contrary to popular belief, psychedelics do not cause addiction (Schlag et al., 2022). The rapid development of tolerance, absence of compulsive use patterns, and lack of reinforcement via the dopamine system all contribute to their low potential for abuse. In fact, psychedelics are increasingly being explored as treatments for substance use disorders. Moreover, recent epidemiological studies suggest that people who have used psychedelics report lower levels of psychological distress, suicidality, and addiction.

Schlag et al. (2022) emphasized that risk is highly dependent on context. Controlled settings—with careful screening, dosing, and integration—are associated with low adverse outcomes. In contrast, unregulated or recreational use can amplify risks. As psychedelics move closer to mainstream medical use, public communication must balance optimism with realism, avoiding both exaggeration and underestimation of risks.

Gearin and Calavia Sáez (2021) explored how the globalized use of ayahuasca has been recontextualized within Western neoshamanic practices. Their ethnographic research illustrates that the traditional, relational, and communal use of ayahuasca by indigenous Amazonian communities has been reframed in Western settings to focus on personal transformation, self-discovery, and individual healing. Unlike traditional Amazonian practices, which view healing as embedded in social, spiritual, and ecological networks, neoshamanic ceremonies often adopt a vision-centric approach. In these settings, visions are interpreted as private revelations and integrated into personal spiritual frameworks, reflecting Enlightenment values of individualism and ownership. Healing becomes an internal, solitary pursuit, rather than a communal or reciprocal process.

A key critique from Gearin and Calavia Sáez (2021) is the Western emphasis on visual phenomena and personal insight, which often overlooks the multisensory and relational dimensions of traditional ayahuasca use. This shift not only reinterprets ayahuasca's function but also commodifies it—turning ceremonies into marketable experiences that can be purchased by spiritual seekers at a high cost. The commercialization of ayahuasca contributes to a consumer-driven model of healing while obscuring the historical and cultural trauma faced by indigenous communities.

Gearin and Calavia Sáez (2021) argued that ayahuasca should not be viewed as a magical solution to individual or systemic issues. Instead, they call for critical awareness of how globalized ayahuasca practices intersect with power, privilege, and cultural appropriation. True transformation, they argue, requires social reciprocity, collective responsibility, and sustained engagement with the relational principles at the heart of indigenous ayahuasca traditions.

Ayahuasca occupies a unique space in the psychedelic landscape—rooted in millennia of indigenous tradition, yet increasingly studied through the lens of modern science and embraced by global spiritual seekers. Research points to its potential in treating psychiatric conditions, reducing inflammation, fostering social connection, and expanding self-awareness. At the same time, its cultural evolution raises important questions about appropriation, commodification, and the shifting meanings of healing. As psychedelic-assisted therapies continue to develop, ayahuasca reminds us that context matters—both the ceremonial setting and the broader cultural and relational frameworks in which these medicines are used. It is not only what we take, but how and why we take it that shapes the outcome. Understanding ayahuasca's full potential requires honoring both its indigenous roots and the complexity of its modern applications.

Clinical Considerations

Ayahuasca is best suited for clients seeking spiritual insight, emotional healing, or a deeper connection to ancestral, relational, or transpersonal layers of experience. Unlike medicines with shorter durations or more predictable arcs, ayahuasca often unfolds as a long, layered process. Clients may encounter intense purging, visionary sequences, and powerful emotional waves that emerge and resolve in nonlinear ways. For this reason, psychological readiness and grounded integration are essential.

This medicine may be particularly helpful for clients struggling with trauma, addiction, anxiety, depression, or meaning-related distress. It tends to soften ego structures, reveal unconscious material, and offer insight that cuts across time, identity, and lineage. At the same time, ayahuasca is not for everyone. It should be avoided by individuals with a history of psychosis, unstable moods, or dissociative tendencies. SSRIs, SNRIs, and medications that interact with MAOIs must be carefully reviewed before proceeding. Therapists should never assume safety; they must engage in thoughtful screening and refer clients to trained medical professionals when necessary.

Unlike clinical psychedelics, ayahuasca is almost always experienced in a ceremonial setting. Whether in a traditional lineage, a syncretic church, or a neoshamanic container, the role of the guide or facilitator is central. The presence of icaros, prayer, and group ritual can shape the entire trajectory of the experience. For this reason, therapists supporting clients around ayahuasca must go beyond assessing readiness. They must help clients discern the safety, lineage, and integrity of the ceremony itself. This includes asking about the facilitator's training, the structure of the space, and the support systems in place before, during, and after the session.

After the journey, clients may feel awe, confusion, heartbreak, or bliss. They may experience a rupture in their worldview or an overwhelming influx of insight. Without integration, these experiences can feel disorienting or fade quickly. Therapists should offer a space for slowing down, connecting language to feeling, and helping clients build meaning from what they saw and felt. Practices such as narrative reflection, dreamwork, expressive arts, or time in nature may be especially supportive after an ayahuasca journey. The goal is not to interpret or contain the mystery, but to allow it to settle into the psyche in ways that serve long-term growth.

Ayahuasca reminds us that healing is relational, layered, and sometimes fierce. Its power lies not only in the visions it brings, but in the humility it demands. For therapists walking alongside clients who engage with ayahuasca, the role is not to lead or explain, but to witness, listen, and trust that what arises—when supported with care—will take root.

Notes

1 Roquet refers here to what is known as ego death. Ego death is a state characterized by the loss of boundaries between the subject and the objective world. All your ideas and identities of who you are, are stripped away. (Grof, 1980)
2 The study did not provide an explanation for the difference in post-treatment follow up.
3 Leary was Pahnke's thesis advisor, and the project was named the Good Friday Experiment (Leary & Penner, 2014).
4 Each group consisted of 4 individuals; half received psilocybin and half received the Niacin placebo.
5 Thorazine (chlorpromazine), an antipsychotic drug, is used to treat mental disorders, such as schizophrenia (NIH, no date).
6 Transient psychotic-like symptoms can be delusions, hallucinations, disorganized speech, grossly disorganized, or catatonic behavior (Stephen & Lui, 2021).
7 For MAPS to get to Phase 3, Phases 1 and 2 were deemed successful and obtained FDA validation (Gillespie, 2020). In Phase 1, healthy volunteers are usually involved, and the goal is to understand what the drug does. In Phase 2, there are smaller pilot studies, which explore the patient population, what doses are being used, what the treatment looks like, and who is excluded and included in the study. The main goal of Phase 2 is to figure out how to design Phase 3—large-scale, randomized, placebo-controlled studies that are required to prove safety and efficacy for patients.
8 In the third session, there was no control group for comparison, but it did lead to more participants experiencing a reduction in symptoms. Phase three trials will include three blinded experimental sessions (MAPS, 2021).
9 All six participants were males, had previous experiences with ayahuasca, and were classified as healthy after being thoroughly assessed. Assessments were in the form of psychiatric interviews (consisting of the DSM-III-R and trait-anxiety scale from the state trait anxiety inventory), medical history, laboratory tests, ECG, and urinalysis.
10 For a full list of symptoms examined, see Barbosa et al., 2009.
11 Using grounded theory approach: Grounded theory is a method for analyzing qualitative data, in which ideas and concepts can emerge from the data and become the basis of a hypothesis or a new theory (Glaser & Strauss, 1967).

Part III

Psychedelics in Practice

The MPIM Model

Chapter 6

The Intake

Setting Client Expectations and Screening

Before We Start . . .

I deeply appreciate Levy and Waldron's concise framing here, as it underscores a vital truth I witness every day in my practice: the medicine alone isn't always enough. The power of psychedelic therapy comes from the intentional, relational, and therapeutic space in which the medicine is experienced. That's why, from my very first conversation with a client, I emphasize relationship-building, preparation, and the careful setting of expectations.

Those conversations take place everywhere. Whenever I am asked what I do for a living and reply that I am a psychedelic integration therapist, I quickly find myself conversing with someone who is full of curiosity, confusion, excitement, or sometimes even terror. I often wind up fielding comments such as, "Aren't psychedelics illegal?" "Aren't they drugs?" "Have any of your clients become psychotic?" "Did you say psychedelics can be therapeutically helpful?!" "What is your part in all this drug stuff?" Some humorous individuals will even ask, "Do you sell any?" and "When can I pick it up?"

Others react with barely concealed horror at the mere mention of psychedelics in therapy. These responses reflect the widespread intrigue and misconceptions surrounding the field of psychedelic-assisted therapy.

These same questions arise in my initial calls with prospective clients. In these calls, I am interested in asking specific questions and begin with inquiring about how the person heard about psychedelic therapy and how they believe it could be helpful for them. I want to make sure that their reasons for inquiry are therapeutic. I make it clear that even though I specialize in psychedelic therapy, I go through a long and structured process before beginning to work with any medicine. I explain that as a marriage and family therapist, my first priority is to form a deep relationship with my clients—one that allows me to clearly understand who they are, how they see the world, what their goals and aspirations are, and what kind of changes they seek. Furthermore, I let them know that it's important for them to get to know

DOI: 10.4324/9781003541639-10

me. Once we've established a relationship, they can decide if I'm someone they would like to work with, if they feel they have chemistry with me, and if they believe I can create a space in which they feel safe and accepted. As I've emphasized many times already, this is vital.

In my initial calls, I also explain that the preparation Phase I guide clients through before introducing psychedelics (e.g., ketamine, ayahuasca, psilocybin, LSD, or MDMA) takes a minimum of four weeks and is an essential part of the psychedelic therapy process. Before each client's initial session, I share that many shamans believe the preparation phase is necessary when working with these sacred medicines, and that it alone accounts for 90% of the psychedelic experience. The pace of this process, and the language I use, comes from my belief that we live in a world where people seek some version of a magic pill that will give them instant gratification.

The underlying tagline for both individuals seeking treatment and therapists working in the industry seems to be: *Take a psychedelic and come out a new and improved version of yourself, with a better life waiting back at home.* This is a great sell, but unfortunately, it couldn't be further from the truth. Not only are statements like these and the belief system behind them wrong, but in my opinion, they're also dangerous. There's a trend in our society of looking for the next quick fix or money-maker that can be commercialized and falsely advertised until, over time, people get frustrated or disappointed when they realize it's not so simple. This trend has gone from being celebrated to being demonized. In the case of psychedelics, the misunderstanding and misuse driven by these false beliefs about them may lead to the abolishing of something that could have been life-changing for many. This is why it's so important for psychedelic therapists to incorporate the MPIM principles I outlined earlier: we intentionally harness expectancy, ensuring that clients have realistic yet hopeful expectations; we engage deeply in utilization, drawing upon each client's unique strengths, history, and resources as essential ingredients for healing; and we cultivate mindfulness as a foundational skill to help clients remain grounded and present throughout their therapeutic journey. These principles collectively create a safe, structured container that allows psychedelics to become meaningful therapeutic tools rather than isolated, potentially overwhelming experiences.

A widely reported case illustrates the stakes of expectation and preparation. In October 2023, off-duty pilot Joseph Emerson attempted to disable a Horizon Air flight's engines midair. Subsequent reports noted a severe mental health crisis in the days prior and psilocybin use roughly 48 hours earlier. While extreme, the case underscores screening and support, not a blanket indictment of psychedelics. These substances are promising but not universally beneficial, and unmet expectations can compound distress when hoped-for relief doesn't materialize (Ross et al., 2022).

Cases like Emerson's highlight the need for practitioners, researchers, and policymakers to advocate ethical standards, comprehensive clinical training, and public education. Psychedelic therapists must clearly communicate that these substances are not shortcuts, but rather tools embedded in a deep, intentional therapeutic process that includes rigorous preparation, guided experiences, and structured integration.

Without clearly reframed expectations, the current resurgence of psychedelics risks repeating the boom-and-bust cycle of the 1960s and 1970s—initial enthusiasm devolving into moral panic and criminalization (Doblin et al., 2019; Pollan, 2019). To avoid repeating history, it is crucial to understand that psychedelics are facilitative instruments within a broader psychotherapeutic context, not standalone solutions.

With the essential nature of clear expectations in front of my mind, I start every psychedelic therapy journey by intentionally challenging clients' culturally ingrained desire for instant transformation. Effective psychedelic therapy isn't about having a singular transformative event that fast-tracks healing, growth, and change. It's an ongoing growth process that happens through self-inquiry, patience, intentional integration, and sustained personal reflection. Practitioners need to make clients aware that progress, setbacks, and uncertainty are natural elements of this journey. The aim of psychedelic therapy is to cultivate a lifelong practice of integrating the insights, skills, and resources gained through the therapeutic process, which involves the psychedelic substance, along with everything surrounding it. Framing therapy as an ongoing engagement with self-awareness and resilience ensures that its benefits endure and become deeply integrated into daily life. However, before guiding any client into this transformative territory, the practitioner has the tremendous ethical responsibility of assessing whether psychedelic therapy is an appropriate intervention for that individual. This process begins with careful screening.

Screening

While research consistently shows that psychedelics can be both safe and potent tools for therapeutic transformation, therapists need to be acutely aware that certain individuals might be at higher risk of being harmed by this therapeutic modality. It is essential to recognize that some medications can have adverse interactions with psychedelics (Johnson et al., 2008). Thus, clients' use of all medications should be thoroughly discussed at the start of the consultation. When a client is taking medication, the therapist should not only make note of the specific drugs but also collaborate with a psychiatrist specialized in psychedelic therapy (Johnson et al., 2008) to ensure that no harmful interactions will occur.

Equally crucial in the screening process is the exclusion of individuals with significant mental health issues. A vital criterion for participant selection in clinical trials is the absence of any prior history of manic disorders or psychotic episodes (Mitchell et al., 2021). This is rooted in evidence demonstrating that psychedelics have the potential to trigger psychotic episodes and even initiate long-term psychosis.

It is imperative to meticulously screen for both personal and familial histories of psychotic disorders, such as schizophrenia or bipolar disorder with psychotic tendencies (Grob et al., 2011). In my first session, I prioritize the exploration of this history. Through an open and relaxed conversation, I gather information about clients' past experiences with psychedelics, the after-effects of those interactions, and any previous manic or psychotic occurrences. I emphasize to my clients that the gravest risks associated with psychedelic therapy are those that emerge when there is a history of psychotic episodes. This highlights the importance of disclosing this pertinent information at the outset of therapy.

I also discern potential risks based on clients' demeanor, being alert to any indications that might suggest susceptibility to a psychotic episode. Moreover, incorporating deep breathwork practices (like holotropic breathwork) into the therapeutic process allows me to gain insight into clients' capacity to navigate altered states of consciousness. If I observe any manifestations of psychosis during the breathwork, I conduct further evaluations before proceeding with psychedelic therapy. One client I worked with offers a clear example of how, through both formal and informal screenings, I identify signs of mental health instability. The assessment I conducted with this client led me to steer her toward a therapeutic approach that didn't involve the use of any psychedelic.

Hannah, a 30-year-old woman, approached me seeking psychedelic integration therapy. She described feeling trapped in a cycle of despair and discontent with her life and told me she was yearning for change. During our initial conversation, Hannah emphasized her belief in the therapeutic potential of psychedelics. She mentioned having previously participated in traditional group sessions involving psychedelics and said that while she felt that those experiences were valuable, having a therapist's guidance might unlock deeper insights. Specifically, she told me she had taken part in two ayahuasca ceremonies and a psilocybin circle, all of which she described as grounding and not particularly challenging.

In our first formal session, Hannah's vibrant personality was immediately apparent—not only through her distinct attire, but also in her animated way of expressing herself. Intriguingly, she referred to her multiple "personalities" by numbering them. Her passion for art shone through as she discussed her ventures into painting, singing, and screenwriting. I found myself wondering if this multifaceted personality was an extension of her artistic spirit. With this in mind, I felt it was too early to rule out the possibility of working with psychedelics and decided to continue assessing her in our next session.

The more sessions I had with Hannah, the stronger our therapeutic bond became. Over time, I began to interpret Hannah's unconventional method of defining herself (using numbers for her personalities) as a form of artistic expression rather than a sign of mental distress. Intrigued yet still wary, I suggested a holotropic breathwork session, to which she enthusiastically agreed.

However, during this breathwork session, Hannah exhibited concerning behaviors: she spoke in various voices, experienced hallucinations, and even displayed moments of paranoia. Most concerning was the extended time it took for her to return to a regular state of consciousness, which typically occurs within minutes. This experience solidified my decision to avoid psychedelics in our therapeutic work. I steered her toward therapy that did not involve these substances and encouraged her to avoid using them on her own.

In our following session, Hannah recounted her breathwork experience, describing it as both unsettling and enlightening. She felt a serenity in the days that followed, despite the initial discomfort. I shared my observations, praising her profound sensory sensitivity and remarkable artistic expression. I highlighted how her unique states of consciousness, rife with creativity, were evident even during the breathwork. I expressed my belief that her innate creativity and depth of introspection meant she could benefit from therapy without the need for psychedelics. Hannah was understandably disappointed and expressed her disagreement with my viewpoint, which I had anticipated. She told me she had clearly stated her desire to work with psychedelics during our initial call and saw me as just a supplement to her exploration with psychedelics. I empathized with her feelings but emphasized my concerns about the potential risks posed by psychedelics, given her heightened sensitivity and creativity. Although she had previous positive experiences with psychedelics, I feared that further exploration might be detrimental. I assured her that there were many other avenues available for us to explore together in therapy, and asked her to trust the process. Fortunately, our strong therapeutic rapport led her to agree, and we scheduled our next session.

Over time, Hannah expressed gratitude, revealing that no one had ever acknowledged her artistic talents and creativity as meaningfully as I had. She began to perceive her unique thought processes and "personalities" as another canvas on which to express herself. I enthusiastically concurred, adding that it takes a genuine artist to interpret and map the world as uniquely and beautifully as she does. Hannah remains a client at my private practice and attends sessions on occasion. Since starting our therapeutic journey, she hasn't felt the need to use any psychedelics, and I believe she derives benefits from therapy alone.

Hannah's journey also beautifully illustrates a vital truth: the therapeutic value of the MPIM framework extends far beyond psychedelic substances themselves. While psychedelics can catalyze profound experiences, the deeper work often arises from the safety, attunement, self-awareness, and creative resilience developed through the therapeutic process itself. Clients like Hannah are a reminder that meaningful therapeutic transformation can occur even without the use of psychedelic medicines, validating and reinforcing the inherent power of mindful, intentional therapy.

For clinicians venturing into the realm of psychedelic therapy, it is essential to rigorously screen clients both before their initial session and throughout the therapy process. This requires the subtle skill of blending formal and informal methods, consisting of both verbal interactions and observational insights. Above all, the client's physical and emotional well-being must be prioritized. The primary aim of the therapeutic endeavor should be to unlock the therapeutic potential of psychedelics while remaining committed to the client's safety and welfare.

Chapter 7

Preparation

Creating Change from the Start

> A teacher points the way. A guru is the way.
>
> —*Ram Dass, 1988, 00:27:00*

In psychedelic therapy, the therapist is the client's teacher, and the medicine is their guru. It is the therapist who points them toward their guru and exposes them to skills that will help them drop into their psychedelic experience safely, with the least amount of mental resistance. Stepping into the role of teacher requires the therapist to adopt a more directive stance and guide clients toward specific practices and tools designed to optimize their psychedelic experience.

These preparatory methods, which I will discuss in detail later, should be implemented in the weeks leading up to the psychedelic session, to ensure that the client enters the experience psychologically, emotionally, and physically prepared. Although this directive approach may initially appear to contrast with the foundational principles of systemic therapy—an orientation rooted in facilitation rather than direct instruction—it represents a careful balancing act. In this context, the therapist must sometimes assume the role of guide, which invites new possibilities and points of caution. For me, being a guide in the psychedelic therapy process allows me to blend shamanic traditions, which emphasize spiritual preparation and intentionality, with the structured, evidence-based framework of systemic therapy. Combining these approaches leaves the therapeutic process both academically grounded and deeply attuned to the transformative nature of psychedelic experiences.

It is vital to always communicate about these practices in a way that empowers the client, emphasizing their autonomy and affirming the choices they make during preparation. When clients feel confident and reassured, they become more receptive and primed for the transformative changes

DOI: 10.4324/9781003541639-11

ahead. Moreover, the preparation process often involves clients making changes—such as limiting their consumption of alcohol or caffeine—that can benefit them independently and potentially create lasting transformation beyond the psychedelic experience.

Beyond what transpires in formal preparation sessions, we encourage our clients to take independent actions in service of their preparation. It is good to offer a range of options for them to consider, based on both your professional experience and the observed therapeutic benefits of these options. These recommendations should be presented as supportive tools rather than rigid directives, allowing clients to explore what resonates most with their individual needs. It's important to emphasize that although we should give suggestions informed by our clinical practice and lived experience, we must help our clients trust their own intuition and self-awareness to decide what helps them feel most prepared. Encouraging this autonomy fosters a deeper sense of agency in our clients, helping ensure that their preparatory work remains personally meaningful and aligned with their unique psychological and emotional landscape.

Clients must be clearly informed that a psychedelic experience can be challenging to interpret, as it involves entering an altered state of consciousness or reality that lacks familiar reference points, conceptual models, or preexisting frameworks. Clients should be prepared for the possibility of encountering novel, abstract, or ineffable perceptions that may require time and reflection to fully integrate. It is unknown territory. And yet, the more the client prepares to work with what they encounter, the less likely they are to experience confusion, fear, or panic. Instead, they are likely to greet the psychedelic experience with a mindset that is conducive to good therapeutic work.

Psychedelics amplify what is going on inside a person's mind (Grof, 1980), so what is in there during the experience influences what the person perceives and interprets, both during and after their journey. The preparation process centers on cultivating what's referred to as the client's *set,* or mindset. To help clients approach the psychedelic experience clearly and ready, we provide comprehensive education on what they might expect before, during, and after their journey. Pre-session discussions should focus on defining and exploring the client's intentions, as well as addressing key factors that can significantly influence their experience. These include breathwork practices, psychoeducation, dietary considerations, mindfulness techniques, sexual habits, and media consumption. Each of these elements plays a critical role in shaping the client's mental, emotional, and physiological state, ultimately contributing to the depth and effectiveness of the psychedelic experience. The short- and long-term therapeutic benefits of a psychedelic journey are largely dependent on those pre-sessions; cutting any of it short would be a disservice to the client.

Pre-session preparation has consistently been shown to facilitate positive changes for clients, even before they engage with the medicine. By fostering intentional shifts in mindset, habits, and emotional readiness, clients can enter the psychedelic experience with greater clarity and a stronger foundation for meaningful transformation. In some cases, clients have found themselves making the change they needed before their psychedelic session, alleviating or even resolving their initial complaints.

One example of this I encountered in my practice was Anne, a 32-year-old Hispanic woman who was raising seven-year-old twin girls and a five-year-old boy with her husband. She contacted my practice, Mindful Psychedelics, hoping to try something other than talk therapy. Anne explained that she had worked with several therapists throughout her adult life, but the lack of improvement she saw from those sessions had her feeling hopeless. She heard about the recent advances in psychedelic therapy, and although she was terrified to try any of them, she was desperately willing to see if they might help her in some way.

During Anne's first session, she complained that she had completely run out of patience for her kids and husband—something she'd been experiencing since her twins were born seven years ago. She added that her husband was a nice man and her children were well-behaved, making it seem as if she was the problem. This was a notion her parents and siblings had often reinforced. Anne shared that recently, she found herself wanting to run away from it all and start a new life—even if it had to be one without her children. On the one hand, that thought scared her, because she loved her children very much. But on the other hand, she believed she was harming them with what she referred to as "verbal and emotional abuse." By the time she came to see me, she'd convinced herself that her family was probably better off without her.

During our initial session, I noticed how uncomfortable Anne appeared, as she sat on the edge of the sofa with her arms and legs tightly crossed. She also spoke quickly and seemed to be constantly out of breath. I told Anne what I noticed about her physical appearance, and she broke down in tears. She said she had felt agitated for a long time, as if something was always wrong, and she was utterly exhausted. I told her I could only imagine how exhausting those feelings must be and that the physical tension must drain her completely, leaving her with no energy or patience for anyone or anything. I told her I believed her body was in a constant mode of flight or fight, which meant that it was prepared for danger at all times. Her mind was telling her body to be ready in case of an emergency. But as helpful as that state of readiness is in a moment of real danger, it's problematic when it becomes a chronic state—especially when there isn't any real, life-threatening danger around.

I asked Anne if it would be okay to try a couple of breathwork exercises to help regulate her autonomic nervous system. She agreed to try. I then demonstrated a simple practice, in which I inhaled slowly through my nose for 4 seconds, held my breath for 7 seconds, and then exhaled through my mouth for 8 seconds. I had her try that breath five times in a row while I guided her through the process. After she finished, I asked her if she felt any different, and she told me she felt a bit calmer. I told her to experiment with using that breathing technique throughout the week, even if she only had time for a couple of those breaths. Again, she agreed.

A week later, Anne came into the session saying she had used the breathing technique throughout the day and found it somewhat helpful. The best part was that it helped her fall asleep quicker than before (a benefit I was aware of but had forgotten to mention in our previous session). I asked Anne if we could work on other mindfulness exercises, and she said that after seeing what a simple breath could do, she was up for anything. During the subsequent few sessions, as we prepared for a psychedelic journey, I taught her other breathing exercises and recommended a mindfulness book.

In the last 10 minutes of every session, Anne and I practiced meditating together. Anne was a disciplined student, so she took the initiative to create habits that resulted in significant change. In what was to be our last preparation session, she mentioned that her sister was impressed to see how different she looked and acted. One of her twins had also told her during bedtime, "Mom, I love you so much"—something she had never said before. Anne credited her new way of being for that beautiful, meaningful moment.

In that same session, Anne told me she wanted to hold off on working with the psychedelic medicine, which we were scheduled to incorporate one week later. She shared that she was happy with how things were progressing and no longer felt the same urgency about working with psychedelics that she had before she called me. Her home life was much calmer, and her desire to run away had mostly disappeared. I excitedly agreed and encouraged her to stay on the path of mindfulness, which she promised she'd never leave. Although Anne was desperate when I first met her, she was hesitant to work with psychedelics in the first place. From the start, I firmly believed that her new practices and tools, including mindfulness and breathing exercises, would be enough to help her create the long-term change she desired.

Anne's case clearly demonstrates how effective preparation practices like breathwork and mindfulness can foster significant personal transformation, even before engaging with psychedelics. This underscores a core principle of Mindful Psychedelics: The beliefs and practices that clients cultivate in preparation for a meaningful psychedelic journey are fundamentally the same as those needed to cultivate a rich and fulfilling life experience.

Harnessing the Power of Expectancy in Psychedelic Therapy

In Chapter 2, I explored how expectancy can shape the initial screening process. Here, I'll delve deeper into its specific role within psychedelic-assisted therapy, where expectations aren't just psychological background noise, but powerful ingredients in the therapeutic process. Studies have shown that when clients approach psychedelic experiences with positive expectations, the likelihood of meaningful insight and emotional healing increases significantly (Carhart-Harris et al., 2018). In this work, how someone prepares for the journey—mentally, emotionally, and even spiritually—can shape the depth of their experience, the way they meet challenges, and the extent to which transformation carries into their daily lives.

To help facilitate this process, early preparation sessions should introduce the idea that change can begin before any medicine is ingested. Clients are encouraged to adopt a broader view of healing—one which includes the possibility that subtle, even mysterious shifts may already be underway. This orientation helps clients see transformation as something that unfolds over time, not something confined to the hours of a psychedelic journey.

To reinforce this perspective, I often invite clients to pay close attention to moments in daily life that feel particularly meaningful or synchronistic. Noticing, writing down, and reflecting on these occurrences can foster a deeper sense of engagement with their inner process, offering opportunities to integrate insights even before the journey begins. This is akin to the miracle question used in solution-focused therapy; it shifts attention away from problems and toward desired changes, allowing clients to begin constructing new internal narratives. The simple act of expecting change can set that change into motion. This kind of expectancy works like a self-fulfilling prophecy: The more clients believe transformation is possible, the more they begin thinking, behaving, and feeling in ways that support it.

Of course, this approach is never one-size-fits-all. Although some clients are moved by ideas of synchronicity or spiritual alignment, others are more skeptical—or even resistant—toward metaphysical language. Ezra, a scientist in his mid-forties, was one such client. Although religious in his daily life, Ezra described himself as "allergic" to anything that sounded too mystical. He came to therapy struggling with deep shame around his experience with erectile dysfunction, and when we began discussing expectancy and change, he bristled at my use of words like "magic" or "energy." For Ezra, transformation needed a foundation in science, not spirituality.

In working with Ezra, I adapted my language to match his worldview. Rather than talking about signs from the universe, I shared findings from neuroscience, explaining that humans consciously perceive only a tiny fraction of available sensory data,[1] due to the brain's built-in filters (i.e., the default mode network I've mentioned in previous chapters). Of the estimated 11 million bits of sensory information processed by the brain each second, we consciously perceive only 40–50. I explained how habits, beliefs, and mental filters shape the highlight reel of what enters awareness, and how intentional practices like mindfulness can rewire these filters to promote a more expansive and optimistic engagement with reality (Davidson & McEwen, 2012).

Ezra resonated deeply with this explanation. It gave him a framework he could trust—one rooted in brain science, rather than abstract intuition. Once he understood that the brain's plastic nature meant he could begin reshaping his experience through focused attention, he fully committed to the preparatory work. By the time he sat with the medicine, Ezra had already experienced significant emotional breakthroughs—not through the medicine itself, but through his preparation for it.

Ezra's case underscores a vital principle: The therapeutic process begins long before the psychedelic is administered. Whether framed in metaphysical or scientific terms, expectancy is a tool therapists can use to help clients step into a mindset of possibility and empowerment. When clients start believing that change is possible, the journey becomes less about seeking something out there and more about discovering what's been unfolding all along.

Preparing Without Priming

Building on the importance of mindset, one of the most delicate aspects of preparation for therapists to consider is finding the right balance between offering guidance and avoiding undue influence. Therapists often wonder how much information is too much, especially when it comes to discussing potentially difficult or distressing experiences. Given how suggestible the mind becomes in altered states, there's a valid concern that even well-intentioned warnings may unintentionally shape a client's experience.

This concern isn't unfounded. Psychedelic states are highly sensitive to both set and setting. When a client hears that they might feel overwhelmed or out of control during their journey, it may lead them to filter and interpret their experience in specific ways. In altered states, even subtle suggestions can ripple into powerful internal narratives that shape the entire experience.

Still, avoiding these conversations altogether can leave clients unprepared. When challenging sensations or unfamiliar states arise, as they often do, clients without context may respond with fear or resistance, which can amplify distress rather than open the door to insight. The key, then, is to prepare without priming.

Rather than offering predictions, therapists can provide a broad, non-directive framework that leaves room for a wide range of experiences. This can happen through simple shifts in language. Instead of saying, "You might feel afraid," a therapist might choose to say, "Some people encounter fear, whereas others describe feelings of deep peace, connection, or awe." Instead of, "You might feel like you're dissolving," they can offer, "Some people describe a sense of merging with everything around them or losing track of their usual sense of self." This language keeps the door open without guiding the client toward any particular outcome. It offers orientation without expectation, equipping clients with enough understanding to navigate intensity while preserving the spontaneity and mystery that often make psychedelic experiences so transformative.

Ultimately, this approach reinforces the client's agency as they enter the open field of possibility that psychedelics offer. By preparing clients with language that supports without shaping, we allow their experience to unfold with integrity. Their insights, then, are more likely to arise from within, rather than being mirrored back from the outside. Preparing without priming is, in essence, an act of respect—for the medicine, for the client's inner intelligence, and for the sacred unknown.

The Role of Mindfulness

Mindfulness serves as a foundational and integrative component of psychedelic therapy, offering clients a structured framework through which they can engage deeply with their inner experiences. As I briefly mentioned in Chapter 2, the capacity for nonjudgmental awareness cultivated through mindfulness is particularly well-suited for the psychedelic process. It supports the work of surrendering to altered perceptions and allowing emergent subconscious material to prompt meaningful contemplation and integration. By fostering psychological flexibility and emotional regulation, mindfulness primes the client for a more intentional and meaningful engagement with their psychedelic journey. More than a preparatory tool, mindfulness becomes a way of being that enhances the therapeutic benefits of the medicine itself.

One of the primary intersections between mindfulness and psychedelics is the ability to suspend habitual patterns of thought, allowing for greater cognitive and emotional openness. Research indicates that both mindfulness meditation and psychedelic substances reduce activity in the DMN, the neural system associated with self-referential thinking and rigid cognitive constructs. When the DMN is quieted, clients are afforded a reprieve from entrenched patterns of negativity, self-doubt, and rumination, facilitating a state of heightened receptivity to new insights. Mindfulness practices, particularly those rooted in Jon Kabat-Zinn's eight foundational attitudes—beginner's mind, non-judging, acceptance, letting go, trust, patience, non-striving, and gratitude—help clients develop the resilience necessary to navigate their psychedelic experience without resistance or fear.

Moreover, mindfulness functions as a stabilizing force throughout the integration process. Although psychedelics can generate profound emotional and psychological revelations, their long-term efficacy depends on the user's ability to translate their insights into lasting behavioral and cognitive shifts. The discipline of mindfulness ensures that these insights get embedded within the client's daily consciousness. Journaling, guided meditations, and breathwork reinforce the themes that arise during the psychedelic experience, allowing the client to engage in ongoing self-reflection and personal growth. The emphasis on non-striving also helps clients manage their expectations, preventing disillusionment if their psychedelic journey doesn't immediately yield clarity.

Many individuals who previously struggled with mindfulness or meditation often find themselves more capable of engaging in these practices after a psychedelic experience. Psychedelics can create a state of heightened neuroplasticity, allowing new neural pathways to form that support sustained attention and emotional regulation. This shift enables clients to access meditative states more easily, sometimes for the first time in their lives. Additionally, the profound sense of presence and interconnectedness experienced during a psychedelic journey can serve as a direct point of reference for what mindfulness feels like in its most embodied form. Clients often report that following one or multiple psychedelic sessions, they are better able to quiet the mind, sustain focus, and remain grounded in the present. Over time, these shifts may become enduring, as the brain reorganizes itself around the new patterns established through psychedelic-assisted introspection. One of my previous clients provides an excellent example of how mindfulness can become vital to a client's transformation in psychedelic work.

Rebecca, who had long been immobilized by the opposing forces of fear and obligation, came to see me after years of rationalizing her unhappy marriage. She described feeling anchored by concern for her children's well-being and terrified about the financial uncertainty a separation might bring. In the weeks leading up to her guided psilocybin journey, I encouraged Rebecca to establish a daily mindfulness practice. Unlike many of my other clients, she connected with the practice almost immediately. She approached it enthusiastically and came to treat it as a lifeline—a way to find herself again. I don't often see someone resonate so deeply with mindfulness, and it played a pivotal role in her process.

Through consistent practice, Rebecca learned to sit with discomfort, observe her inner dialogue, and soften the harsh self-judgments that had long shaped her experience. Over time, she developed the ability to notice her thoughts and emotions without being overwhelmed by them—an awareness that would soon become essential.

During her journey, Rebecca confronted the full weight of her emotional pain. She described it as falling into an abyss—a deep and inescapable descent into the sadness, resentment, and fear she had long suppressed. But instead of resisting or retreating, she drew on the skills she had practiced. She stayed present with the discomfort. She breathed. She observed. And slowly, she began to see clearly. She saw how much of her life had been shaped by fear—whether the fear of conflict, rejection, or abandonment.

She lamented the countless years she'd spent carefully managing her husband's moods, trying to preempt his anger, and walking on eggshells to maintain peace. What once felt like a rational way to keep her family together now appeared as a survival mechanism rooted in anxiety and self-sacrifice.

In the midst of her clarity, Rebecca experienced something unexpected: self-compassion. The mindfulness practice she had built over the weeks leading up to her journey had allowed her to respond to her own suffering with gentleness instead of blame. That shift opened the door to a deeper truth for Rebecca. She shared:

> I do love him. I always have. But I thought loving him meant staying. I thought it meant suffering. Now I see—I can still love him, and choose to leave. I can love him, and love myself, and not betray either one.

Rebecca was grounded and clear. The psychedelic experience hadn't given her something new; it had revealed what she had known all along but never felt strong enough to face. And it was mindfulness that gave her the strength to face it. Later, Rebecca shared with me that without the preparation she did leading up to her journey, that insight would have made her panic. But because she had practiced staying with discomfort, noticing without judgment, and bringing kindness to herself, she was able to meet this revelation with courage and insight.

In psychedelic therapy, the medicine opens the door, but it's mindfulness that teaches clients how to walk through it. It anchors them in presence, strengthens their resilience, and helps them stay connected to themselves when everything else dissolves. For Rebecca, that anchor made all the difference.

Intention Setting

One essential difference between a therapeutic psychedelic journey and a recreational one is the setting of intentions prior to receiving the medicine. Setting a clear intention is one way that clients can start preparing their mindset, or set. Intentions help focus their energy and attention toward a desired goal. Furthermore, the intention can help clients navigate their psychedelic journey, especially if it becomes difficult or chaotic at certain points.

Following the initial call with a potential client, the first step is to ask, "What are you hoping to gain from a psychedelic experience?" Their response to this question becomes the foundation of the first session. It prompts our exploration into their goals, aspirations, and challenges, and it helps shape the process of identifying and refining their intentions for the journey.

When guiding clients in the process of setting their intentions for the psychedelic journey, therapists must keep several things in mind. First, it is essential that a client's primary intention be rooted in trust and acceptance. This helps ensure that they approach their experience with openness, allowing them to deeply engage with the therapeutic process and facilitate meaningful transformation through the journey.

Therapists should strongly encourage clients to incorporate a primary intention that reflects openness and surrender, such as, "I surrender to the medicine. I allow it to give me what I need, not necessarily what I think I want." Establishing this type of intention serves two critical functions in the preparation process. First, it reinforces key mindfulness principles, including trust, letting go, non-striving, and acceptance. These principles help clients cultivate a receptive mindset, reducing resistance to the experience and fostering a deeper sense of presence. Second, it broadens the range of possibilities during the psychedelic experience, allowing clients access to more fluid and adaptable interpretations of the insights they gain, which, in some cases, may not immediately emerge. This openness becomes particularly valuable in post-integration sessions, where meaning is explored and framed in a way that supports long-term personal growth and understanding.

Some clients may undergo a psychedelic session without experiencing any noticeable changes in thought patterns, body sensations, or visual perceptions. This can happen for a variety of reasons. Most often, it can be attributed to the participant's mental resistance. Some individuals, despite being well-prepared, will experience high levels of anxiety during the administration of the psychedelic, which can cause a fight-or-flight response that interferes with the medicine's hallucinogenic effects (Winkelman & Sessa, 2019). The mind and body's perception that a threat is present will make it difficult for the client to surrender to the experience. In this way, the client's mind and body can be more of a force than the medicine itself. The key to these individuals' post-integration process is to utilize the primary intention of allowing the experience to give them what they need. This intention gives the therapist great flexibility, allowing them to frame the experience in a way that shows the client the medicine has revealed something subtle but essential.

This was the case for Milton, who, in his mid-twenties, was hoping to process and let go of some childhood trauma, having been mercilessly bullied in elementary school. He took part in an ayahuasca circle and came out of it disappointed. He believed that the medicine hadn't done anything for him, because the effects he felt were too subtle and fairly uneventful. He didn't come away with any clear insights or emotional shifts. When Milton arrived at my office for his first post-journey session, he was devastated. During that post-integration session, I focused on his primary intention and the mindfulness themes we had worked on previously. I suggested that maybe the medicine was letting him know he'd already let go of more than he realized, and there wasn't much more to process or release. We spoke about the importance of accepting and trusting the process, and we agreed that if he had more to let go of, a new opportunity would arise for him to have a different experience with the medicine. He left that session feeling differently about his ayahuasca journey than when he first arrived. More importantly, he left with the idea that maybe he was more healed than he knew, something he later told me was significant for his healing process.

In another post-integration session with a client who also didn't experience much in her psychedelic journey, I offered the metaphor of the psychedelic experience as a mindfulness "life test." Collaboratively, the client and I determined that the medicine was giving her an opportunity to practice letting go of expectations and working toward acceptance of what is—a teaching that was relevant to her therapeutic goal of exploring the exhausting tendency to try controlling every outcome of her daily experience.

The second component of the intention-setting process involves developing secondary intentions that align with the client's primary goals and desires. Several key factors should be considered when guiding clients through this process. First, their intentions should be framed in a positive orientation, emphasizing the presence of something rather than the absence of something else (de Shazer et al., 2007). For example, if a client expresses a desire for the medicine to help decrease self-hate, the intention should be reframed as, "I hope the medicine helps me connect to love for myself." This approach fosters a constructive mindset that encourages growth, healing, and openness to transformative experiences. Changing a negatively oriented intention to a positive one ideally helps make the journey smoother and keep the client's mindset positively oriented.

Reframing intentions in a positive, presence-oriented way is crucial. It helps direct the client's focus toward growth, connection, and constructive outcomes, rather than keeping them fixated on what they wish to avoid. Research in solution-focused therapy suggests that positively framed goals are more actionable and empowering, encouraging clients to engage with the process in an open and optimistic way (de Shazer et al., 2007). Additionally, this positive reframing aligns with the principles of neuroplasticity. Focusing on desired outcomes strengthens neural pathways associated with those experiences, potentially enhancing the therapeutic benefits of the psychedelic journey.

The next consideration in the intention-setting process is to avoid what can be referred to as *crystal ball intentions*. Clients often want to set intentions that are ultimately requests for answers about their future, such as whether they should remain in a romantic relationship or leave their current job. These types of intentions should be discouraged, as psychedelic experiences rarely provide direct answers to binary questions. When clients expect a definitive resolution, they risk perceiving the experience as unsuccessful if they don't get the clarity they anticipated. Naturally, this hinders the post-integration process, making it more difficult for the client to extract meaningful insights from their experience.

Instead, therapists should guide clients toward setting deeper, more open-ended intentions that allow for personal exploration rather than seeking direct answers. It's important to explain that the subconscious—or the broader universe—doesn't operate in linear, transactional ways. Instead, psychedelic experiences often present wisdom in abstract, symbolic, or emotional forms, requiring interpretation and reflection. Integrating mindfulness principles—such as acceptance of the present moment and trust in the process (Kabat-Zinn, 2019)—can help clients shift their approach to intention-setting.

For example, if a client initially formulates an intention such as, "I want the medicine to show me if I should stay in my marriage," it should be reframed to address the core of their desire. A more effective intention would be, "I want the medicine to show me love and connection." This adjustment allows for a broader, more meaningful exploration of the client's needs and values. Clients typically accept and appreciate this shift, as it helps them engage with the experience in a way that fosters deeper self-understanding.

Once the client feels confident and satisfied with both their primary and secondary intentions, the therapist should have them write the intentions on paper and take them home, where they will place them somewhere visible. This ensures that the client will consistently see their intentions. This will prompt them to regularly reflect on them and integrate them into their daily mindfulness practice. The goal is for clients to internalize their intentions so much that once they enter their psychedelic journey, the intentions shape their mindset and allow them to navigate the experience with clarity and purpose.

Breathwork as a Somatic Tool for Psychedelic Preparation and Integration

Breathwork is one of the simplest and most powerful tools available to both therapist and client. It acts as a bridge between body and mind, giving clients a direct way to regulate arousal, calm anxiety, and reconnect with presence. Slow, exhale-emphasized breathing reliably shifts the nervous system toward parasympathetic balance and increases heart-rate variability, creating a more resilient baseline for the intense experiences that psychedelics often evoke (Zaccaro et al., 2018; Shaffer & Meehan, 2020). Even short, exhale-heavy sighs have been shown to reduce distress within minutes (Balban et al., 2023). In the psychedelic space, where large-scale networks such as the default mode network (DMN) are in flux (Tagliazucchi & Carhart-Harris, 2014a), the breath provides a steady anchor that keeps clients tethered to the body while navigating altered states of consciousness.

In preparation, breathwork helps prime the nervous system. Practicing steady, paced breathing in the weeks leading up to a session teaches the client how to find stability when emotions intensify. Techniques like resonance or coherence breathing—about five seconds in, five seconds out—create a reliable sense of balance and can be introduced as a daily practice. Exhale-dominant patterns, such as 4–7–8 breathing, are especially valuable for clients prone to anxiety. These methods do more than calm; they cultivate familiarity with surrender. Each exhale becomes a rehearsal for letting go, training the client's body to soften into uncertainty rather than resist it.

During the journey itself, the breath often becomes the most accessible guide. Psychedelics can swing the nervous system between sympathetic activation—racing heart, shallow breath, tremors—and parasympathetic collapse—immobility or derealization. Clients who have practiced breath awareness can meet these shifts without interpreting them as danger. A long, slow exhale can downshift a spiral of panic. A series of short inhales followed by an extended sigh can interrupt acute overwhelm. Even breathing in rhythm with a therapist, when appropriate and consensual, can restore safety and coherence, particularly for trauma survivors who benefit from co-regulation.

Breathwork is not only for moments of distress. It can also help a client stay embodied during profound states such as ego dissolution. A steady rhythm of inhales and exhales allows the client to remain anchored in the body even as identity and perception expand. In this way, the breath does not pull the client out of the experience but offers a non-fragmented way of moving through it.

Once the journey has ended, breathwork supports integration. Returning to simple, paced breathing helps stabilize the nervous system and reestablish equilibrium. When paired with reflection, the breath can also act as a doorway back into the journey: clients often find that breathing in a particular way allows them to recall the emotional tone of their psychedelic experience and revisit it safely. This somatic recall helps insights take root. Over time, incorporating breath practices into daily life—morning resonance breathing to begin the day balanced, or an extended exhale sequence before bed—creates continuity between the peak event and everyday life. The insights of the session are thus not left behind but woven into the client's nervous system and routines.

Of course, therapists must be mindful of limitations. Certain practices, especially fast cyclical breathing or prolonged hyperventilation, are contraindicated for clients with cardiovascular disease, epilepsy, glaucoma, or other medical vulnerabilities, and should not be introduced during the height of a psychedelic session. Intensive methods such as Holotropic Breathwork belong to a different context, requiring their own screening and supervision (Grof & Grof, 2010). What is most useful in psychedelic work are gentle, accessible practices that can be taught in minutes and recalled when needed.

In practice, the breath becomes a language in itself. Sometimes a simple cue—"Exhale longer than you inhale. Soften the jaw"—is enough to help a client find ground. At other times, the therapist may remind: "Let the out-breath carry what you cannot hold," or "Even inhales and exhales—feel your feet on the floor." These phrases, simple and embodied, anchor the client in the here-and-now.

Breathwork, then, is not an add-on but a foundation. It offers continuity across all three phases of psychedelic therapy: it prepares the body to surrender, steadies the mind within the journey, and helps translate insights into daily rhythms of regulation and presence. When integrated in this way, the breath allows what unfolds in the medicine space to be not only felt but also lived.

It is worth saying that the potential of the breath extends far beyond what can be captured here. An entire book could be devoted to its role in therapy, medicine, work, and everyday life. What I have offered in this section is only a glimpse—a way of honoring the breath without attempting to do it full justice. To truly explore the depth and importance of this practice would require another volume altogether.

Still, even a few simple practices can serve as anchors. Here are three that I often introduce:

Steady Breathing

Find a comfortable position, with your feet grounded and your spine long. Place one hand lightly on your belly, the other on your chest. Begin by inhaling gently through your nose for a count of five, allowing the belly to rise. Exhale for five, letting the body soften as the air leaves. Continue at this rhythm, five in and five out, for several minutes. Notice how the steadiness of your breath begins to steady your thoughts. If your mind wanders, simply return to the count and the sensation of the air moving in and out. This practice is like tuning an instrument—it brings your whole system back into harmony.

Calming Exhale

Sit or lie down somewhere you feel safe. Take a slow inhale through your nose for four counts, then let the exhale lengthen to six counts. If that feels comfortable, you can gradually move toward a 4–7–8 rhythm: inhale for four, hold gently for seven, then release in a long exhale for eight. With each extended exhale, imagine letting go of the tension you no longer need. Feel your shoulders drop, your jaw soften, and your heart slow its pace. Continue for two or three minutes, allowing the longer exhale to teach your body how to settle into calm. This is especially helpful before sleep, or whenever anxiety feels close at hand.

Reset Sigh

When you feel a sudden wave of overwhelm or panic, pause and take a short, deep inhale through the nose, then add a little "top-off" inhale, as though you are filling the lungs to their edge. Exhale fully through the mouth with a long sigh, as though you are letting the weight of the moment leave with the breath. Repeat this one to three times. You may notice your heart rate slowing, your chest loosening, and your mind clearing enough to reorient to the present. Think of it as a way of pressing "reset," giving your body permission to release what it cannot carry.

These are humble practices, yet they open profound doorways. They remind us that healing is not always found in the extraordinary but often in the simplest of gestures: a steady rhythm, a longer exhale, the soft release of a sigh. In these small moments, the body remembers how to return home.

The Dieta: Food, Sex, and Media

This section examines the insights I've gained from my interactions with plant medicine shamans and facilitators, highlighting their perspectives on the essential components of preparation for engaging with the medicine. The three key areas of emphasis include dietary habits, sexual activities, and media consumption.

Shamans have long played a central role in preparing individuals for psychedelic journeys, drawing on indigenous traditions that emphasize the importance of intention, ritual, and community support. Preparation often involves creating a sacred context through ceremonies, dietas (restrictive diets designed to cleanse the body and mind), and guided meditations (though they aren't referred to as such). All of these elements serve to align the participant with the spiritual and therapeutic purpose of the experience (Tupper, 2009). In indigenous tradition, preparatory practices are designed to foster a calm and receptive mindset, helping participants enter the experience with clear intentions and reduced fear or resistance. Though they are unlikely to use those terms, shamans emphasize the importance of set and setting, which means ensuring that the physical environment is safe and spiritually attuned. Modern psychedelic research echoes this, asserting that attention to set and setting is critical for positive outcomes (Carhart-Harris et al., 2018; Schmid & Liechti, 2021). By integrating symbolic rituals, songs (icaros), and prayers, shamans help participants prepare to navigate the altered states of consciousness induced by substances like ayahuasca or psilocybin.

An individual journeying to the Amazon for an ayahuasca ceremony would typically undergo days, or even weeks, of preparation. Shamans often suggest that 90% of the therapeutic benefits derived from these medicines emerge from the preparatory phase itself, which is largely centered around specific lifestyle adjustments (Anonymous, 2012).

Although clients may not be traveling to the Amazon, adhering to traditional guidelines regarding food, sex, and media consumption has been shown to provide significant benefits. However, within a Western professional context, offering such recommendations—particularly concerning diet—may be perceived as exceeding the boundaries of therapeutic expertise. As neither a nutritionist nor a medical doctor, a therapist providing dietary guidance falls outside the scope of conventional professional qualifications in Western practice. Nonetheless, the influence of these preparatory measures on the psychedelic experience remains well-documented, requiring therapists to be thoughtful and ethically grounded when discussing them with clients[2].

Navigating between two distinct cultural paradigms requires an awareness of the deep reverence traditional societies hold for shamans and plant healers. These individuals aren't merely regarded as spiritual guides; rather, they are seen as holistic healers who address all aspects of well-being, including physical health. Serving in the role of guide, therapists must act as conduits for deep wisdom while maintaining clear ethical and professional boundaries. Therapists should always encourage clients to consult with their healthcare providers before taking medicine, to ensure that their preparatory practices are consistent with their individual health needs and medical considerations.

From the very first session, it is essential to assess the client's dietary habits as part of the preparation process. Clients should be advised to eliminate processed foods and refined sugars, with the exception of natural sugars found in fruit. This guidance aligns with the shamanic perspective that artificial chemicals in processed foods and sugars may interfere with the body's natural equilibrium and inhibit an individual's connection to inner wisdom. They suggest that a body with fewer chemical residues can interact more potently with the medicine, thereby enhancing its therapeutic properties.

Furthermore, shamans caution against consuming meat. They believe that meat carries residual negative energies and emotions that might disrupt the clarity and focus of a psychedelic experience. The rationale is that the animals, having experienced significant trauma, carry distress in their DNA and tissues. When a person consumes that meat, they can inadvertently integrate the animal's trauma into their psyche. During a psychedelic journey, they might confront and process these traumas, mistakenly interpreting them as their own. Beyond these dietary guidelines, clients should also be strongly encouraged to abstain from alcohol, caffeine, and certain medications. The specifics concerning medication depend on the psychedelic in question and should always be discussed with a medical professional.

The second key area is sexual activity. Abstinence from sex in the weeks leading up to a psychedelic journey is a practice rooted in both traditional and contemporary wisdom. Its purpose is to conserve physical, emotional, and spiritual energy in preparation for the psychedelic journey. Modern practitioners also recommend sexual abstinence, to minimize distraction and avoid emotionally entangling experiences that might cloud the participant's intentions or bring unresolved relational dynamics into the session (Carhart-Harris et al., 2018). Furthermore, sexual activity can involve a significant exchange of energy and emotions. According to some traditions, this can dilute the clarity of the participant's inner work or integration process. Although little scientific research has been conducted to explore the direct impact of sexual abstinence on psychedelic outcomes, many facilitators and participants report that this practice enhances focus, introspection, and the overall depth of the journey.

During the first preparation session, therapists should inform clients that it's recommended for them to abstain from sex and masturbation for at least two weeks before taking the medicine. They should explain that according to traditional teachings, sexual energy is a powerful force that can be harnessed during the psychedelic journey. The more this energy is contained, the more readily it can flow and be utilized throughout the experience. Many clients will even notice that energy flowing through them during their altered state.

The third and final key area of lifestyle preparation is media usage. The pervasive use of screens and smartphones has created a culture of collective addiction. If we were to apply the CAGE questionnaire—commonly used to screen for alcohol addiction—to phone use, most people would likely qualify as addicted. The four questions—"Have you ever felt you should Cut down your use?", "Have people Annoyed you by criticizing your use?", "Have you ever felt Guilty about your use?", and "Have you ever used it as an Eye-opener in the morning?" (Ewing, 1984, pp. 1905–1906)—are alarmingly relevant to our relationship with screens. Being connected 24/7 exposes users to a barrage of influences—ranging from social media comparisons to the negativity of doom scrolling. Being mindful of media consumption in advance of a psychedelic journey is, therefore, pivotal.

Evaluating a client's media consumption—including television, social media, and other information platforms—should be an integral part of the preparation process. Clients should be strongly encouraged to implement a media detox in the weeks leading up to their psychedelic experience, eliminating exposure to news and social media. This recommendation is based on the principle that the mind should be oriented toward internal reflection rather than external distraction, as preoccupation with world events can shape emotional states and significantly influence the trajectory of the psychedelic journey.

The impact of media exposure on the psychedelic experience is well-documented, with numerous cases illustrating how external stressors can dominate the psychedelic state. One such case involved Emma, a 42-year-old journalist who had spent years covering international conflicts and political instability. Highly analytical and deeply invested in global affairs, Emma had developed a habit of consuming news updates throughout the day, particularly in the morning and before bed. Despite her commitment to the therapeutic process, she found it difficult to disengage from her work, often carrying the weight of current events into her personal life.

Leading up to her ayahuasca journey, Emma continued her routine of reading daily geopolitical analyses and immersing herself in discussions about escalating international tensions. She entered the ceremony hoping to understand why she struggled to be emotionally available in relationships, but instead, she found herself trapped in a harrowing, hyper-realistic vision of being inside a nuclear warhead, within the chaos of impending global catastrophe. Every attempt to redirect her focus toward her personal healing was overtaken by the intrusive imagery of destruction and existential dread. After the journey, she expressed frustration, feeling as though she had wasted a critical opportunity for self-exploration. It became evident that her emotional and cognitive state at the time of ingesting the medicine had been significantly shaped by the content she had been consuming in the days prior.

Emma's experience serves as a clear example of how media exposure can shape the subconscious landscape of a psychedelic journey. Rather than facilitating deep personal insight, her session had been consumed by external anxieties, limiting its therapeutic potential. Although she ultimately used the experience as a lesson in curating her mental environment, her case underscores the need to do internal preparation. Clients should be guided to approach their psychedelic experience with mental clarity and receptivity, helping to keep external concerns from overshadowing the deeper personal work the medicine is intended to facilitate.

In our post-integration session, Emma sat across from me with a look of quiet frustration. "I thought I was coming to heal myself," she said. "But instead, I lived through the end of the world." I gently reminded her of the emotional goal she had entered with—to explore the walls she'd built in her personal life. I asked what she thought had kept her from getting there. Without missing a beat, she replied, "The world got in the way. Or maybe I let it in too much." That insight shifted the tone of the session. Emma began to reflect on how often her identity had been tied to knowing everything, staying ahead of the news cycle, carrying the weight of global crises as a badge of honor and a shield. "It's like I've outsourced my inner life to the headlines," she admitted.

Together, we explored the idea that curating her internal environment could be an act of self-respect, rather than one of avoidance. She agreed to begin a media fast, checking the news only once a day, and substituting her morning doomscrolling session with a short mindfulness practice. Three weeks later, Emma reported that she was feeling lighter. "I'm starting to hear myself again," she said. "It's quiet, but it's there."

Just as the inner landscape must be tended to with care, so must the social and relational environment in which the client is embedded. Psychedelic healing doesn't happen in a vacuum; it unfolds within complex systems that can either support or hinder integration.

Systems in Psychedelic-Assisted Therapy

In psychedelic-assisted therapy, the client's social context—including their family, intimate relationships, and broader support system—plays a crucial role in the integration process and overall therapeutic outcomes. A systemic lens requires the therapist to assess not only the individual's readiness for the experience, but also the relational dynamics that may support or hinder their process. Clients don't exist in isolation. They are embedded in relational networks—families, partnerships, and communities—that carry specific beliefs, biases, and power dynamics. These systems inevitably influence the therapeutic process. Thoughtful preparation is essential to ensure that these external forces support, rather than derail, the client's healing.

One critical consideration is the moral, religious, or ideological stance that close family members—especially spouses and parents—may hold toward the use of psychedelics. In many cultural and religious traditions, the use of psychoactive substances—even in a therapeutic context—is viewed as dangerous, immoral, or indicative of personal failure. A spouse or parent with such beliefs may respond with disapproval, judgment, or even active opposition, particularly if they perceive the client's engagement in psychedelic therapy as reckless or unethical. This can generate internal conflict for the client, who may struggle with guilt, secrecy, or the fear of disappointing loved ones. In these cases, therapists should take care to help their clients thoughtfully consider how much to share about their psychedelic experience, and with whom.

Beyond ideological resistance, some family dynamics introduce more overt risks. Clients in abusive or controlling relationships must carefully consider the potential for coercion, blackmail, or manipulation stemming from their engagement with psychedelic substances, particularly in jurisdictions where use of these substances remains legally precarious. In high-conflict separations, divorces, or custody disputes, a vindictive partner may exploit a client's psychedelic use as leverage—either as a legal or moral argument against their fitness as a parent, or as a means of exerting control over their decisions. In such cases, the therapist must work collaboratively with the client to strategize how disclosure happens, ensuring that their participation in psychedelic therapy won't expose them to additional vulnerability. This may involve selectively sharing information; establishing discreet and secure support networks; and intentionally planning when and how they'll do their integration work, to minimize external interference.

Even in less extreme circumstances, unsupportive or skeptical family members can complicate the post-experience phase. Clients often emerge from their psychedelic journeys with heightened emotional sensitivity and openness, making them particularly susceptible to the influence of others' words, attitudes, and energy. Dismissive attitudes, persistent questioning, or outright hostility from family members can erode a client's trust in their experience, triggering doubt, defensiveness, or emotional contraction at a critical moment in their integration. Therapists should guide clients in anticipating and managing these interactions. This may include setting intentional boundaries around post-experience conversations, rehearsing non-confrontational responses to skeptical inquiries, or planning a temporary retreat from critical influences in the days following the experience.

Conversely, some family members may respond to the client's psychedelic experience with curiosity and openness, leading to meaningful shifts in relational dynamics. A client's healing and transformation can serve as an entry point for family members to explore their own psychological and spiritual growth. In these cases, the therapist may support the client in navigating these evolving relationships, helping them discern what to share, when to share it, and how to do so without feeling pressured to become a guide, teacher, or evangelist. The impact of psychedelic therapy can extend far beyond the individual client, influencing the broader systems in which they exist.

Ultimately, an effective therapist must balance these systemic considerations with a client-centered approach, empowering their clients to make informed decisions about disclosure, boundary setting, and support seeking. Psychedelic-assisted therapy doesn't take place in a vacuum; its success depends on the client's ability to navigate the complex web of relationships in which they are embedded. Creating a support map during preparation—which involves identifying safe confidants, likely skeptics, and potentially harmful influences—can help clients feel more grounded and empowered as they navigate the ripple effects of their transformation. By proactively addressing these challenges, therapists can help clients maximize the benefits of their work while safeguarding their well-being in the broader social context.

Psychedelic Psychoeducation

Educating clients about psychedelics—what they are, how they work, and what the experience might feel like—is a foundational part of preparing for therapeutic use. Psychoeducation builds trust, addresses fear, and supports clients in stepping into the unknown with confidence.

The abundance of well-researched resources—books, films, podcasts, and articles—available today makes it easier than ever to access information about psychedelics and their therapeutic potential. At the same time, this influx of material can be overwhelming or even misleading if it isn't carefully curated. Therefore, it's critical that therapists initiate structured conversations during preparation, to introduce key concepts that support their clients' psychological readiness and emotional resilience. Some of the core topics that should be part of this psychoeducation include:

- The physiological safety of most classic psychedelics.
- The importance of turning toward challenging emotions.
- How to engage with ego dissolution and altered states.
- The futility of resisting or attempting to "turn off" the medicine once it begins.
- The importance of trust—in the therapist, the process, and the medicine itself.

Introducing these themes ahead of time helps clients cultivate flexibility, surrender, and trust—three capacities essential for transformative engagement.

At the end of the first session, therapists should offer clients some thoughtfully selected materials, so they can begin engaging with these concepts on their own. The resources should be tailored to each client's existing knowledge, experience, and preferred learning style (e.g., auditory, visual, and experiential). Engaging clients in follow-up discussions about the material not only reinforce their learning, but also offers them an opportunity to clear up misconceptions and deepen their understanding. Therapists are encouraged to fully review resources before sharing them with clients, to ensure that what they share aligns with their values and clinical orientation. Below is a curated list of recommended resources.

Books

- *How to Change Your Mind* by Michael Pollan (2019)
- *The Psychedelic Experience* by Timothy Leary, Ralph Metzner, and Richard Alpert (1964)
- *Psychedelic Medicine* by Dr. Richard Louis Miller (2017)
- *Breaking Open the Head* by Daniel Pinchbeck (2003)
- *The Doors of Perception* by Aldous Huxley (1963)

Documentaries, Videos, and Podcasts

- *Fantastic Fungi* (2019)
- *How to Change Your Mind* (Netflix series, 2022)
- *The Healing Trip*—The Goop Lab with Gwyneth Paltrow (2020)
- *The Tim Ferriss Show*: Michael Pollan (2018)
- *The Tim Ferriss Show*: Stan Grof (2018)
- *Ayahuasca*—Aubrey Marcus & Mitch Schultz

These materials serve as helpful companions on the client's path toward expanded awareness, deepening their preparation for the journey ahead.

Additional Pre-session Conversations

Safety

One of the most common reasons people panic at the peak of a psychedelic journey is because they believe something is physically wrong with them. They may fear they're losing control, overdosing, or in danger. This is why it's so important to educate clients about the proven safety of psychedelic substances. The more they understand the pharmacology and mechanisms of action, the more they can relax into the experience.

One effective way to build trust is by introducing clients to relevant medical research, including the studies I write about in this book. Reviewing scientific literature helps clarify the consistently low toxicity and high physiological tolerability of psychedelics (Passie et al., 2002). These data points, grounded in decades of research, can offer clients the reassurance they need to let go into the process.

Most people need some form of validation from science or medicine to feel safe. Providing information on how psychedelics impact the brain—such as by modulating activity in regions like the DMN—also helps normalize the experience. Psychedelics temporarily reduce activity in this region, which is associated with self-referential thought and egoic processing. This shift opens space for increased emotional insight; but it can also create a sense of losing control, which the mind often interprets as danger. In response, the nervous system may initiate a fear-based, protective response, activating thoughts like:

- "Something bad is happening."
- "Why did I do this? Make it stop."
- "I think I overdosed."
- "I need to go to the hospital."

Letting clients know in advance that these thoughts are common gives them a psychological reference point. If fear arises during the journey, they can recall this conversation and recognize the thoughts as normal, not urgent signals of danger.

It also helps to frame these physiological changes as part of the nervous system's fight-or-flight response. When the mind feels it's losing control, it may generate frightening thoughts in an effort to reestablish a sense of safety. Understanding this mechanism ahead of time gives clients tools to navigate the moment. Therapists should also provide strategies for calming the mind if fear arises, reminding clients that feelings of fear aren't evidence of actual danger.

I often share with clients a quote from Timothy Leary's *The Psychedelic Experience that* illustrates this point:

> You must remember that the experience is safe (at the very worst, you will end up the same person who entered the experience), and that all of the dangers which you have feared are an unnecessary production of your mind. Whether you experience heaven or hell, remember that it is your mind which creates them.
>
> (Leary et al., 1964, p. 5)

Clients should know that even if they encounter terrifying imagery or enter what feels like Hell, these are mind-created states. They aren't in real danger. The worst-case scenario is returning to the integration session afterward feeling like nothing happened—which can still be worked with therapeutically.

This perspective helps relieve anxiety by reframing the journey as a temporary state that will be followed by structured support for reflection. Reminding clients that they will soon be sitting in a room with their therapist discussing whatever unfolded can be deeply grounding.

Still, no amount of preparation can fully eliminate the possibility of a profoundly challenging or disorienting experience. What we *can* do is teach the critical skill of meeting difficulty without resistance—a lesson that extends well beyond the psychedelic session. As explored previously, Young's equation—Suffering = Pain x Resistance—reminds us that resisting discomfort only amplifies it.

Learning to move through pain without resistance is one of the most important practices we can offer our clients. The heightened neuroplasticity of the brain during a psychedelic session makes it an especially potent time to install new mental habits—like meeting fear with breath, stillness, and curiosity instead of panic. By normalizing fear, educating about physiology, and providing frameworks for responding to distress, we prepare clients not just for the medicine, but for life itself.

To help clients internalize these safety principles, I provide them with a client-friendly handout titled *What to Remember if Fear Arises During Your*

Journey. It covers key affirmations, breathwork strategies, and reminders about the nature of fear and resistance. Many clients find it helpful to re-read the handout in the days before the journey, sometimes even keeping it nearby during their session:

Turning Toward the Dark

Clients preparing to work therapeutically with psychedelics may encounter difficult psychic material during their journey. In fact, many seek out these experiences precisely to address unresolved trauma, challenging life events, or entrenched emotional pain. Helping clients learn to turn toward what arises, rather than resist it, is a vital part of the preparation process. Mindfulness skills are among the most effective tools for this work.

It is essential that clients enter their psychedelic journey with at least a foundational understanding of the breathing and mindfulness techniques introduced earlier in this book. Being familiar with these practices and having embodied experience with them prior to the journey is critical, as it increases the likelihood of clients effectively accessing them when the experience becomes emotionally intense or disorienting.

The human nervous system is biologically wired to protect itself through fight-or-flight responses (Cannon, 1929; Mobbs & Kim, 2015). It isn't instinctive to turn toward something frightening. This makes it especially important for clients to understand that what they may see or feel during a psychedelic journey is a product of their mind, not an external threat. If distress arises, there isn't anything to fear or escape; rather, a manifestation of something within them is asking to be seen, understood, and integrated.

Therapists should remind their clients that psychedelics grant access to deep inner wisdom, and whatever shows up during the journey—no matter how uncomfortable—is part of the healing process. As Grof (1980) famously taught, these experiences are meaningful and necessary. He advised clients to approach challenging material directly, saying things like: "If you see a dark staircase, go up it," or "If you encounter a monster, go toward it." His thousands of sessions showed that immense healing often lies just beyond these moments of fear or resistance.

Importantly, Grof (1980) also warned against using tranquilizers to interrupt a difficult psychedelic journey, as doing so can keep clients from accessing the insight they're seeking. Clients should know this in advance. They should understand that encountering darkness doesn't mean something's gone wrong; it's an invitation to move through that darkness toward something greater. There is always light on the other side. They just have to keep moving with the experience, rather than pushing against it.

Leary et al. (1964) offered another helpful metaphor, encouraging clients to "go downstream" with the journey and let the music[3] guide them. Therapists can share a version of this metaphor with clients during preparation, tailoring it to their unique goals and emotional style:

> During your psychedelic experience, imagine that the music is a winding river. Let yourself float with its current. There's no need to swim—with it, or especially against it. Instead, surrender to the flow. Watch, listen, feel. If the waters become choppy and it feels like you might drown, turn toward the music and use your breath as your floating device. Your breath will carry you—gently and reliably—until you arrive at calmer waters.

This image helps clients understand the dual role of music and breath. The music is the river that carries them, and the breath is a tool that helps them stay grounded and steady. They don't need to steer the experience or hold on tightly. Even if part of the journey feels like a death, it is temporary—and it often leads to something that feels like a rebirth.

Ego Death

Many individuals describe experiencing a particular phenomenon under the influence of psychedelics that is commonly referred to as ego death, ego dissolution, or ego-loss (Gorman et al., 2021; Krupitsky et al., 2002; Russ et al., 2019). Scientifically, ego death corresponds with decreased activity in the DMN, the brain region responsible for self-referential thought and ego-driven perceptions (Carhart-Harris & Friston, 2010; Carhart-Harris et al., 2012; Carhart-Harris et al., 2014a). In other words, when the DMN shuts down, a person's commonly held sense of themselves ceases to exist. This ego death experience results in an absolute disappearance of the typical identifications with who one is (i.e., name, family, religion, home, and body). It's as if their form is extinguished completely. Grof (1980) believed that the process of ego death is vital for therapeutic change, because what dies in the process are those negative thought processes that trace as far back as childbirth and strongly influence a person's identity. Ego death is often a therapeutic goal and should be recognized as a fundamental component of profound and transformative psychedelic experiences. In clinical practice, it has been consistently observed as a state that facilitates deep personal insight, emotional healing, and lasting psychological change.

Clients frequently inquire about the nature of ego death and how they will recognize if it's happening. Though individual experiences vary, many people report that it starts with an uncomfortable physical sensation.

Leary et al. (1964) identified the key characteristics of ego dissolution. This synthesized list helps clients better understand and contextualize the experience, allowing them to approach it with greater awareness and preparedness:

- Intense bodily pressure.
- Quick back-and-forth changes in body temperature (from hot to cold or cold to hot).
- The feeling of body disintegration.
- Intense pressure in the head and ears.
- Tingling in the extremities.
- Feelings of the body melting or flowing like wax.
- Nausea.
- Trembling or shaking that begins in the pelvic regions and spreads up to the torso.

According to Leary et al. (1964), these physical reactions should be recognized as both ego death and the start of a possible mystical experience. He explained that the physical reactions shouldn't be considered symptoms of illness; rather, individuals should accept them, merge with them, and even enjoy them. Approaching the ego-loss experience this way holds potential for beneficial change and introduces the potential for rewiring the brain, thereby altering ways of seeing, understanding, and acting in the world.

Several researchers have explored the therapeutic benefits of ego death experiences during psychedelic-assisted therapy, particularly within the treatment of depression, anxiety, and addiction. Griffiths et al. (2006) found that participants who underwent psilocybin-assisted therapy reported mystical experiences, including ego dissolution, which were strongly correlated with enduring positive changes in mood and attitudes. Carhart-Harris and Friston (2019) proposed the REBUS model (Relaxed Beliefs Under Psychedelics), suggesting that ego dissolution allows for a temporary relaxation of rigid, self-referential thought patterns, enabling new insights and emotional processing. These studies suggest that the dissolution of the ego may create a cognitive and emotional reset, fostering therapeutic outcomes by breaking maladaptive thought loops.

However, ego death isn't required for positive therapeutic outcomes to emerge from psychedelic therapy. In their study of LSD-assisted psychotherapy for patients with anxiety, Gasser et al. (2014b) found that although some participants reported experiencing ego dissolution, others experienced healing without it, through more conventional emotional processing or enhanced introspection. Based on their own findings, Watts and Luoma (2020) assert that although ego dissolution can amplify therapeutic potential for some individuals, the broader therapeutic context—which includes the quality of preparation, the integration process, and the therapist-client relationship—more significantly influences the outcome of therapy.

These findings imply that while ego dissolution can be transformative for some people, it may not be a necessary ingredient for achieving therapeutic benefits during psychedelic-assisted therapy. Russ et al. (2019) investigated how specific states experienced during psychedelic sessions predict the effectiveness of therapy. The researchers analyzed data from individuals who had undergone psychedelic-assisted therapy and found that the quality of the acute experience—especially states associated with emotional release, relaxation, and inner peace—strongly predicted long-term therapeutic outcomes. Although transformative experiences like ego dissolution and mystical states were beneficial for some participants, the study highlighted that feelings of safety, connectedness, and emotional openness during the session were more consistently associated with positive outcomes. These findings underscore the importance of creating a calm, supportive environment during psychedelic therapy, to optimize its therapeutic potential.

Do Not Turn on Your Guide

During a psychedelic journey, the guide plays a crucial role in supporting the process; therefore, it is essential for an individual taking psychedelics to trust and allow the guide's involvement. While on psychedelics, a person can become confused about their surroundings, including anyone in proximity to them, such as the guide. Whether the therapist or another facilitator is guiding the session, it's essential to establish the fundamental rule that clients must not turn against their guide. Psychedelic experiences can induce significant perceptual and cognitive distortions, leading clients to momentarily forget who their guide is or perceive them as physically transforming. Such experiences may trigger distrust or fear, disrupting the therapeutic process.

Preparing clients for these possible distortions helps them maintain the correct perspective if they arise, reducing resistance and fostering trust in the process. By understanding that these perceptions are temporary and a natural part of altered states of consciousness, clients are better equipped to stay grounded, reframe their experience, and continue engaging meaningfully with their journey.

Clients have reported perceiving their guide in various forms during psychedelic experiences, often seeing them as entities beyond their ordinary identity. These perceptions have included figures such as an angel, a princess, a snake, a witch, and even a monster. Such transformations reflect the mind's altered state of consciousness, where symbolic and archetypal imagery can shape the way individuals interpret their surroundings. Understanding that these distortions are a natural aspect of the experience helps clients maintain perspective and reduces fear or resistance if such visions arise. It is therefore essential to prepare individuals for the possibility of having disorienting experiences like these during their psychedelic journey. This helps to keep them from taking these experiences as literal or real. A fundamental guideline to emphasize before the journey is, "Trust your guide fully." Reminding participants of this principle helps them feel secure and supported, allowing them to explore and accept whatever arises during the process.

You Can't Turn off the Medicine

Another essential point to address with clients is that they can't turn off the medicine. During the journey, some clients may wonder whether it's possible to stop the experience. Generally speaking, the answer is no. Once a psychedelic has been ingested, the experience must be allowed to run its natural course.

As I mentioned in previous sections, feelings of anxiety, confusion, discomfort, and fear are common during a psychedelic journey. Clients need to understand that these sensations, although intense, are normal and temporary aspects of the altered state of consciousness.

During the experience, they may lose track of linear thought or encounter perceptions they don't immediately comprehend. This is unfamiliar territory, and the mind's instinct may be to resist or try interpreting what's happening. But this tendency to figure it out often escalates into panic or distress. If clients aren't adequately prepared, such confusion can snowball into fear, prompting a desire to escape the experience. It's vital to emphasize that **resistance intensifies discomfort.** Trying to fight the journey will likely make it more difficult.

Some people believe that certain sedatives—such as benzodiazepines—can cancel out the effects of psychedelics. This is a common misconception. Oral sedatives are typically ineffective once the medicine is active, and seeking emergency care to receive intravenous sedatives is rarely a desirable option. Clients must, therefore, enter the experience with the clear understanding that they are safe—even if the experience temporarily convinces them otherwise. If fear arises, they can recall our preparatory conversations and remember that the experience isn't physically dangerous. Any feelings of threat or chaos are projections of the mind, not objective reality. As Timothy Leary (1969) once wrote:

> You must remember that the experience is safe (at the very worst, you will end up the same person who entered the experience), and that all

> of the dangers which you have feared are an unnecessary production of your mind. Whether you experience heaven or hell, remember that it is your mind which creates them.
>
> (p. 5)

Clients should know that even the most challenging moments will pass. They will return to their normal state of consciousness and soon be sitting in their integration session, unpacking what the experience revealed—whether subtle or profound.

The importance of preparation can't be overstated. Clients who commit to learning, practicing mindfulness tools, and engaging earnestly with the process give themselves the best chance for a healing and transformative journey. Although psychedelics can open doors to deep insight and growth, they must be approached with reverence, clarity, and readiness.

What to Remember if Fear Arises During Your Journey

1. You Are Safe

At the very worst, you will return to being the same person who started the experience. Every feeling—no matter how intense—is temporary:

> Whether you experience heaven or hell, remember that it is your mind which creates them.
>
> —*Timothy Leary, The Psychedelic Experience*

2. Your Mind May Resist Letting Go

Fear is normal. It is often your mind's way of trying to stay in control. Remind yourself that this is just part of the process. Try not to fight the experience—breathe and allow it to unfold.

3. Resistance = More Suffering

Remember this equation: **Suffering = Pain × Resistance**

Instead of pushing away discomfort, invite it in. Get curious. Ask: *What do you want to show me?*

4. Breathe

Slow, conscious breathing is your anchor.

Try this:

- Inhale for 4 seconds.
- Hold for 7 seconds.
- Exhale for 8 seconds.

Repeat this a few times until you feel calmer.

5. *You Can't Stop the Medicine—But You Can Soften into It*

Trying to make it stop only increases fear. Say to yourself:

- *I surrender to this moment.*
- *I trust the process.*
- *This is happening for me, not to me.*

6. *You Will Be Supported*

You are not alone. Your guide is here for you. And afterward, you will have an integration session to talk through whatever came up.

7. *Bring a Reminder*

Feel free to bring this handout with you. Some clients fold it and keep it in a pocket or under a mat—just knowing it's there helps them feel safe.

Notes

1 The assertion that the human brain processes approximately 11 million bits of sensory information per second, with conscious awareness limited to about 40–50 bits per second, is brought forth as an example of a scientific theory that less spiritually inclined clients may find compelling and applicable within therapeutic contexts. This concept is widely discussed in the fields of information theory and physiology. According to the Encyclopædia Britannica, the human body sends around 11 million bits of sensory data per second to the brain for processing, whereas the conscious mind is estimated to handle only about 50 bits per second. This dramatic discrepancy suggests that the brain performs substantial compression and filtering of sensory input, allowing conscious awareness to focus on select critical elements. Although the general principle of limited conscious capacity relative to the vast sensory input is well accepted, the exact figures are likely influenced by differing methodologies, assumptions, and the specific context of measurement. Despite being widely cited in literature, identifying a single empirical study that definitively establishes these precise values remains challenging, as the figures have been reiterated and interpreted across multiple sources over time without a clear original reference.

2 In the specific context of ayahuasca, however, research conducted in Western settings has demonstrated the necessity of following an MAOI-compatible diet (Callaway & Grob, 1998). This dietary restriction is essential to avoid hypertensive crises and other adverse reactions that can occur due to the interaction between monoamine oxidase inhibitors (MAOIs) present in ayahuasca and certain foods, such as those high in tyramine.

3 Music is one of many important tools that help guide individuals during a psychedelic journey and serve to create meaning and direction during the session (Kaelen et al., 2015).

Chapter 8

The Journey

This chapter explores the role of the guide and offers guidance for therapists to create a warm, grounded, and safe container for their clients' psychedelic journeys. In the evolving landscape of psychedelic-assisted therapy in the United States, ketamine remains the only legally accessible psychedelic in many clinical settings, making it a primary tool for therapeutic exploration. As a result, much of the knowledge presented in this chapter has been shaped through direct experience guiding clients through ketamine journeys in collaboration with experienced colleagues. Although the discussion here draws primarily from work with ketamine, the principles outlined are broadly applicable to therapeutic work with psychedelics of all kinds.

It's essential to emphasize that therapists should never guide their clients through a psychedelic experience alone—except in the case of a low, psycholytic dose. A two-guide model is strongly recommended to ensure that the client receives comprehensive support throughout their journey. One guide is primarily responsible for attending to the client's physical and emotional well-being, while the second works to keep the environment safe and comfortable, addressing logistical concerns and responding to questions as they arise. This dual-guidance approach enhances both the depth and safety of the therapeutic experience by offering structure, attunement, and reassurance.

Having two guides also ensures that all ethical and moral boundaries are upheld throughout the process. The presence of a second facilitator provides important protection—not only for the client, but for the guides themselves—ensuring that both parties observe therapeutic boundaries and remain accountable. In this way, the two-guide model isn't just about optimizing care; it's also about maintaining professionalism, transparency, and mutual safety at every stage of the process.

Additionally, having two people available to provide guidance and reassurance can be particularly beneficial for those clients who experience strong emotions or unexpected challenges during the psychedelic

DOI: 10.4324/9781003541639-12

experience. If an unforeseen situation arises, it can be handled more efficiently and safely with two facilitators present.

Both guides should have established a strong therapeutic rapport with the client prior to the session. Preparatory meetings should be scheduled with each of the individuals who will be present during the journey. These sessions help establish the trust and safety the client needs to surrender to the process, while also allowing for intention-setting, logistical planning, and clarification of expectations. A well-prepared and relational foundation makes all the difference when guiding clients through a profound and often vulnerable experience.

Day-of Preparation: Guiding Clients at the Threshold of Their Journey

After many weeks of preparation and consistent mindfulness practice, the client is ready to meet the medicine. This moment is often accompanied by a complex blend of excitement, anticipation, curiosity, and fear. For many clients, it is the culmination of much emotional and mental preparation. From the moment they arrive at their psychedelic journey, the environment should be carefully curated to promote a sense of emotional safety, warmth, and grounding.

Before administering the medicine, the guide should invite the client into a brief, structured conversation. They should begin by asking how the client is feeling in the moment and normalize any strong emotions that are present. This is an important time to reassure the client that whatever they're feeling—nervousness, excitement, tension, or even doubt—is entirely natural. This establishes a compassionate presence from the start of the journey, helping the client step into their experience with greater ease and trust in the process.

It's also important for the therapist to acknowledge and affirm the client's effort, reminding them that they have prepared thoroughly for this moment, and that the skills, insights, and lifestyle changes they've integrated in recent weeks will support them throughout the experience. The therapist should use this time to review and repeat key themes and messages from their preparation—especially those related to trust, surrender, and the importance of turning toward whatever arises.

At this point, one final reminder should be gently emphasized—one that will likely have been repeated many times throughout preparation:

> No matter what arises while on the medicine—whether it feels easy or difficult, beautiful or terrifying—it isn't real in the physical sense, nor is it dangerous. At the end of the session, you will return to yourself.

The experience will pass, but it may leave behind something beautiful, meaningful, or transformative.

Final Preparations Before Administration

Before the medicine is administered, the therapist should review a final list of logistical concerns:

- **Confirm session readiness**: Ensure that the client has brought any items discussed in preparation sessions, such as extra layers to stay warm (i.e., sweaters and socks), a blanket or eye mask, and a written copy of their intentions. Physical comfort and symbolic reminders can greatly enhance the depth and resonance of the journey.
- **Review dietary and substance restrictions**: Confirm that the client has fasted for at least eight hours and has abstained from caffeine, alcohol, and recreational drugs for a minimum of 48 hours. These steps aren't just physiological safeguards; they're symbolic gestures of commitment to the work.
- **Confirm post-session care**: Make sure the client has arranged for a trusted companion to pick them up after the session and stay with them for several hours. Clients should be reminded that they are not permitted to drive themselves home, regardless of how lucid they may feel.
- **Collect emergency contact information**: Confirm that the name and phone number of the designated post-session support person are on file. The client should confirm that this person is aware of their role and ready to support them.
- **Confirm integration session**: Schedule and confirm the time and date of the integration session—ideally 24–48 hours after the journey. Integration is essential to help the client process and embody what arose during the experience. Knowing from the start that this container exists can help reduce anxiety and reinforce a sense of support and continuity.

The Final Words Before the Medicine

Once all safety and logistical matters have been addressed, the therapist or guide should revisit the themes of trust, surrender, and non-resistance. They can then offer a short, grounding conversation that helps the client cross the threshold from ordinary consciousness into sacred space. This conversation should reinforce the therapeutic frame and offer comfort and orientation as the client prepares to let go.

The following is a real-world example of a pre-journey conversation that my fellow guide, Isaac, and I had with one of my clients. It illustrates how to offer structure, reassurance, and practical guidance without disrupting the client's autonomy or the organic unfolding of the experience:

Vanessa: This medicine works every time in the same kind of way at the onset. Within 10 to 15 minutes or so, you will feel it. When you do, let us know you are feeling it. At that point, we recommend that you put on the eyeshades, and your goal is to just drop into the playlist.

Client: Okay.

Vanessa: The playlist is designed for the ketamine experience. It will take you on the journey, and you don't have to do anything. Remember, just float. No need to swim or hold on to anything.

Client: Okay, Okay.

Isaac: You are letting go and surrendering. Let's talk again about what that means. What I do, I literally say, take me over. I'm going to give you again the guarantee that you will leave here; this human being will leave here today. If you die in your experience or something like that, that's just your ego dying. You will be with your wife later; she will be here picking you up. You will return safely to your everyday world. I guarantee you that. So, the best strategy is, okay, let's rock and roll and let go. The medicine will guide you and your subconscious will guide you. Okay?

Client: Okay.

Isaac: It is very common that there will be a little bit of a push or a pull, a little bit of a struggle to let go of your conscious mind (ego). Your conscious mind is going to be there. I don't know if you will get to a point where you will lose all sense of reality on ketamine like you will on ayahuasca, but on ketamine it often seems like if you have a watcher. Let that conscious mind be the watcher, but don't engage with it. "What are the lessons?" "What do I need to find?" "How do I make sense of it?" All that kind of stuff is what that watcher does. Don't try to make sense of anything. If it's weird and wild, or beautiful and amazing, whatever it is, just experience this psychedelic experience. Do not try to make lessons of it in the moment. We will generate lessons over time. Maybe at the end of the session, maybe later when we are integrating, maybe in talking to your wife this weekend, the lessons will come out.

Client: Okay, I understand.

Isaac: You have some beautiful intentions here, and you can always remember them whenever you find it necessary to do so. Just have fun. This is a fun, funky experience. It is very busy; it has a lot of movement. It can be in the stars, it can be in the ground, it can be in the mountains. Some people have visuals. Just have fun. You just worked your butt off. You put so much time and energy into this process. Now it is time to reap the benefits.

Client: Oh, yes.

Isaac: You have already grown so much. From the day that I met you to this day right here, your relationship with alcohol is so different, your mindfulness with your kids, the way you are dealing with your wife, the way you are relating to work . . . . So much is different already.

Client: Oh, yes!

Isaac: Awesome!

Vanessa: Wow, awesome stuff. I want you to remember, if you see a door, walk through it. If you see a window, look through it. If you feel like you are melting, dying, exploding, embrace it. If you see something scary, such as a monster or a beast, go towards it. All of it will pass. There will be an opposite to every experience, so if there is death, there will be a rebirth, or if there is something ugly or scary, something beautiful will be waiting for you on the other side.

Client: Yes.

Vanessa: If at any time you feel it is too much, remember we are here next to you. You can ask either of us to hold your hand or any other support. I also want you to remember the power of your breath. If the music is the river you will be riding on, then your breath is what will help you float seamlessly on it. Use it.

Client: Okay.

Isaac: Vanessa will be breathing with you throughout the journey. You will hear her breathing, and she will be sending you breaths. Your breath is your friend. All you must do is find it.

Client: Okay.

Vanessa: Let's go over the three main rules. We are your guides; you don't turn against us.

Client: [laughing]

Isaac: If you are in your psychedelic experience, and me and her are sitting here chatting or handing her a paper, we are just here. If we are looking at our phones, we are just looking at the playlist. Does that make sense?

Client: Perfect.

Vanessa: We are here completely present with you. Rule number two: The dosage you are taking is perfect for you. There is no questioning it. The conscious mind might form ideas in its efforts to not lose control, such as, "Maybe I took too much" or "They gave me the wrong amount because something feels wrong with me." Remember, it is the perfect amount, and you are incredibly safe.

Isaac: Yes.

Vanessa: And the last rule, there is no turning off the medicine. Once you take the medicine, you will allow time to pass for the effects to diminish.

Isaac: Yes. No one here wants to end up in an emergency room getting injected with tranquilizers due to a panic attack. Remember, we will take care of your physical body and make sure that everything is absolutely safe. You have practiced trusting this experience completely.

Client: Yes.

Isaac: Okay. So, during the experience, talk if you want and then don't talk if you want. If you start talking and get lost, leave it alone.

Vanessa: Yes. If you think that you are not making sense, don't worry about it.

Isaac: If I tell you, "Sue, this is a good time to not talk and drop in," no ego. Just listen and drop in. It's not because we don't want you to talk. It's not because we don't want to hear you. It's just because we want you to drop in and have the best experience. Does that make sense?

Client: Yes, I got it.

Vanessa: Thank you for trusting us and allowing us to share in this space with you. There is nowhere else we'd rather be than here with you. This is our favorite work. I will add something that I have learned from a shaman who provided wonderful insight when working with the medicine. He comes from a tribe that believes words carry different types of energy. He explained that I could ask the medicine to be gentle with me and I would have a gentle experience and to also let it know my intentions. Furthermore, he said that if at any time the experience feels too heavy or dark, there are two mantras I could use to guide me through it: "I am light," "I am love." They are mantras that carry a high vibration, and they would assist me during challenging times. You, too, can ask the medicine what you need and use the mantras throughout the journey.

Client: Okay, I will.

Vanessa: Please allow yourself to say or do anything. You are in a super safe space.

Client: I feel it, I feel it. Thank you. I feel safe.

Isaac: And listen, do not hold back anything. If you think it sounds weird. If you want to cry, if you want to fart, if you want to make sounds. Don't hold anything back. That is what can create a stuckness and makes the conscious mind get involved.

Client: Okay.
Vanessa: Anything!
Isaac: So, anything that wants to come out, if you want to laugh your ass off, cry your ass off, say the weirdest shit in the world. We want to hear your weird shit, and we are not judging any of it. Okay?
Client: Okay.
Isaac: I've seen you very mindful, very chill, very relaxed. I'm going to now give you the ketamine. Whether the ketamine tastes good or the ketamine tastes bad, just let it be.
Vanessa: It just is.
Client: Okay.
Isaac: Can you read the intentions to us please?
Client: Yes.

This pre-journey conversation demonstrates how guides can weave together structure, safety, and spiritual permission without overwhelming the client or disrupting the organic flow of the experience. The dialogue provides containment through the repetition of three core agreements: trust your guide, trust the dosage, and remember that the medicine can't be turned off. At the same time, it normalizes common fears and offers tools like breath, mantra, and surrender. The language is both firm and deeply compassionate, balancing humor with reverence and offering both science-informed and intuitive guidance. By modeling nonjudgment, offering full permission, and maintaining a steady presence, the guides create a relational field in which the client can begin to let go, even before the medicine takes effect. After reading her intentions aloud, the client placed the ketamine on the inside of her cheek and allowed it to dissolve naturally. Again, we reminded her one last time that she was safe, that we would be there with her the entire time, and that she could let go and surrender. This exchange serves as a blueprint for how to hold space with integrity, humility, and clinical skill.

The following sections outline the core skills and guiding principles that support effective facilitation during psychedelic sessions. In addition to the interpersonal and clinical tools a guide brings into the space, we will also explore best practices for shaping the physical and psychological environment. Together, these elements—presence, skill, and setting—form the foundation of a safe, transformative, and deeply supported psychedelic experience.

Guiding

> The role of a psychedelic guide is perhaps the most exciting and inspiring role in society. He is literally a liberator, one who provides illumination, one who frees men from their life-long internal bondage.
>
> —Timothy Leary et al. (1964, p. 17)

The role of the guide is one of the most significant determinants of a client's success in psychedelic-assisted therapy. As such, it is essential that the therapist understand and embody the therapeutic philosophy best suited to this unique and vulnerable phase of the work.

At this point in the process, the therapist's role shifts. While the preparation phase often requires a more active, teaching-oriented stance, the journey phase calls for the opposite. Now, the therapist adopts a non-directive, receptive presence—less a teacher and more a witness and gentle anchor. This quieter role is grounded in patience, attunement, and trust in the client's inner healing intelligence. It is about holding space.

This approach is founded upon a combination of Carl Rogers' principles of non-directive therapy, Douglas Flemons' techniques in hypnosis and hypnotherapy, and the wisdom of traditional healers referenced earlier in this book. Together, these perspectives offer a robust framework for guiding psychedelic experiences in ways that encourage safety, surrender, and deep exploration. The guide's presence must convey warmth and stability, offering the client an internal and external environment in which anything that arises can be met with openness and curiosity. In this space, the medicine and the client's subconscious are regarded as the experts. The guide simply walks alongside the client as a sturdy and compassionate witness to their process.

Between Everything and Nothing: Systems Thinking

Psychedelic experiences often challenge our sense of self, dissolving the boundaries we rely on to define who we are. In the absence of those familiar constructs, clients may find themselves standing at the edge of what feels like total disintegration. This moment—raw, terrifying, and potentially transformative—invites an encounter with what lies beneath identity: a deeper truth that connects the individual to something larger than the self. In this part of the process, systems thinking becomes essential. It supports the understanding that identity isn't a fixed entity, but rather a living system shaped by relationships, beliefs, culture, trauma, and resilience.

Identity isn't fixed; it is fluid, shaped by the unseen currents of culture, faith, relationships, and history. It feels solid and tangible, until altered states of consciousness blur or shatter the roles and boundaries of identity. In the absence of those familiar constructs, a person is forced to confront what remains. *Who am I when the world I trusted no longer reflects me? Who am I when the shape I have always taken no longer fits?*

Dovid had never questioned these things. He had lived comfortably within the framework of his Orthodox Jewish community, where meaning was clear, belonging was certain, and life followed a rhythm that had existed for generations. But the night he was attacked while walking home from synagogue, everything shifted. The men who beat him did more than break his jaw and leave him with a traumatic brain injury—they left him with a rupture in his sense of self. Once steady in his identity, he now felt unmoored, watching the world from the outside. His body recovered, but inside, he was unraveling. He stopped going to synagogue. He stopped praying. He was no longer sure who he was.

Ketamine therapy wasn't something he had ever imagined for himself. Psychedelics belonged to a world far from his own. Yet here he was, hoping that somehow, this unfamiliar medicine might grant him a way back to himself.

As the ketamine took hold, the boundaries of his body softened. The weight he had carried—the fear, the anger, the suffocating smallness of victimhood—began to dissolve. At first, it terrified him. He had been holding on tightly to his suffering, to the proof that what had happened to him was real. *If I let go, what remains? If I am not this pain, then who am I?* He saw himself from above, as though he were simply a presence in space—untethered. He felt nothing. *I am nothing.*

Then, something shifted. In the stillness, he sensed he wasn't separate from anything. He was woven into something vast and enduring—a network of love that had existed long before this suffering and would continue long after. He was nothing and he was everything.

Dovid felt himself stretched between those two truths. He had been swallowed by pain, convinced it was all he was. But now he saw: He was more than his suffering. He was also the hands that had held him, the prayers whispered in his name, the resilience of his ancestors, and the life that was still waiting for him. He was nothing, and he was everything. The moment passed, but something in him had shifted. His pain was still there. His fear was still there. But so was everything else.

Dovid's journey mirrors the way identity can be shaped, broken, and re-formed. He had believed himself to be one thing—a man of faith, of family, of tradition—until an act of violence took that certainty from him. For a time, he became only his suffering, unable to see beyond it. But through this altered state, he glimpsed something deeper: Identity isn't fixed, and it isn't erased by trauma. It moves. It adapts. It expands.

His community had once been his anchor, his faith his foundation. After the attack, everyone felt distant and unreachable. But in the dissolution of the self, he saw that they had never been separate from him at all. His healing wasn't about returning to who he had been. It also wasn't about abandoning his past. It was about stepping forward with a new understanding. He could hold both. He could be both.

Between nothing and everything, his life moved forward.

Trusting Clients' Inner Wisdom

Psychedelics facilitate an internal process that taps into unconscious material in the mind. Throughout the process, the mind manifests the inner wisdom needed to support the change clients seek. In other words, therapists must understand that they aren't the ones teaching, sorting out, understanding, or coming up with information and insight. Furthermore, they aren't in a position to know what is best for their clients. Instead, clients will explore these avenues on their own.

Rogers' (1957) non-directive approach works seamlessly with psychedelically induced, inner-directed work. Many psychedelic integration therapy models incorporate non-directive techniques (Carhart-Harris, 2016, Gorman et al., 2021; Griffiths et al., 2016). Therapists should be fully present and supportive as they accompany clients on their therapeutic journey, never telling them where to go.

The therapist believes in the client's inner abilities and expertise, trusting that they have everything they need to change and heal. This belief influences the therapist to direct the client inward when exploring, describing, or even questioning their lives during the psychedelic journey. Additionally, the therapist should know how to encourage the client to direct their questions inward, as they possess all the answers they seek.

This philosophy—that the client is an expert in their own life—leads therapists to instill confidence in their clients that they know what they need to reach their goals. The therapist invites the client to learn how to heal, change, and live a fulfilling life through the guidance of their inner wisdom.

To illustrate the profound importance of trusting a client's inner wisdom, consider the experience of Eli, a 32-year-old transgender man who had spent much of his life navigating the complexities of his identity. From an early age, Eli had felt disconnected from his body, struggling with a misalignment between his internal sense of self and the way the world perceived him. After years of emotional and physical transition, he had finally arrived at a place where his external presentation matched his internal identity; yet a lingering sense of detachment and unresolved tension remained.

Hoping a more profound healing experience might offer the insight he sought, Eli traveled to Peru for an ayahuasca ceremony led by a highly respected curandero from the Shipibo tradition. The gathering included individuals from various parts of the world, each arriving with their own histories, traumas, and hopes for healing. Eli's main goal was to reconnect with his body—not in the physical sense, as his transition had allowed him to do that, but on a deeper, more spiritual and emotional level.

As night fell, the participants gathered in the ceremonial space. The curandero moved around the circle, offering each individual a cup of the ayahuasca brew. As he approached Eli, he paused. Unbeknownst to those around him, Eli had fallen into a deep sleep, his body completely still. To everyone's surprise, the curandero simply walked past him, without offering the medicine.

When Eli awoke the next morning and realized what had happened, he was filled with disappointment. During the integration session, he asked the curandero why he hadn't been awakened. The curandero explained that in the Shipibo tradition, nothing happens by accident. Falling asleep was no mistake—it was an act of deep inner wisdom. The medicine had worked on Eli, even if it wasn't the way he'd expected. His soul had received what it needed: rest, stillness, and surrender.

The curandero shared that psychedelic healing doesn't always occur through direct ingestion; sometimes, it happens through energetic presence, absorption, and simply being in the field of transformation. Eli was reminded that healing can unfold in ways that defy logic and expectation.

At first, Eli struggled to accept this perspective. But over time, he came to see that he was receiving an important lesson about allowing. His entire transition had been about shaping his identity through will. But here, in this space, his healing came through surrender.

This experience serves as a powerful reminder of the importance of trusting the client's inner wisdom, particularly in psychedelic-assisted therapy. Just as the curandero had trusted Eli's process, therapists must resist the urge to interfere or impose their own ideas. Psychedelic work doesn't always happen in the moment; it often unfolds gradually, in subtle and unexpected ways.

Another example of this same idea arose in a ketamine session that Isaac and I facilitated for Mathew, a man in his late forties who had been diagnosed with bipolar disorder and had recently survived a suicide attempt. Because his situation was urgent and required us to act quickly, we weren't able to conduct a thorough preparation phase as usual, but we intentionally moved forward nonetheless.[1]

In the first half of the session, Mathew struggled to let go. He kept trying to talk, ask questions, and remove his eyeshades. Every attempt we made to help him drop in worked only briefly. Then, at the peak of the experience, Mathew asked, "What is wrong with me? What do I need to do to heal?" Isaac gently suggested that he ask his subconscious. "Sometimes the answer takes a moment," Isaac added. "Just be still and curious."

Surprisingly, Mathew became quiet. A few minutes later, he shared two memories, one at age three and another at age six, when he nearly drowned. He vividly recalled the fear and powerlessness he felt, the panic of not being able to breathe, and the feeling of his father finally pulling him out of the water.

This memory marked a turning point in the session. It seemed the medicine had touched a long-buried trauma, inviting it into Mathew's awareness for the first time in decades. Grof (2008) wrote extensively about the healing power of revisiting early traumas during psychedelic sessions, noting that even birth trauma can surface and catalyze meaningful change. Mathew's resurfaced memories gave us material for integration and offered possible clues toward healing his bipolar symptoms. Most importantly, the session marked a shift. Following it, Mathew's suicidal ideations disappeared. He continued therapy and, until the time of this writing, reports many positive changes.

Both Eli and Mathew's stories illuminate the same truth: The client's inner wisdom leads the way. As therapists and guides, our role isn't to steer, but to support and witness. The less we try to control, the more space we create for true healing to emerge. These stories serve to remind us of the humility required to be a psychedelic therapist. In this capacity, we are not the drivers of change; we are protectors of a space in which change becomes possible.

Reflecting the Experience

Reflection is an essential therapeutic tool during a psychedelic journey, in which heightened emotional sensitivity and perceptual shifts can make experiences feel overwhelming, disorienting, or profoundly revelatory. In this altered state, the therapist or guide's role is to be a steady, attuned presence who reinforces the client's trust in their own unfolding process. By reflecting the client's experience back to them in simple, direct language, the therapist helps anchor them in their awareness, providing a sense of containment without interference. This approach reassures the client that their perceptions and emotions are being witnessed exactly as they are, without distortion or external influence.

Because psychedelic states often amplify internal material—bringing deeply personal insights, memories, or sensations to the surface—reflection ensures that the client remains oriented within their own experience, rather than being subtly pulled into the therapist's framework. If, in the midst of an intense emotional or visionary experience, a client says, "I feel like I am dissolving," a therapist might attempt to be soothing and offer, "You are safe; just let go." Although well-intended, this response subtly directs the client to interpret the dissolution as something to surrender to. A more precise reflection—"You feel like you are dissolving"—simply mirrors the experience without imposing any specific meaning. This allows the client to explore what the dissolution means for them, rather than being told how to engage with it. Rule of thumb: mirror first, orient second, reassure last—in that order—so you protect the client's meaning-making while staying supportive.

Reflection also plays a critical role in regulating emotional intensity during difficult or disorienting moments. Psychedelics can heighten emotional and sensory perception, sometimes amplifying fear, confusion, or existential distress. If a client says, "It's so dark, and I feel like I'll never get out," an instinctive response might be to offer reassurance: "You will come through this; you're not stuck." However, such a statement, no matter how true, moves the client toward an outcome, rather than keeping them in the moment. Instead, reflecting back something like, "It feels dark, and it seems endless," acknowledges their immediate experience and keeps them inside it. The therapist's role isn't to fix, but to witness—to provide a steady, relational anchor that allows the client to remain present with their own process.

Reflection isn't a mechanical process. It requires the therapist to be emotionally attuned, grounded, and fully present, even as they refrain from imposing meaning. In moments of awe or beauty, reflection enhances the client's ability to fully engage with the expansiveness of their experience. If a client exclaims, "It's so beautiful! I can feel the whole universe breathing," rather than analyzing or inquiring, the therapist might say, "Yes, you feel the whole universe breathing." This simple mirroring validates and amplifies the client's own perception, without layering it with external concepts. In this context, reflection serves as a gentle affirmation that keeps the client centered in their unfolding awareness, reinforcing their agency in the meaning-making process.

Although reflection is a core element of many Western therapeutic models, it can also be adapted to align with a wide range of cultural and spiritual frameworks. Regardless of approach, the key remains the same: to preserve the client's internal authority and autonomy during the psychedelic process.

Ultimately, reflection during a psychedelic journey isn't a passive process. It's precisely attuned to the client's moment-to-moment experience, serving as a means of ensuring that the therapist remains fully present to the client's subjective reality as it unfolds. By mirroring rather than interpreting, the therapist supports the client's deepening awareness of their own process, thereby reinforcing the foundational truth of psychedelic therapy: that the most profound healing comes from within.

Checking in

Hypnosis and psychedelic work share the common goal of establishing a safe, supportive space that allows clients to explore their inner world. One essential practice in both fields is checking in—periodically ensuring that the client remains engaged, comfortable, and supported. In hypnosis, facilitators do this to maintain rapport and adjust the session to the client's responses. Similarly, in psychedelic sessions, where clients may become deeply immersed in their experience, gentle check-ins help maintain a sense of connection and ensure the client's well-being.

However, in most cases—especially during journeys with higher doses—the therapist should avoid applying any hypnosis-based practices during the actual psychedelic journey. Since the client is in an altered state—highly suggestible and not fully in touch with ordinary reality—there is a risk of unintentionally influencing or redirecting the client's experience. The primary focus during the journey should be to provide non-intrusive support, rather than active guidance. Practices such as anchoring, suggestion-based guidance, and integration prompts are more appropriate to implement in the integration sessions following the journey, when the client can more clearly reflect on their experience.

Anchoring is a hypnosis technique through which the facilitator helps the client establish a grounding mechanism, such as a breath pattern or small physical gesture. It is often introduced before a psychedelic session, to help the client navigate intense moments independently. However, reminding a client to use their anchor during the experience itself may unintentionally interrupt their natural process. Similarly, therapists should avoid using suggestion-based guidance—which, in hypnosis, involves gentle prompts like, "You can allow yourself to relax into whatever comes up"—as it could shape the client's perception in ways that aren't authentically their own. Instead, such suggestions can be helpful before the experience, to establish a framework, or afterward, to support reflection.

Incorporating integration prompts—another tool commonly used in hypnosis—can be especially useful after the journey, when the client is grounded and processing their experience. In hypnosis, the facilitator often asks, "What part of this feels important to you?" or "What did you notice shifting?" These same questions can help clients recall and make sense of their psychedelic insights, without imposing an external narrative.

With this in mind, let's now explore the role of checking in—one of the few direct facilitator interventions that is appropriate during the psychedelic journey. In hypnosis, facilitators regularly check in with the client to ensure they remain engaged, comfortable, and supported. This practice is equally valuable during psychedelic sessions, where clients may become deeply immersed in their experience. Since it isn't uncommon for individuals to remain silent and still—appearing to an outside observer as if they are in a meditative state or even asleep—periodic check-ins help maintain connection and provide reassurance throughout the journey. Clients are often deeply engaged in their internal experience, processing emotions, memories, and insights. Clients who remain silent during their psychedelic journey are often effectively accessing their inner wisdom. These individuals frequently return from their experience with a wealth of insights and reflections to process during integration. However, it is advisable to incorporate gentle, periodic check-ins to ensure their well-being and maintain a supportive presence throughout the session.

As a general rhythm, if a client has remained quiet and still for a substantial stretch, offer a gentle check-in: "Just checking in with you, where are you now?" It is best to agree on phrasing in advance during preparation so it fits the client's preference. Provide an opportunity for the client to share their experience without disrupting their internal process. This technique helps maintain therapeutic connection while allowing the client to remain immersed in their journey.

In some cases, checking in may be especially meaningful for clients who appear calm on the outside but are struggling internally. Once, when I checked in with a client who was looking completely blissful, to ask what was going on, he quickly responded, "Oh! You are here! Thank you. I did not want to be alone." Although he looked peaceful from the outside, he was going through a challenging experience. Later, he expressed that my checking in on him helped move him through the difficult moment. Some clients will respond to the check-in by briefly describing what they are experiencing, then going back to being silent; others will give vivid explanations.

The process of checking in can also be adapted according to how the client appears to be doing. For clients who are actively speaking, physically restless, or showing agitation, the therapist can use a check-in to gently reorient the client or assess whether they need more supportive interventions. When working with clients who have trauma histories or come from cultural backgrounds that view authority figures through a certain lens, it is especially important to establish in advance how they would like to be checked in on. This collaborative agreement respects their autonomy and ensures that they feel safe.

Nonverbal check-ins—such as a light touch of the hand or soft breathing sound—can be powerful ways of communicating presence without words. These methods can be especially effective for clients who are nonverbal during their journey, or those for whom language feels too far away. A simple, unobtrusive check-in might sound like, "Just checking in with you gently—where are you now?" This invites clients to share without imposing pressure to respond.

Another benefit of checking in is that brief descriptions or vivid explanations give the therapist information they can utilize and explore in the integration sessions. During integration, clients often highlight the parts of their journey that were transpiring in the moment they were checked in on. Since they often don't remember much of their experience, that reference point allows the therapist and client to recall more of the psychedelic journey later.

After the session, therapists can use notes from check-ins as anchor points in integration conversations. Prompts like "Do you remember what came up when I asked where you were?" can reconnect the client to important insights. Still, it is essential to balance the benefits of check-ins with the risk of interrupting deep processes. Checking in too often could limit the client's ability to fully surrender and immerse themselves in the experience. As with all interventions in psychedelic work, timing, attunement, and consent are key.

Touch

Therapeutic touch can be a valuable and ethically sound component of psychedelic-assisted therapy, when it is applied with clear intention and professional boundaries. Notably, what constitutes therapeutic touch varies significantly depending on the guide's worldview and therapeutic training. In practice, clients often find it soothing to hold the guide's hand or receive other forms of nurturing touch, such as a gentle hand on the shoulder or a reassuring pat on the back during their journey. These forms of contact can provide grounding, emotional reassurance, and a sense of safety, reinforcing the therapeutic alliance and supporting the client's process. At times, this form of touch can give them the strength or sense of safety they need to turn inward or toward uncomfortable material.

Ethical Touch and Consent

Before we turn to one of the most sensitive parts of this work—touch—I want to be plain about the ground we stand on. Safety is not only clinical; it is moral and ethical. Touch carries power. It can comfort and regulate, and it can also confuse or harm. In psychedelic-assisted therapy—where consciousness opens and boundaries can soften—we cannot rely on good intentions alone. We need clear agreements, explicit consent, thoughtful documentation, supervision, and organizational guardrails. Codes of ethics exist for a reason. Our field has learned, sometimes painfully, that when boundaries are unclear, the impact can be deep and lasting. Boundaries are part of the method, not an afterthought.

A difficult lesson comes from the case of Meaghan Buisson. In 2015, while enrolled in a MAPS-sponsored Phase II MDMA trial in Canada, Buisson reported that one of her therapists, Richard Yensen, engaged in sexual contact during and around the course of care, and that his co-therapist, Dr. Donna Dryer, knew of boundary violations. Yensen later acknowledged a sexual relationship but framed it as initiated by the client—an argument that ignores the basic duty of care and the power imbalance of this setting. MAPS condemned the conduct as unethical. The matter was settled outside of court and professional consequences followed. Whatever the legal language, the human truth remains the same: people come to us vulnerable, and the responsibility to protect them is ours.

Psychedelic sessions place unusual influence in the hands of the therapist. Clients may have altered judgment, heightened suggestibility, and a body that remembers in powerful ways. What might be a neutral gesture in ordinary therapy—a quiet tone, sustained eye contact, and a gentle pause—can carry immense meaning here. Small slips can become large wounds. Coercion is obvious harm, but so are ambiguous touch, inappropriate self-disclosure, and any collapse of role clarity. When the frame wavers, the session stops being a place of repair and becomes a reenactment of old pain.

Because sessions are immersive and often long, our presence must be warm and disciplined at the same time. We track our own pull to rescue, to merge, to be the answer. If a grieving client reaches for contact, we ask whether grounded, consent-based, non-sexual touch would truly help regulation or risks entanglement. If a client pours out love and gratitude, we receive it with care and return authorship to them: the transformation belongs to their system. We are there to hold the container, not to become the source.

Transference is not a problem to be erased; it is information. If a client experiences us as the parent they always needed, we explore the need that is being contacted and how they can internalize that steadiness for themselves. If anger or disappointment appears, we stay curious. When have you felt this before? What does this moment echo? In this way, the relationship becomes a place where old patterns are seen and new choices are practiced.

Afterward comes integration, where boundaries matter even more. Some clients want to stay very close to the person who witnessed their inner world. They may seek frequent contact or reassurance, or ache for the intensity of connection felt in the session. We normalize the longing and keep the frame intact. We offer scheduled integration, clear communication channels, and a steady redirect to practices, relationships, and supports outside of us. The task is to help the client metabolize the experience into a life, not into a bond with the therapist. This is not rigidity; it is devotion to a structure that protects dignity and sovereignty. When boundaries are firm and kind, the room feels safe enough for depth. When boundaries are loose or inconsistent, confusion and dependence grow. Boundaries are not walls; they are scaffolding. They allow the experience to remain the client's own and their healing truly theirs.

The MAPS MDMA-AT Code of Ethics (2019b) offers concise guidance for therapeutic touch:

> "It is necessary to obtain consent before using any therapeutic touch; discuss consent for touch during the preparation sessions, detailing its purpose and how or when touch might be used during the psychedelic session. Only offer touch if it falls inside your scope of practice and competence, and it should be clear to the client that touch is always optional. Absolutely no sexual touch is initiated or allowed in any way with the client; maintaining clear professional boundaries must be held at utmost importance at all times."
>
> (p. 3)

It is helpful to briefly revisit this conversation just before the session to reinforce informed consent and create space for any changes in comfort or preferences. A simple check-in—"As we discussed in our prep sessions, I'm here if you want a hand to hold or need grounding touch, but only if you ask for it"—reestablishes agency and safety.

Human connection extends beyond words. Physical touch, when used with intention, sensitivity, and clear ethical boundaries, can foster safety, deepen trust, and support regulation. In psychedelic-assisted therapy, where clients often navigate intense somatic and emotional states, a reassuring hand on the shoulder or a brief, well-timed touch on the hand or forearm may help a client reconnect with their body. Touch should never be all-or-nothing; it is a spectrum guided by the client's history, preferences, culture, and explicit consent.

Virginia Satir intentionally incorporated physical touch into therapy, viewing it as a tool for amplifying positive communication, reinforcing new learning, and consolidating change (Andreas, 1999). She held that the energy transmitted through touch could support embodied shifts, challenging psychotherapy norms that over-privileged verbal interventions. Satir's stance—use touch with clear intent and strong boundaries—resonates in psychedelic contexts, where nonverbal attunement can be as clinically significant as words.

There is an active debate about touch in therapy. Used appropriately, with defined boundaries and consent, touch can enhance trust and facilitate healing, particularly when clients are reliving trauma or deep psychological pain and need help regulating their nervous system (Grof, 2012). Broader research also suggests that ethical, culturally attuned touch can promote emotional regulation, reduce stress markers, and strengthen interpersonal trust (Zur, 2007). The standard remains the same across approaches: touch is never sexual; it is never about the therapist's needs; and it is always optional, time-limited, and purpose-bound.

Cross-cultural differences matter. Western mental health professionals tend to use therapeutic touch more readily than traditional healers. In many Indigenous settings, facilitators maintain physical distance even in the face of distress, relying on chanting, icaros, or other energetic methods to guide the process. Some religions and cultures limit cross-gender touch or minimize physical contact in general. Orthodox Judaism observes laws of Shomer Negiah that prohibit touch between unrelated men and women; many Islamic contexts discourage physical contact between unrelated adults; and traditional Japanese culture often favors minimal touch in favor of bowing. These norms do not render touch universally "off-limits," but they require that we ask, listen, and adapt. Preparation sessions are the place to discuss all of this—what touch could look like, when it might be offered, and whether it is wanted at all. Any touch with sexual connotation is unacceptable and harmful.

Energetic implications also deserve attention. Incorporating deep emotional presence and physical touch can have unintended consequences for the guide. In one psilocybin ceremony, I supported a client in intense distress for hours and later became physically and emotionally depleted, even vomiting during the session. A shaman later framed this as an energetic entanglement—an unguarded closeness that risked absorbing aspects of the client's process. Whether one uses that language or not, the clinical lesson is clear: connection without boundaries can overwhelm the therapist and does not serve the client. Flemons (2022) offers a useful remedy in "empathetic enclosure": fully attune to the client and then deliberately disengage to re-establish a distinct sense of self. For moments of deep attunement, we may even experience "one mind" (Flemons, 2002); the enclosure is what allows us to return to grounded separateness. Intentional disengagement is not abandonment—it is containment. It protects both parties and sustains the work.

A brief vignette illustrates the clinical nuance. Rachel, a woman in her thirties whose parents fled the Bosnian war, struggled to receive care as a child and later as a mother herself. During an ayahuasca journey, she called me over, laid her head in my lap, and I gently stroked her hair. She settled. As the effects waned, she recalled a childhood memory of her mother caressing her in the same way. The touch served as a catalyst, opening grief and love. In integration, Rachel revisited painful incidents with her mother from a new vantage point—seeing imperfect love where she had only known absence. She traveled to New York to repair their relationship and began mothering her own children with more tenderness. In classical terms, this was transference: the redirection of feelings from earlier figures to the therapist, surfacing material that could be processed and re-authored with support (Freud, 1958). The work succeeded not because of touch alone, but because touch occurred within a clear frame of consent, purpose, and post-session integration.

Clinical considerations: discuss touch during preparation, including purposes, limits, and explicit opt-in; document agreements and revisit just before dosing; offer only what is within your scope of practice and competence; keep all touch non-sexual, time-limited, and client-initiated whenever possible; monitor your own countertransference and rescue impulses; maintain energetic and psychological boundaries through deliberate disengagement; consider cultural, religious, and gender norms and adapt accordingly; use supervision and organizational guardrails; in integration, normalize longing while redirecting toward the client's practices and supports outside the therapy relationship.

Ultimately, therapeutic touch is neither a necessity nor a universal approach. It is one possible tool within a well-defined ethical frame. Used sparingly and with cultural humility, it can anchor a client in moments of intensity and help translate insight into embodied safety. Its power lies not in the contact itself but in the disciplined, attuned presence that offers it, and in the boundaries that keep the experience the client's own.

Taking Notes

Clients often have difficulty recalling their psychedelic experience in full, as these journeys can be dense, nonlinear, and hard to articulate. For this reason, the guide's role in documenting the session is critical. Careful note-taking preserves key moments, emotional shifts, and insights that may later support integration. It also helps the therapist track patterns and themes across sessions.

The following elements should be documented throughout the journey:

- Client's primary and secondary intentions.
- Time and dosage of medicine administration.
- Time of reported onset.
- Client's verbal expressions, including words, stories, and notable phrases (this can begin before the client ingests the medicine).
- Items or thoughts the client brings into the space, such as photos, songs, or symbols.
- Therapist responses or interventions.
- Client's body language, such as hand gestures, posture, or facial expressions.
- Therapist check-ins and client responses.
- Emotional states before, during, and after (e.g., fear, calm, joy, and anxiety).
- Physiological responses, including breathing changes, tears, trembling, or temperature shifts.
- Shifts in vocal tone or pacing, including whispering, sudden loudness, drawn-out pauses, or altered cadence.
- Nonverbal vocalizations, such as humming, moaning, laughter, or crying.
- Breakthroughs or insights voiced by the client.
- Periods of silence or stillness, and the shifts that follow.
- Responses to music, light, or other environmental stimuli.
- Guiding tools such as breathwork, verbal prompts, consensual touch, or grounding techniques.
- Distress or difficult moments, and how they were met or held.

- Client's closing reflections and emotional state at session's end.
- Therapist's notes on integration themes to revisit in follow-up.
- Significant changes from prior sessions, if relevant.

Guides should discreetly take concise notes, using shorthand or keywords to minimize distraction and keep them fully present with the client.

Patience and Calm Through the Chaos and Silence

Clients respond to psychedelics in highly individual ways, influenced by their psychological makeup, personal history, and emotional readiness. Guides must be prepared to navigate a wide spectrum of responses, from complete stillness to intense emotional expression.

Some clients may remain quiet and still throughout most of their journey, whereas others may move frequently, cry, or vocalize. Because psychedelic sessions can last many hours, the therapist must embody patience, steadiness, and presence.

When a client is mostly silent or still, the guide should maintain a calm, grounded, meditative state, periodically checking in while attuning to subtle cues, shifts in breath, posture, or facial expression. Silence can reflect deep inward processing, but it may also indicate emotional shutdown or dissociation. The therapist's steady presence and moment-to-moment discernment help create a safe, responsive container. Taking notes during these periods preserves details that may later support integration.

In more active sessions, clients may cry, shake, scream, or engage in primal expressions. The therapist's role is to remain centered and nonreactive. Any expression of fear, discomfort, or judgment can disrupt the client's process, which is often unfolding beneath their conscious awareness. Maintaining a regulated nervous system—through grounding breathing patterns, silent mantras, or simple internal resourcing—allows the therapist to remain open, calm, and supportive.

These intense expressions are especially common in ayahuasca ceremonies, where clients may embody animalistic energies—flicking their tongue like a snake, roaring like a lion, or producing deep, guttural sounds. Though striking, these behaviors are well-known to experienced facilitators, who understand them as instinctual releases—unconscious material rising for resolution. One facilitator I sat with in Costa Rica described them as a reconnection to something primal and long-buried that is emerging for healing.

These expressions may carry different meanings in different cultural contexts. Therapists must, therefore, approach them with humility, cultural sensitivity, and reverence for the mystery of the process. What matters most is the quality of presence the guide offers—steady, nonjudgmental, and attuned to the sacred unfolding of whatever needs to be seen and moved.

Setting the Stage

The setting in which a psychedelic journey takes place profoundly shapes the client's experience. When therapists understand and honor the power of setting, they can create environments that feel safe, supportive, and conducive to transformation. This section outlines the essential elements of designing an optimal setting for psychedelic-assisted therapy. Since most clinical sessions occur indoors, the focus will be on creating a therapeutic indoor space.

External Setting

Early psychedelic researchers in the 1950s quickly realized that cold, clinical medical rooms were not the ideal environment for healing to take place. They began redesigning their spaces to feel more like comfortable living rooms, and this approach remains commonplace today (Johnson et al., 2008). A well-prepared room should be warm, calm, and visually soothing. Soft lighting, thoughtful décor, and a clean environment all help signal safety. Incorporating elements from the natural world—plants, flowing water, stones, or artwork inspired by nature—can support grounding and connection, especially since many clients naturally long for a return to nature while under the influence of psychedelics.

There should be a reclining chair, couch, or bed available so the client can lie down comfortably, along with warm blankets and eyeshades. The lighting should be dim enough to create a gentle atmosphere, but bright enough for the therapist to safely move around the space. The room should be free of sharp or fragile objects, as clients may risk getting injured if they move around. A quality sound system is also essential, as music plays a central role in shaping the journey.

Music

> If psychedelics erase the individual's map of who they are and the world around them, music provides much-needed direction.
>
> —*Bonny and Pahnke (1972, p. 70)*

Music is one of the most significant components of the setting during the client's psychedelic journey. Music can significantly influence the individual's subjective experience and is vital in providing direction within the experience (Kaelen et al., 2018). As I shared previously, I tell clients that the music is the river that will transport them on their journey. I inform them that it ebbs and flows, depending on the track that is playing at any given moment. At times, the river's movement will be fast. Other times, it will be slow. Nevertheless, it will constantly bend and transition in different directions. Therefore, the client's job is to "relax and float downstream" (Leary et al., 1964, p. 3). Attempting to swim in a different direction can become exhausting, perhaps even resulting in the client feeling as if they are drowning.

Utilizing familiar music during a psychedelic therapy session can be a double-edged sword; while it may provide comfort, it might also distract the client from immersing in the novel, abstract experience. Therefore, adhering to well-established guidelines is crucial. One of the foundational resources in this field is a set of guidelines developed in 1972 by Pahnke and Bonny, which continues to be widely used in the field of psychedelic therapy today. They wrote that the proper use of music is essential for accomplishing five vital therapeutic objectives:

1. Help the patient relinquish control and enter more fully into their inner world.
2. Facilitate the release of intense emotionality.
3. Contribute to a peak experience.
4. Provide continuity in an experience of timelessness.
5. Direct and structure the experience (pp. 66–72).

According to the authors, the right kind of music is an effective stimulus that complements the medicine's function. It is a tool that facilitates opening the doors to the unfolding content of the subconscious mind. Furthermore, it aids in guiding and organizing highly unorganized psychedelic information.

Bonny and Pahnke (1972) explain that the two most important variables when choosing a psychedelic playlist are appropriateness and timing. In my experience, these two factors determine a successful playlist. My colleague, Isaac, has taken the job of creating the playlists we use with our clients. He successfully structures them so that the melodies follow the intensity of the medicine, from pre-onset to onset, then to peak intensity, and, finally, to come down. He has even become exceptional at noticing when the client is entering the peak of their journey and then playing songs that have shown to be the most successful in eliciting deep and meaningful experiences.

Bonny (1969) interviewed seven psychedelic integration therapists and asked them to vote on which songs were the most effective in producing psychedelic peak experiences for their clients. Through these interviews, she created a six-phase outline of characteristics that should be kept in mind when creating an appropriate playlist. I want to note that the therapists she interviewed mainly worked with LSD. Therefore, I will not include the time frames, which vary depending on the psychedelic (e.g., LSD takes around 8–12 hours, while psilocybin takes 4–6 hours). The therapist should decide on a time frame based on the medicine and its standard trajectory (i.e., times of pre-onset, onset, peak intensity, and comedown).

In Phase One (pre-onset), the music should be pleasant and neutral, of the nonspecific, quieting variety. Isaac prefers relaxing piano pieces, such as *BlueBird* by Alexis FFrench. One of my choices is a selection from the neutral guitar concertos by Antonio Vivaldi. In Phase Two (onset), the drug begins to have an effect. This is when the client will usually alert the therapist that they are starting to feel something. The goal in this phase is to choose music that allows for a smooth entry into the experience—music that encourages the client to remain relaxed and positive. Again, guitar concertos by Antonio Vivaldi are a good choice, or light binaural beats, such as *Introspection* by Laraaji.

Phase 3 (building toward a peak experience) is when the effects of the medicine are increasing, guiding the client toward their peak experience. At this time, the client will often begin to resist or turn away from what they are experiencing. During Phase 3, music plays a vital role in helping to stabilize the client and move them forward. Music with insistent rhythms and long, flowing phrases is best. Some recommendations are Bach's *Come, Sweet Death* or *Arioso*. Phase Four (peak intensity) is achieved when the client reaches the peak action of the medicine. The peak period is the most critical, and having the right music is crucial. Isaac often plays *Sound of Invisible Waters* by Deuter, and we have seen it evoke powerful emotions in many clients.

In her study, Bonny (1969) found that therapists selected their music based on what they observed in their clients' psychological state. If they noticed that a client was stuck or blocked, they chose music that was stronger with insistent rhythms, such as *Winter* from Vivaldi's *The Four Seasons*, or Beethoven's *Symphony No. 5*. Once the therapist believes the client has reached their peak experience, some good selections are Gounod's *Cecilia Mass*, Richard Strauss's *Death and Transfiguration*, or Faure's *Requiem*, parts III and IV.

In Phase Five (comedown), the effects of the medicine are beginning to diminish. The client will usually find themselves more stabilized, sometimes beginning to exhibit a sense of peace and tranquility. Music that reflects this mood, such as *Morning Mood Variations* by Grieg and Scheps, Brahms' *Violin Concerto*, or music geared toward Zen meditation, is all excellent choices. Finally, Phase Six is when the client has returned to ordinary consciousness. This is a time primarily used to talk with the client about their experience and highlight any significant insights. This is also a time when lyrical music can be played. Sometimes, clients will ask if they can listen to music they find enjoyable, and it is perfectly acceptable to allow this. In the other phases, using music the client is familiar with can be risky, as it might distract them from an abstract and new experience.

Ultimately, the more experienced the therapist becomes in guiding their clients' psychedelic journeys, the more proficient they will be in knowing how and when to play certain songs and ensembles. The outline I have provided is just a stepping stone toward exploring the vast and important elements for creating the correct type of playlist for a client's psychedelic journey.

In conclusion, the role of a guide and creating a warm and safe setting are essential components of a positive and therapeutic psychedelic journey. The guide is important in providing support, guidance inward, and safety throughout the journey. Additionally, the guide is responsible for creating a space that allows the client to feel trust and openness to explore whatever arises in their journey. By creating a strong therapeutic relationship, maintaining healthy boundaries, and providing a safe space, therapists can help guide their clients through the complexities of a psychedelic experience and help them access unconscious material that allows them to create lasting positive change in their lives.

Note

1 Although I encourage therapists to conduct thorough preparation in most cases, there are some exceptional cases in which the benefits of expedited entry into a psychedelic session outweigh the potential drawbacks.

Chapter 9

Integration

The term *integration* has its roots in the Latin word *integratio*, which is derived from the verb *integrare*, meaning *to make whole* or *to unite*. In a more general sense, integration involves the process of combining disparate parts or elements to form a cohesive whole. In the context of psychedelic experiences, integration refers to the ongoing process of incorporating insights, learning, and personal growth from the journey into daily life (Bathje et al., 2022). The process of integration isn't limited to the time right after the experience; rather, it can continue long afterward.

During the integration process, the client explores their experiences and consciously reassembles different pieces of it. In collaboration with the therapist, they identify ways to put their insights and learnings into useful contexts and daily practices. The window of neuroplasticity that remains open soon after a psychedelic experience offers a rich opportunity to make meaningful and lasting changes. Effectively integrating psychedelic experiences is crucial for individuals who want to fully realize the benefits of their psychedelic experiences in their daily lives. It allows them to translate their insights and learnings into positive changes in their perspective, behaviors, attitudes, and relationships.

The process of psychedelic integration can be defined in multiple ways, but I'm partial to this comprehensive and flexible definition from Bathje et al. (2022):

> Integration is a process in which a person revisits and actively engages in making sense of, working through, translating, and processing the content of their psychedelic experience. Through intentional effort and supportive practices, this process allows one to gradually capture and incorporate the emergent lessons and insights into their lives, thus moving toward greater balance and wholeness, both internally (mind, body, and spirit) and externally (lifestyle, social relations, and the natural world).
>
> (p. 4)

DOI: 10.4324/9781003541639-13

In essence, psychedelic integration is an ongoing, dynamic process that bridges the gap between insight and lasting transformation. It involves actively working with the psychedelic experience, making sense of emotions, shifts in perception, and newfound understandings in a way that fosters meaningful change. By engaging in intentional reflection and incorporating supportive practices, individuals can move toward greater coherence and wholeness in their inner and outer lives. Ultimately, integration is what allows a psychedelic journey to become a catalyst for growth, healing, and deeper alignment with one's values and purpose.

All Reality Is Psychedelic

The idea that *all reality is psychedelic*—a paradigm coined by my colleague, Isaac Farin—offers a powerful reframing of both psychedelic experiences and everyday life. It suggests that the perceptual flexibility so central to altered states is not unique to those moments, but is rather a fundamental feature of consciousness itself. From this perspective, life is both the *medicine* and the *journey*, constantly offering opportunities for healing, transformation, and growth.

As previously discussed, psychedelic experiences are marked by heightened neuroplasticity, expanded awareness, and a capacity to perceive reality in new ways. These shifts are associated with changes in brain activity, especially within the DMN, which typically filters perception and reinforces habitual patterns of thought. Psychedelics loosen this filtering system, opening the door to a more fluid and expansive experience of reality. Yet even in non-psychedelic states, perception remains inherently malleable. Our attention, emotions, conditioning, and unconscious expectations are constantly shaping how we engage with the world around us. This means that although psychedelics may magnify these shifts, they aren't creating something foreign—they are illuminating the very nature of perception.

Beyond what we consciously register, an immense amount of sensory and emotional data is filtered and simplified by the brain. Each person's reality is essentially a highlight reel shaped by personal history, cognitive biases, and neurological limitations. Most of what exists in the external world never makes it into conscious awareness. What we do perceive is a narrow, idiosyncratic slice of a much larger reality. In this sense, human consciousness always operates within a psychedelic frame—subjective, shifting, and deeply personal.

Recognizing that perception is already fluid dissolves the boundary between ordinary and psychedelic states. Both are part of the same continuum. Reality isn't fixed; it is an ever-unfolding process of perception that can be consciously influenced through awareness, intention, and integration. This means that the practices an individual might rely on to navigate a psychedelic session—mindfulness, emotional regulation, surrender, and reflection—are just as powerful when applied in daily life. Setting an intention before a psychedelic journey helps guide and anchor the experience. In other aspects of life, our goals and values serve the same purpose. Choosing to surrender in the face of overwhelming feelings is essential on psychedelics, but it's just as vital when navigating life's inevitable uncertainties. Whether we're in an altered state or not, emotional regulation, presence, and the willingness to integrate what we learn can serve us well.

In many ways, preparing for a psychedelic journey is a way of preparing for life itself. When clients approach their inner world with care and curiosity, tune into subtle patterns, listen deeply, and respond consciously, they are strengthening the same muscles that will help them navigate their relationships, challenges, and growth in the outside world. Integration, then, is a way of relating to life. Every moment becomes an opportunity to apply what was learned, to stay present, and to invite transformation.

Every experience, whether joyful or painful, can serve as a catalyst for healing. Relationships, challenges, and moments of insight offer opportunities just as profound as those accessed in ceremony. The psychedelic session simply reveals this more vividly. When clients learn to treat life with the same reverence they bring to a session, their integration deepens. Instead of compartmentalizing their experiences, they begin to carry them forward in how they live, love, and relate to themselves and others.

Therapists can support this process by encouraging clients to remain open to ordinary moments of insight—those flashes of meaning, synchronicity, or emotional clarity that arise unexpectedly. These subtle shifts often mirror the kinds of revelations experienced in ceremony. Teaching clients to recognize and honor these moments reinforces the integration process while tapping into the well-researched power of expectancy and the placebo effect (Kirsch & Lynn, 1999). When clients believe that change is possible and ongoing, they are more likely to notice and embody it.

Unfortunately, many training programs focus heavily on preparation and the session itself, offering minimal instruction on integration (Ali et al., 2021). This gap can significantly undermine the effectiveness of psychedelic therapy. Without proper support, the insights gained during a journey may fade or become sources of confusion and emotional fragmentation. Integration is where the healing takes root. It's what allows insights to solidify into new patterns, behaviors, and ways of being.

As described in Chapter 1, the metaphor of the hill covered in snow illustrates this clearly. Psychedelics can carve new paths—fresh grooves in the neural terrain, but those paths are shallow at first. Without reinforcement, they can melt away, making it easier for the mind to slide back into well-worn patterns. Integration is what keeps those new tracks alive. It prevents the return to automatic habits and invites clients to consciously choose who they want to become.

Clients should be encouraged to understand this: The work doesn't end when the session ends. Integration allows the momentum of transformation to continue. When practiced with intention, it reinforces the new pathways created during the journey, helping them become lasting parts of the client's worldview and identity.

This chapter offers a comprehensive approach to integration, beginning with the utilization technique—drawn from Milton Erickson's work—as a foundational method for helping clients engage with their experiences. It then explores three essential domains of integration: body, mind, and soul. Each domain offers a unique path for translating psychedelic insight into embodied, meaningful change. Through this multidimensional approach, therapists can help clients understand what happened during their journey, and learn to live differently because of it.

Integration Process

The idea that all reality is psychedelic reminds us that integration is more than just a post-journey task; it's an ongoing process of translating insight into lived experience. Psychedelic journeys may open the door to profound shifts in awareness, but it's integration that renders these shifts sustainable and transformative. Jesse Gould and Paul Austin (n.d.) emphasize that while psychedelics may open the door to profound insight and transformation, the real impact depends on the individual's willingness to take action and integrate those insights into their daily lives, through meaningful and often difficult choices.

One of the most common questions clients and therapists ask is when the integration process should begin. Ideally, it starts as soon as the client returns to a baseline state after the journey. At this point, the experience is still fresh—emotionally, physically, and cognitively. This is a valuable window for capturing key impressions, insights, and emotional shifts before they fade or become distorted. If the therapist is present during the journey, they can begin this process through gentle conversation and observation. If the client journeys independently, they should be encouraged to record their reflections—through journaling, voice notes, drawing, or movement—as soon as possible.

It's important to remember that integration isn't confined to the hours or even days after the experience. Insights often unfold in layers. Some are immediate, whereas others emerge gradually in the weeks that follow. Clients may feel joy, clarity, or renewal; but they may also encounter disorientation, grief, or resistance as old patterns are confronted. These moments aren't setbacks; they're invitations to trust what's unfolding and allow space for the experience to ripen over time. With therapeutic support, clients can engage with these waves as part of the larger movement toward wholeness.

Stolaroff (1993) captured this beautifully:

> Many people believe that a profound psychedelic experience provides all the answers and changes everything. While such experiences can be transformative, they primarily show us what's possible and point us in a new direction. There is a brief grace period following these experiences where we're infused with the power and wonder of new information and can make rapid changes. However, if we fail to act on this opportunity, old habits quickly reassert themselves, and we slip back into our previous state.
>
> (p. 3)

This grace period reflects a time of enhanced neuroplasticity. The brain is more open to rewiring, and change is easier to initiate. If approached intentionally, this period offers a powerful chance to begin building new habits, restructuring thought patterns, and living in alignment with the insights received. But if left unattended, the old grooves tend to reassert themselves, and the deeper potential of the experience may be lost.

Therapists play a key role in helping clients seize this opportunity. Through active listening, reflection, and collaborative meaning-making, they can guide clients to identify what felt most true, powerful, or moving during their journey. With these significant aspects of the experience identified, the integration process can then be focused on translating insights into concrete, meaningful changes.

The remainder of this chapter outlines a flexible yet structured approach to integration. It includes practical tools for helping clients process their journey, identify key themes, and move from insight to action. By engaging body, mind, and soul—and building sustainable daily practices—clients can preserve the energy of their psychedelic experience and use it as fuel for long-term growth and healing.

Identifying Learnings

Identifying meaningful insights from a psychedelic journey can be challenging. Clients often emerge feeling overwhelmed or uncertain about how to articulate what they've experienced. Expressions like, "I can't explain it," or "It was everything and nothing," reflect the nonlinear, complex nature of these journeys. In these moments, the therapist's primary role is not to extract clear answers, but to gently guide clients toward recognizing what resonates most deeply for them.

Therapists can initiate exploration by asking broad yet purposeful questions: "What moment from your journey feels most vivid or significant to you right now?" or, "Is there an image, sensation, or insight you feel drawn to explore further?" Revisiting the client's original intentions is also especially beneficial. Even when experience feels chaotic or unclear, returning to these intentions can illuminate underlying themes or insights.

Insights first tend to surface as bodily sensations or emotions, rather than clear narratives. Softening breaths, unexpected tears, or subtle shifts in posture often indicate deeper meanings. Therapists should gently notice and reflect these somatic cues. For example, "I noticed tears coming up as you spoke about that moment. What might this emotion be trying to communicate?"

Clients may resist interpreting their experience, perceiving it as random, frightening, or abstract. In such cases, therapists can validate and contextualize these feelings, reassuring clients: "It's completely natural to feel uncertain or overwhelmed right now. Let's remain patient and curious, allowing meaning to unfold gradually."

Creative expression provides another powerful pathway for integration when language alone won't suffice. Encouraging clients to engage in activities like drawing, movement, or collage can help reveal symbolic dimensions that words might not access. For instance, a client struggling to articulate a confusing vision might discover deeper meaning through a drawing or collage that reflects emotional themes from their journey.

Central to this process is the Ericksonian principle of utilization—meeting clients precisely where they are, using their own language, imagery, and experiences as the raw material for growth. Rather than imposing external interpretations, therapists draw directly from clients' lived experiences, highlighting and amplifying their natural insights. For example, if a client describes feeling "lost at sea," the therapist might reflect, "You're feeling lost at sea. What might the ocean represent in your life right now?" Similarly, if another client describes feeling "weightless and free," a therapist could gently inquire, "In which areas of your life might that sense of freedom be valuable?"

By thoughtfully reflecting somatic cues, revisiting intentions, inviting creative exploration, and utilizing clients' metaphors, therapists can help clients gradually unpack and integrate the richness of their psychedelic experiences into lasting, meaningful change. Sarah's story illustrates this effectively. Struggling with persistent nightmares, Sarah hoped ayahuasca might resolve these distressing dreams. Instead, the ceremony intensified her nightmares. Despite initial disappointment, gentle utilization allowed Sarah to see her experience symbolically. By reframing her journey as a metaphor, her difficult nights became analogous to the ayahuasca journey itself. Sarah found a new way to relate to her suffering. The phrase "daytime is playtime" became her anchor, helping her shift her focus. Instead of trying to stop the nightmares, she decided to embrace how she wanted to live in spite of them. This subtle yet profound shift changed her relationship to the issue, offering emotional resilience and practical healing.

Sarah's story demonstrates how utilization can help clients create unique meaning from their own experiences. Using this approach, the therapists can guide their clients to recognize what they inherently know, supporting them in experimenting with new meanings. By returning to the images, emotions, and insights that linger, integration becomes an ongoing conversation—an unfolding of insight that invites presence, patience, and compassion. In this way, clients become the primary source of their transformation, and therapists serve as guides, facilitating awareness and fostering self-generated healing.

Using the Client's Intentions

An effective application of the utilization technique involves returning to a client's intentions—both primary and secondary—as reference points during integration. Intentions serve as a kind of internal compass, helping orient the client amidst the often abstract or overwhelming material that emerges during a psychedelic journey. By revisiting these intentions, the therapist can help the client frame their experience in a way that connects directly to their therapeutic goals.

As described in Chapter 3, clients are encouraged to set two kinds of intentions before their journey. The primary intention is open-ended: to surrender to the process and trust that the medicine will offer whatever is needed. This flexibility is crucial, especially when the journey unfolds in unexpected or confusing ways. If a client comes out of their journey feeling disappointed or unclear about what they got from it, the therapist can gently remind them of their intention to surrender and trust that they received what they needed.

When a client struggles to remember parts of the experience or feels disoriented by what emerged, returning to this primary intention can be deeply grounding. It allows the client to trust that even in the absence of conscious understanding, something meaningful is occurring beneath the surface. Drawing from Carl Jung's work, the therapist can reinforce that the unconscious profoundly influences thoughts, emotions, and behaviors—often in ways we can't see right away. Reminding clients of this can help them release the pressure to make sense of everything and, instead, stay open to the idea that meaning may unfold gradually.

This perspective also gives clients permission to label parts of their journey as mysterious. Doing so can be liberating. The need for certainty often creates distress, but accepting the unknown can foster trust in the process. When clients come to believe that they don't need to have all the answers, they can move forward with more ease and openness.

While the primary intention offers spaciousness, secondary intentions—the more personal and specific goals clients bring into the experience—can also be deeply useful. They may not carry the same therapeutic flexibility, but they often serve as valuable reference points for understanding what the medicine may have been pointing toward.

For example, one of my clients entered a psilocybin journey with the intention to reconnect with the feeling that "everything is perfect," even though his conscious mind found that notion threatening. During the session, he recalled a seemingly insignificant memory from childhood: winning a giant chocolate Easter bunny at a church fair. At first, he was confused by the image. But when we explored it together, he remembered how strongly he had known he would win. This was a rare moment of clarity and confidence during a time in his life that was marked by instability and poverty. As we unpacked the memory, he realized the journey had taken him back to a version of himself who could trust life, even when the future was uncertain. This opened the door to reconnecting with the carefree resilience he had once known.

Another client, Maya, emerged from a ketamine session describing a cracked ceramic bowl. "No matter what I did, I couldn't fix it," she said. "It just stayed broken." She interpreted the image as a failure—a symbol that she was damaged beyond repair. Rather than challenging her directly, I leaned into her metaphor. "What if the bowl wasn't meant to be fixed?" I asked. "What if it's more like *kintsugi*, the Japanese art of filling cracks with gold? Could the medicine have been showing you where your beauty lives now?" Maya paused, her expression softening. "I never thought of it that way . . . that's interesting," she said, a note of curiosity entering her voice. The reframe seemed to gently open her to new possibilities.

This is a simple example of Ericksonian utilization. It involves working with what the client brings—a symbol, a language, an emotional state—and gently reframing it in a way that opens new meaning. I didn't offer Maya something foreign. I used what was already present, and followed her metaphor into a new possibility.

That's the heart of utilization. As therapists facilitating psychedelic work, we don't need to analyze our clients' journeys or interpret the symbols that emerge for them. Instead, we listen closely for what feels alive in the client's story—an image, a phrase, a moment of emotional charge—and use that to guide insight. Intentions become part of this process, serving as themes that live inside the client and often resurface in some symbolic form, both during and after the journey.

When therapists help clients reflect on how their journey related to their intentions, both directly and indirectly, they reinforce the idea that the client's system is always moving toward healing. Whether through a childhood memory, a cracked bowl, or a mysterious moment of silence, the journey often brings what was most needed. Utilizing the client's intentions helps them see that even when the medicine's intervention doesn't make sense, it may still be right on track.

By drawing on both primary and secondary intentions, therapists can support clients in integrating their experience with greater trust, clarity, and alignment with who they are becoming.

Finding Mystical Experiences

Another vital dimension of integration is the exploration of spiritual or existential elements that often emerge from psychedelic journeys—what are sometimes called mystical or peak experiences. As discussed in Chapter 2, these experiences have shown profound potential for facilitating lasting transformation and enhancing a client's sense of meaning, purpose, and connection. When they arise, it is essential to gently lean into them during the integration process, helping clients understand and embody the depth of what they encountered.

Common mystical themes include an expanded awareness of the self, a felt sense of unity or oneness, and a deep interconnection with all life. These moments are often imbued with a quality of sacredness (Pahnke, 1963), which is why clients frequently describe them as more real than everyday consciousness. It isn't uncommon for clients to rank such experiences among the most significant of their lives.

Interestingly, mystical experiences also tend to deepen clients' engagement with mindfulness. Clients who have these types of experiences often develop a renewed or intensified connection to the mindfulness practices introduced during preparation. The journey itself can serve as a crash course in presence, surrender, and awareness—qualities that are central to mindfulness. After their journey, clients may find themselves more receptive to sustaining those states through daily practice. Rather than mindfulness being an abstract concept or therapeutic tool, it becomes something they've lived, felt, and come to trust.

Mystical experiences often anchor clients in essential principles of mindfulness, such as wholeness, acceptance, surrender, trust, gratitude, and beginner's mind. These elements offer not only a way to integrate the psychedelic experience, but also a framework for living. As Kabat-Zinn (2019) explains:

> [These elements are] balm and medicine for our anguished hearts and agitated minds, as windows on the inner and outer worlds through which to see with eyes of wholeness. In that seeing, that realizing, we finally do come to our senses, not as an end in itself, but as a way of being, as a new beginning, a reaffirmation of our wholeness as human beings, of our potential for living wisely and for loving what is here for us to love, in the midst of the messiness.
>
> (p. 48)

The work of integration involves gently piecing together the fragments of the journey into a coherent whole. When mystical or sacred moments arise, they often serve as guiding lights in the integration process, inviting clients to see themselves—and life itself—through new eyes. By weaving these experiences together with the mindfulness practices introduced in therapy, clients can begin to live from a deeper sense of truth and alignment. They aren't just integrating a single event; rather, they're stepping into a new way of being.

To effectively facilitate this process, therapists can gently encourage their clients to revisit and describe the most significant moments of their mystical experience. Simple, guiding questions such as, "Was there a particular moment when you felt a deep sense of unity or sacredness?" or, "What aspect of your experience continues to feel especially meaningful or alive for you?" can help clients engage more deeply with these moments.

Therapists can also suggest practical ways for clients to nurture and maintain a connection to their mystical insights. These can include journaling or creating expressive art, building simple rituals or daily practices that evoke their mystical experience, or identifying specific mindfulness exercises that resonate deeply with the qualities they encountered. Therapists might ask, "What daily or weekly practices could you introduce that would help you keep connected to this sense of sacredness or unity?" or, "How might you embody the insights you've gained from this mystical experience in your daily interactions or life choices?"

In this way, mystical experiences become integrated through a combination of intellectual understanding and embodied, intentional actions and practices. Therapists can thus help clients translate their profound encounters into tangible changes, guiding them toward a life that reflects the deeper truths and connections illuminated by their psychedelic journeys.

Contextualizing Difficult Experiences

As previously discussed, psychedelic journeys can contain highly impactful themes, sensations, and insights. On one end of the spectrum, journeys may be mystical, awe-filled experiences that are positive, transformative, and inherently therapeutic in nature. Integrating such experiences is generally a natural and easy endeavor. On the other end of the spectrum are those psychedelic experiences that are deeply challenging or unsettling, as they may involve disturbing visuals, overwhelming sensations, or scary revelations. To effectively integrate these experiences, therapists must first contextualize and reframe them—shifting from literal interpretations toward symbolic understandings. Doing so provides emotional safety and helps clients harness their therapeutic insights rather than remain trapped in fear or distress.

Pam's story provides a clear example of how disturbing material can be integrated. Pam was experienced with psychedelics and had generally found them to be beneficial. However, during one particularly intense session, she encountered a terrifying vision of a beast telling her she would develop cancer and die young. The experience was traumatic, leaving her fearful, disoriented, and convinced that the vision was a literal prophecy.

When Pam arrived at my office, my initial goal was to validate the intensity of her experience without pathologizing it. By acknowledging that such frightening experiences are common and understandable, I helped Pam feel less isolated and ashamed. In the following weeks, I worked with her to reframe the experience as a symbolic event. Rather than accepting the vision as a literal truth, we explored it as a metaphor representing something within her that needed to change or be released—perhaps an outdated identity or buried emotional wound. This reframing transformed her fear into an invitation for introspection and growth.

Due to ongoing anxiety, Pam consulted a psychiatrist and began a short-term medication regimen, which reduced her panic and allowed her to engage more effectively in therapy. As Pam confronted memories, challenged limiting beliefs, and began to reconnect with herself, she gradually moved from feeling haunted to making peace with her experience.

This therapeutic reframing and contextualization isn't aimed at minimizing the intensity of the experience, but at offering a compassionate container within which even the most terrifying content can be explored safely. By viewing the vision symbolically rather than literally, Pam gained agency over her previously overwhelming experience. Her journey demonstrates how powerful healing becomes possible when therapists approach difficult psychedelic experiences with openness, empathy, and the flexibility to consider multiple interpretations.

Holistic Integration: Nurturing the Body, Mind, and Soul After Psychedelic Therapy

The insights and realizations gained during a psychedelic experience can profoundly impact an individual's perspective, purpose, and way of being. These openings often bring glimpses of truth, connection, or healing that feel life-changing. But unless they are meaningfully integrated, even the most powerful experience may fade into memory rather than lead to lasting transformation. This is where integration begins. As therapists, one of our central responsibilities is to guide clients in weaving their psychedelic insights into embodied, sustainable change. A key part of this is helping them develop integration practices that give structure and form to what was felt or seen—practices that support long-term shifts in behavior, emotion, and spiritual alignment.

Through my work and personal experience, I have found that the most effective integration practices address three fundamental and inseparable aspects of being: the body, mind, and soul. Each of these domains plays a vital role in our well-being. When one is neglected, the whole person suffers. When all three are nurtured, a sense of wholeness becomes possible.

Psychedelic integration supports a total rebalancing of the human system. This is why I teach clients to build their integration work in a way that meaningfully engages all three domains. Although every practice naturally touches more than one aspect, I present them in this framework to offer clarity, intentionality, and structure. By organizing integration this way, clients are more empowered to personalize their process while maintaining a holistic view of their healing.

This model was born from a personal ketamine journey that shifted the way I understood healing. In that space, I experienced something beyond thought—an embodied realization of how intricately the body, mind, and soul are woven together. It was as if I could perceive myself as a constellation of energies and systems working in exquisite relationship. I felt my consciousness stretch beyond its usual borders, dissolving into a field that seemed to contain both my physical form and something far greater. I sensed that what I had previously seen as separate aspects of myself—my emotions, my thoughts, my spiritual awareness—were interconnected frequencies within a larger field of being.

There was a moment when I felt the atoms of my body vibrating with the same rhythm as the earth beneath me. I couldn't quite explain it, but I knew it: I wasn't just *in* the world, I *was* the world. In this space, the distinctions between "my" body and the land, "my" mind and the collective mind, "my" soul and the soul of the universe began to blur. The more I surrendered, the more I recognized that healing doesn't occur in isolated parts, but in the coherence of the whole.

This insight became the foundation of my integration model. I clearly saw that the body isn't just physical; it's consciousness in form. The mind isn't just cognition; it's a tool for meaning-making and transformation. And the soul isn't something abstract; it's the guiding intelligence that animates our being. When these parts are aligned, we become conduits for truth, healing, and deeper purpose.

In the following sections, I will share the specific body-, mind-, and soul-based practices I recommend to clients. Although each practice can affect all three domains, I've organized them separately for clarity. This framework is intended to serve as a living structure that honors the uniqueness of each person's journey while grounding the integration process in the truth that we are all comprised of body, mind, and soul. Our deepest healing work asks us to tend to them together.

The Body

The body isn't merely a vessel we inhabit—it is the ground of our lived experience, the place where trauma imprints, healing takes root, and integration becomes real. In psychedelic therapy, the body plays a central role both during and after the journey. Clients often return from expanded states with heightened physical sensitivity, energetic shifts, or a sense of disconnection from their somatic self. Grounding through the body is often the first and most vital step in reclaiming integration. This stage requires listening, restoring, and cultivating a renewed relationship with embodiment.

Psychedelic insights may spark a desire to care for the body in new ways. The following practices support the development of lasting habits that nourish physical well-being while anchoring the client's transformation in the tangible, sensory world.

Connection to the Land

One of the most powerful and ancient ways to return to the body is through reconnection with the earth. I often speak of nature as the land from which we came from and to which we will return. In today's fast-paced, hyper-digital world, many clients have become estranged from nature—yet psychedelic experiences often rekindle that connection. The integration period is an ideal time to strengthen it.

Contact with nature has been strongly correlated with psychological well-being, including increased life satisfaction, reduced stress, and a deepened sense of meaning (Bowler et al., 2010; Nisbet et al., 2011). I encourage clients to build simple grounding practices that connect them with the natural world:

- Walking Barefoot: Direct contact with the earth (often called earthing) has been shown to reduce anxiety and improve mood. Walking barefoot in a park, forest, or on the beach supports grounding and nervous system regulation.
- Outdoor Movement: Gentle hikes, jogging, swimming, or dancing outside can help clients integrate movement, breath, and rhythm with the elements around them.
- Gardening: Caring for plants offers a daily dose of connection, responsibility, and growth.
- Mindful Observation: Simply sitting outside and observing the world—trees swaying, birds singing, clouds drifting—can awaken awe and presence.

Yoga and Somatic Movement

Yoga offers a powerful entry point for reinhabiting the body after psychedelic work. It promotes presence, flexibility, emotional release, and energetic flow. The practice is not about performance—it's about reconnection. It can help the client reestablish safety in the body, support detoxification, build self-trust, and develop a deeper awareness of subtle energetic and emotional shifts.

Yoga can also awaken new insight. I've had clients describe a sudden emotional release while in a long-held posture or receive a flash of clarity while seated in meditation after a movement flow. The body holds memory, and movement can unlock what words cannot.

I recommend clients explore styles based on their current needs:

- Restorative Yoga: Gentle yoga postures, held for extended periods of time, encourage deep relaxation, parasympathetic activation, and emotional release. This practice is ideal for clients recovering from intense journeys or those prone to overwhelm.
- Ashtanga or Vinyasa: This more dynamic style of yoga can help stimulate energy, strengthen boundaries, and support reintegration for clients feeling stuck, lethargic, or disconnected.

Even a few minutes a day of intentional movement can make a significant difference. When paired with breathwork or meditation, yoga becomes a bridge between the physical and the subtle—between body and mind, matter and energy.

Nutrition and Supplementation

What we consume during the integration phase has a profound impact on physical healing and emotional balance. Psychedelic experiences can be physically and energetically demanding, and nutritional support helps replenish the system, fortify the nervous system, and support the emotional shifts underway.

Although direct evidence of nutrient depletion from psychedelics remains limited, it is widely accepted that emotionally intense or energetically taxing journeys can strain the body's metabolic and hormonal systems. Staying hydrated and nourished during this time supports clients in anchoring their insights and recovering a sense of resilience[1].

A nutrient-rich diet based on whole foods balances energy levels, supports emotion regulation, and promotes optimal brain function. I encourage clients to:

- Avoid processed foods, refined sugars, and inflammatory ingredients.
- Prioritize whole, colorful fruits and vegetables, healthy fats, and high-quality proteins.

- Drink plenty of clean water and support electrolyte balance, especially if the client has fasted or purged.

Many of these nutritional recommendations echo the traditional teachings of Eastern medicine, indigenous systems, and shamanic wisdom—all of which view food as a sacred extension of life-force energy.

Some of the supplement recommendations (to be considered with guidance from a licensed health professional) I make include the following:

- Vitamin D, Omega-3 fatty acids, Magnesium, and Folate: These vitamins may support mood stabilization, nervous system repair, and cognitive clarity.
- Adaptogens such as ashwagandha, rhodiola, and holy basil: These supplements can help support adrenal balance and recovery from intense emotional experiences.

The compound 5-HTP, naturally produced from the amino acid L-tryptophan, was previously recommended to aid in the replenishment of serotonin after taking MDMA. However, recent research findings suggest that supplementing with 5-HTP too soon after MDMA could interfere with natural recovery or neurotransmitter balance. As modern psychedelic research continues to progress, it is best to approach matters of supplementation with caution and professional oversight, ideally recommending and incorporating supplements only when they are clearly indicated and well-timed within a broader post-journey care plan.

Guides working with MAOI-containing psychedelics like ayahuasca should urge clients to follow strict dietary protocols, to avoid adverse interactions with tyramine-rich foods or contraindicated medications (Frecska et al., 2016). Clients should be educated about the importance of pre- and post-dietary adherence in these cases.

Additional Somatic Supports

These optional but powerful practices can further help clients feel grounded, rested, and restored:

- Massage Therapy: Encourages circulation, releases physical tension, and soothes the nervous system.
- Acupuncture: Helps rebalance energy and regulate emotional flow.
- Infrared Sauna or Traditional Sauna: Promotes detoxification, muscle relaxation, and clarity.
- Rest and Napping: Often overlooked, rest is an essential component of nervous system integration.

Integration through the body is about more than just physical care; it's about creating safety and presence from the inside out. As clients begin to feel more at home in their bodies, they can more fully anchor the emotional and spiritual insights gained in their journey. The aforementioned practices serve as portals through which insight becomes embodiment, and healing becomes lived experience.

The Mind

The mind plays a central role in shaping how we perceive, process, and respond to the world. After a psychedelic journey, the mind often enters a rich and complex process of integration—where thoughts, insights, questions, and sometimes confusion surface in ways that may feel unfamiliar or difficult to organize. Cognitive integration is about helping clients make meaning of their experiences by creating space for reflection, mindfulness, and active engagement with the stories they tell themselves about what they've seen, felt, or realized.

Mind-based integration practices allow clients to further explore and digest the psychological content of their journey. These practices help expand awareness, soften mental rigidity, and establish clarity around insights gained.

Mindfulness

Mindfulness is the foundation of mental integration. It provides the internal spaciousness necessary to observe, rather than react, to one's internal landscape. Clients who practiced mindfulness or breathwork prior to their journey are often more equipped to navigate the waves of insight that follow it. Ongoing mindfulness practice helps clients regulate emotional reactivity, deepen self-inquiry, stabilize nervous system shifts, and reconnect with inner stillness. I encourage clients to choose one or more of the following practices:

- Body Scan Meditation: Bringing awareness to physical sensations throughout the body, helping to identify areas of tension, emotion, or insight stored somatically.
- Drink Meditation: Slowly savoring a warm beverage with full sensory awareness—sight, smell, taste, and temperature—as a daily ritual for grounding and presence.
- Mindful Walking: Focusing on the sensations of the feet touching the ground, the rhythm of breath, and the surrounding sights and sounds. This practice is especially helpful when feeling overstimulated or mentally scattered.

These simple practices, when done consistently, offer profound access to presence and gentle witnessing—skills that become essential when navigating post-journey mental processing.

Journaling

Journaling is an effective tool for helping clients begin unpacking and processing their psychedelic experience. It's a practice I encourage clients to incorporate into their daily integration process, as a way to enhance their mindfulness and self-awareness. An extensive body of mental health-related research supports the healing potential of journaling. Studies indicate that expressing, in writing, one's thoughts and emotions about significant events can catalyze improvement in numerous areas, generate understanding about oneself and one's lived experience, and support general well-being (Alexander et al., 2016).

As a tool for post-psychedelic integration, journaling also provides a space for clients to reflect on their experience and capture any insights or realizations that arise for them. It allows them to continually unpack their psychedelic experience and construct a narrative that benefits their therapeutic outcome. Clients should be encouraged to write freely, allowing their thoughts to flow without concern for cohesiveness or content. I encourage clients to write down anything that comes to mind, without worrying about the cohesiveness or content. The goal is to create a safe and nonjudgmental space for the client to explore their thoughts and emotions after the psychedelic experience. I have found that clients often recall and understand their experience more clearly as they write their thoughts and reflections down on paper.

During the integration sessions, the clinician should regularly review and discuss clients' journal entries with them, exploring any themes or insights that emerge from their reflections. By revisiting their journal, clients can gain a greater understanding of their experience and magnify the positive meanings associated with their insights. Clients should be encouraged to explore various journaling styles as part of their integration process. Some of the journaling styles I encourage clients to practice include the following:

- Daily Journaling: Write for at least 10 minutes each day during the week following the psychedelic journey. This practice helps capture immediate reflections, emotions, and insights while the experience is still vivid, fostering deeper self-exploration and integration.
- Bullet Points: Create bulleted lists of key insights and takeaways. This can be an incredibly helpful tool in the integration process, as bullet points extract the most significant information in a clear and concise

form. Clients can refer to the bullet points whenever they need to be reminded of the insights they gained during their journey. This helps them stay focused and motivated as they work to integrate the experience into their lives.

- Quotes: On a separate piece of paper, write the key insights or meaningful quotes from previous journal entries or bulleted reflections, and place them in a visible location. This quoted material can then serve as a continuous reminder of what emerged from the journey, reinforcing integration and supporting long-term personal growth.

I once had a client who came to her first post-journey session feeling overwhelmed by the recent mushroom ceremony she had attended. She felt she had "seen too much" and couldn't explain it. However, through the practice of journaling for five minutes each morning, she began to identify singular, meaningful aspects of the experience—a dream-like memory, a visual, a feeling in her chest—and by the end of the week, she had formed a clear insight. The powerful realization she arrived at, that she had abandoned a part of herself years earlier, became the central focus of our work together.

Additional Practices

- Letter Writing: This might include the client writing a personal gratitude letter, in which they acknowledge the courage and commitment it took to participate in a psychedelic journey. It could also take the form of a letter to a loved one, in which they describe their journey or any other messages they would like to convey.
- Storytelling: This practice involves the client sharing the story of their journey with trusted individuals. It can provide a space for sharing experiences, gaining new perspectives, and finding connection and support.
- Reading: This involves engaging with literature on meditation, spiritual teachings, and personal empowerment, as these readings can provide valuable insights, reinforce mindfulness practices, and support the integration of their psychedelic experiences. I often encourage clients to read books related to meditation, spiritual teachings, or personal empowerment.

Therapists should educate their clients about the nature of post-journey mental fluctuations, normalizing the tendency for the mind to revisit doubts, fears, or looping thoughts during the integration process. Rather than pathologizing this mental noise, mindfulness helps contain and soften it. In my experience, clients also appreciate understanding the adaptive quality of this rumination. I explain to them that from a neurological perspective, the integration window is marked by heightened neuroplasticity, which offers a valuable opportunity to rewire old patterns and anchor new ways of thinking, feeling, and relating.

By tending to the mind with curiosity and care, clients can more effectively transform their psychedelic experience from a singular event into a meaningful chapter of their healing story. As the integration process deepens, the mind learns to begin relating to life with more fluidity, presence, and openness.

The Soul

The soul is often considered the spiritual dimension of our being—the part of us that connects to something greater than ourselves and anchors our sense of meaning, belonging, and purpose. In psychedelic integration, tending to the soul isn't about promoting a particular belief system; rather, it is a way of honoring the mystery, transcendence, and existential awakening that often emerge through altered states.

Although the concept of the soul may fall outside the purview of traditional medical models, it remains a cornerstone of many healing systems, including indigenous traditions, transpersonal psychology, and spiritual lineages across cultures. Psychedelic journeys often open clients to experiences of awe, unity, timelessness, or sacredness that can't be easily explained with logic or understood intellectually. Integrating these experiences requires a container expansive enough to hold what feels ineffable.

Many clients, regardless of whether they would describe their experience as mystical, emerge from their journey with new spiritual questions or a deep desire to live more authentically aligned with their values. Whether the intention is to reconnect to their intuition, experience a sense of divine love, or confront their mortality, spiritual integration allows clients to translate the ineffable aspects of their experience into something deeply and personally meaningful.

Clients may also confront existential themes like death, rebirth, and the search for purpose. Integrating these aspects of the experience requires care, containment, and reverence. Spiritual practices can provide structure for clients to continue nurturing these dimensions:

- Spiritual Learning Centers and Communities: Engaging with a spiritual group or community—whether rooted in a specific faith, mystical practice, or psychedelic integration circle—can offer belonging, perspective, and continuity. Clients often find it reassuring to know that others are walking a similar path.
- Creating an Altar: Clients may benefit from creating a small altar or sacred space filled with personally meaningful objects—stones, photos, candles, handwritten intentions, or symbols. Spending a few quiet moments at the altar each day can foster presence, reflection, and a felt sense of connection.

- Reading Spiritual Texts: Books on mysticism, mindfulness, Kabbalah, Taoism, or other frameworks can help clients expand their worldview and continue exploring spiritual questions. Reading often helps clients realize that they aren't alone in their experience.

Spiritual integration is also a deeply personal process. For some, it's about reconnecting with God or Source. For others, it's about accessing the sacred through nature, creativity, or silence. There is no singular path. Therapists can help clients define what soul nourishment means for them.

Psychedelic journeys often leave clients feeling porous, humbled, and more aware of their place in the cosmos. But just as a biologist thinks and works beyond the microscope, the client must eventually return to their everyday life, hopefully viewing it through new eyes. As Alan Watts (1965) wrote, "psychedelic drugs are simply instruments, akin to microscopes, telescopes, and telephones. The biologist does not remain permanently peering through the microscope; he steps away and reflects on what he has observed" (p. 26).

The therapist's role in the integration process is to help their clients step away from their journey, without forgetting what they've seen. By helping them develop practices that address the body, mind, and soul, we support their transformation. Spiritual integration anchors a sense of meaning into daily life and allows the soul's voice to be heard long after the journey concludes.

The process of integrating the insights that emerge from a psychedelic journey is just as crucial for clients as what transpires in the preparation and journey phases. Integration is a pivotal period during which clients internalize their newfound understanding and use it to discover new ways of being and interacting with the world. Therapists should encourage the integration process by helping their clients implement practices that address their unique spiritual, physical, mental, and social requirements. This becomes part of an all-encompassing, balanced strategy for integration that incorporates the client's body, mind, and soul. Such a holistic approach can enable clients to fully utilize the transformative potential of their psychedelic experiences, fostering enduring benefits and positive transformations in their everyday lives.

Note

1 Clients should be strongly advised to consult with a qualified healthcare professional, such as their primary care physician or a registered dietitian/nutritionist, before implementing any of the following recommendations to ensure they align with their individual health needs and medical considerations. I strongly recommend to clients that before they consider implementing any of the following advice, they consult with a qualified healthcare professional, such as their primary care doctor or a registered dietitian/nutritionist, to ensure that it is suitable for their specific health needs.

Chapter 10

Conclusion

A Return to Wholeness

> There will come a time when you believe everything is finished; that will be the beginning.
>
> Louis L'Amour, 1980, p. 79

The Challenges That Remain

Despite the promise of psychedelic-assisted therapy, several significant challenges continue to impede its widespread integration into the field of psychotherapy. These challenges stem from historical stigma, regulatory complexity, gaps in research, insufficient education and training, accessibility issues, and ethical uncertainties. Addressing these barriers is essential to ensuring the ethical, safe, and effective inclusion of psychedelic therapies in mainstream mental health care.

One of the most enduring obstacles is the historical and legal stigma associated with psychedelics. The classification of substances like LSD and psilocybin as Schedule I drugs in the 1970s not only criminalized their use, but also stalled decades of scientific progress. This prohibition fostered public fear, media sensationalism, and deep-seated institutional bias. Although today's renewed interest—driven by groundbreaking studies and increasing media coverage—has begun to shift the narrative, many therapists and healthcare systems still hold onto outdated beliefs about psychedelics. These stigmas continue to shape institutional policies, insurance coverage, research funding, and client attitudes.

Although scientific research on psychedelics has advanced significantly in recent years, the field remains in a relatively early stage of development. Phase II trials on MDMA and psilocybin have yielded promising results, but the lack of large-scale phase III studies and longitudinal outcome data presents a challenge to broad regulatory approval and public trust. Questions about standardized protocols, population-specific effects, long-term safety, and the durability of outcomes remain unanswered. Additionally, the

DOI: 10.4324/9781003541639-14

population with which psychedelics have been studied lacks diversity, raising concerns about the generalizability of findings across ethnic, cultural, and socioeconomic groups. If the psychedelic renaissance is to truly serve collective healing, future research must be inclusive and expansive in scope.

Another considerable challenge is the lack of standardized education and certification for mental health professionals. Few graduate and doctoral programs in psychology, psychiatry, and social work include coursework on psychedelic-assisted therapy. This leaves many clinicians unprepared to offer integration support or understand the ethical nuances of guiding altered states of consciousness. In the absence of widely recognized standards, training programs vary greatly in quality and focus, and few are regulated or accredited. The Mindful Psychedelics™ Integration Certificate Course and other similar programs attempt to fill this gap, offering structured curricula that combine neuroscience, somatic practices, ethical frameworks, and clinical skills. However, there remains an urgent need for broader adoption of curricula on psychedelics in academic programs, as well as professional regulation in clinical settings.

Legal ambiguity further complicates the picture. The regulatory landscape for psychedelics is in constant flux. Although some states, such as Oregon and Colorado, have taken bold steps toward legalization and the implementation of clinical infrastructure, others remain restrictive. Therapists are often caught between enthusiasm and caution, unsure of how to responsibly engage with psychedelic work while adhering to their legal and professional boundaries. Researchers face delays in approval and restricted access to these substances. Clients are left navigating underground circles or traveling abroad to experience these substances in unregulated settings. Until more uniform policies are established, the field will remain fragmented and its progress precarious.

In addition to legal and institutional barriers, there are several ethical complexities to consider. Power dynamics, boundary violations, inadequate screening, and cultural insensitivity are all serious and relevant concerns related to the implementation of psychedelic research and therapy. Psychedelic states heighten vulnerability, and without rigorous safeguards, clients can be harmed, retraumatized, or misled. The integration of indigenous knowledge and sacred traditions into Western frameworks also raises critical questions about cultural appropriation, reciprocity, and respect. Ethical practice in psychedelic therapy must include ongoing education, self-inquiry, consultation, and a commitment to decolonized and justice-oriented standards of care.

Finally, there is the issue of accessibility. The cost of psychedelic-assisted therapy—especially when offered outside of research settings—remains prohibitive for many people. Socioeconomic disparities threaten to reproduce the same inequities that exist in other areas of mental health. If psychedelic healing is to become truly transformative, it must be accessible to diverse communities, particularly those most impacted by trauma and systemic oppression.

Although these challenges are significant, they are not insurmountable. They are invitations to move forward with greater awareness, accountability, and collaboration. By advancing rigorous research, expanding ethical and inclusive training, reforming policy, and committing to cultural humility, we can build a future where psychedelic-assisted therapy is not only effective, but equitable. The road ahead is long, but the groundwork has been laid. What remains is the collective will to walk it together.

As this manual draws to a close, I invite you to pause—to reflect on what you've read, and to feel into the deeper essence of this work. What we have explored together is far greater than a clinical method or a therapeutic innovation. It is a return—to the body, to the earth, to the soul, to community, to presence. A return to remembering that healing is not a destination, but a practice of becoming.

This book has attempted to build a bridge—between science and spirit, between ancient wisdom and modern research, between the measurable and the mysterious. We have traveled through the history of psychedelics, their suppression and reemergence, and the compelling evidence of their clinical efficacy. But more importantly, we have entered the sacred territory of human transformation. Through case studies, practical tools, and integrative frameworks, this manual has presented a dynamic invitation to engage with these powerful tools ethically, reverently, and humanely.

From the neuroscience of the DMN and neuroplasticity to the art of guiding, I have attempted to capture the full arc of psychedelic-assisted therapy—from preparation, to the journey itself, to the integration that follows. Together we've explored the body's sacred intelligence, the mind's plasticity, and the soul's yearning for reconnection. We've revisited the historical roots of these medicines, from indigenous ceremony to early Western psychiatry, and acknowledged the cultural harms caused by both appropriation and criminalization.

We've considered the importance of preparing clients with intention-setting, mindfulness, and the dieta. We've explored the subtle skill of guiding—how presence, patience, touch, music, and attunement shape the field. We've emphasized integration as the phase where meaning is made, where insight is applied, and where healing becomes sustainable.

The stories of clients throughout this book are a reminder that the journey is often nonlinear, unexpected, and deeply personal. Whether it was Pam's post-ceremony terror, Sarah's shift in perspective about her nightmares, or Sofia's transmission of love through touch, these stories are more than examples. They offer archetypes of transformation that reveal how we, as therapists, must listen with our full being.

Psychedelics are not the answer; they are an amplifier. They do not heal us; they help us see more clearly what we already know how to heal. They soften the veil, reorganize perception, and connect us with deeper truths. But the real work begins after the journey ends—when we wake up the next morning and ask, "What do I do now with what I've seen?" Integration is the soul of psychedelic therapy. It's where insight becomes embodiment, where visions become values, where the extraordinary gets woven into the ordinary. In a world fractured by disconnection, trauma, and spiritual starvation, integration is our path back to coherence. It's how we translate sacred insight into relational repair, service, creativity, and justice.

To the therapists, guides, and space-holders: You are midwives of a new paradigm. Your responsibility is profound, and so is your privilege. You are holding sacred space for healing and remembrance—for a deeper truth that lives in each client's body, memory, and soul. May you always stay connected to your own inner work, your own humility, your own connection to something greater. May you remember that this work is not about being the expert, but about becoming a clear and compassionate mirror.

To the clients and seekers: You are courageous. You are whole even when you feel shattered. There is nothing wrong with you that presence, compassion, and integration can't touch. Your pain is not pathology; it's part of your calling. Your visions aren't illusions; they're maps. Trust that your journey is unfolding with purpose, even when you can't yet see the horizon.

To those on the margins—those whose stories have been silenced or overlooked, those whose cultures carried this wisdom long before it was legitimized by science: This work honors you. We aren't here to appropriate, but to remember. Your traditions, your language, your rituals, your cosmologies must be protected and uplifted as we move forward. True integration includes justice.

And to all of us—as a collective humanity standing at a threshold: We must choose how we walk into this new terrain. The promise of psychedelics is more than therapeutic; it's planetary, ecological, existential. These substances remind us of our interconnectedness; of the fragility and sacredness of life; of our potential to live in alignment with truth, beauty, and reciprocity.

Along the way, we have drawn on the insights of many brilliant minds—pioneers such as Stanislav Grof, who taught us to trust the intelligence of non-ordinary states; Michael Pollan, who has humbly helped bring these ideas back into public awareness; Robin Carhart-Harris, whose neuroscience research and REBUS model have offered a modern language for what mystics and shamans have long known: that healing often begins when rigid patterns soften, when control dissolves, and when the unknown is allowed to speak. Their contributions have helped legitimize and illuminate the mystery—not to explain it away, but to better serve it. We are being asked to remember that healing moves in spirals. It contracts and expands, humbles and reveals. It demands patience, accountability, and love. It isn't separate from justice, community, or the earth. It's all connected.

May this book be a companion and a catalyst. May it offer structure, language, and guidance, inspiration, reverence, and soul. May it remind you that healing is holy, and that each journey is a prayer. As Alan Watts reminded us, psychedelics are like microscopes or telescopes. We don't stare into them forever. We step back. We reflect. We integrate. And ideally, we live differently because of what we've seen. This is the heart of integration—not a task to check off, but a way to walk in the world. A way to live with eyes wide open, heart softened, body grounded, and spirit awake. May we walk gently. May we remember who we are. May we return to wholeness—not just as therapists or clients, but as a human family reclaiming the sacred art of healing.

Final Thoughts

The future of psychedelic therapy holds immense promise, signaling a profound transformation in the landscape of mental healthcare. This ongoing renaissance offers a paradigm shift that invites us to rethink how we treat psychological suffering and how we understand the nature of healing, consciousness, and the human experience.

What we are witnessing is the emergence of a more integrative, more compassionate, and more expansive model of care—one that draws from ancient healing traditions, modern neuroscience, transpersonal psychology, and relational therapy. Psychedelic-assisted therapy represents an evolutionary step that bridges the clinical and the mystical, the evidence-based and the intuitive, the individual and the collective.

Throughout this book, we have explored how seemingly disparate paradigms—structured methodologies from Western psychotherapy and the deep, symbolic language of psychedelic journeys—can converge to support profound transformation. We have looked at how systemic therapy, mindfulness-based interventions, somatic practices, and spiritual frameworks complement and enhance the psychedelic experience. This intersection challenges conventional diagnostic frameworks by inviting them into a wider context—one in which healing is about integrating, making meaning, and returning to a sense of wholeness.

At its best, psychedelic therapy does more than just alleviate symptoms; it changes people's relationships with themselves, with others, and with the world. It reconnects individuals with forgotten parts of themselves, loosens entrenched patterns, and invites a deeper inquiry into purpose, belonging, and truth. The tools offered by psychedelics—when supported by rigorous preparation, skilled facilitation, and careful integration—allow for deep emotional release and a reweaving of the inner world.

And yet, we must tread carefully. As this field evolves, our work must be guided by ethical clarity, cultural humility, and an unwavering respect for the indigenous communities and spiritual lineages that have stewarded these medicines for centuries. As Western clinicians and researchers bring psychedelics into the medical mainstream, we must guard against the temptation to reduce them to mechanistic tools or commodified services. Psychedelic therapy is sacred work, and it must be held with reverence.

The future will require new frameworks of collaboration. Psychologists must learn from shamans. Scientists must dialogue with mystics. Therapists must become students again. Only through an interdisciplinary, intercultural, and heart-centered approach can we unlock the full potential of this work. What lies ahead is more than an opportunity to advance clinical practice; it's a chance to shift our foundational understanding of suffering and healing. Psychedelics open a door, but it's up to us—as clinicians, educators, advocates, and seekers—to walk through it with discernment, vision, and care.

May this book serve as the beginning of a deeper inquiry into how we facilitate healing and hold space for transformation. May it be an ongoing reminder of how we, as guides, must be transformed in the process. The realm of psychedelic work is one of the most important frontiers of our time. May we venture through it with courage, speak with clarity, and hold space with love—as guides, as seekers, and as stewards of the sacred. The revolution ahead is not only in neuroscience or policy. It is in the heart. And it begins here.

References

Alexander, J., McAllister, M., & Brien, D. L. (2016). Exploring the diary as a recovery-oriented therapeutic tool. *International Journal of Mental Health Nursing, 25*(1), 19–26. https://doi.org/10.1111/inm.12179

Ali, I. L., Bathje, G. J., Hallisey, R., Booher, L., Novick, B., & Feduccia, A. (2021). Practical and ethical considerations for psychedelic therapy and integration practices. *Journal of Psychedelic Psychiatry, 3*(3), 1–20.

Almond, K., & Allan, R. (2019). Incorporating MDMA as an adjunct in emotionally focused couples therapy with clients impacted by trauma or PTSD. *The Family Journal, 27*, 293–299. https://doi.org/10.1177%2F1066480719852360

Anderson, H., & Goolishian, H. (1992). The client is the expert: A not-knowing approach to therapy. In S. McNamee & K. J. Gergen (Eds.), *Therapy as social construction* (pp. 25–39). Sage Publications.

Andreas, S. (1999). *Virginia Satir: The patterns of her magic*. Real People Press.

Anonymous. (2012). *Ayahuasca manifesto: The spirit of ayahuasca and its planetary mission*. https://worldonayahuasca.files.wordpress.com/2015/09/ayahuasca-manifesto_anonymous.pdf

Apud, I. (2023). Ayahuasca and personality: A systematic review and meta-analysis of cross-sectional studies with long-term participants. *Studies in Psychology, 44*(1), 27–49. https://doi.org/10.1080/02109395.2022.2163776

Arrieta, O., Angulo, L. P., Nuñez-Valencia, C., Dorantes-Gallareta, Y., Macedo, E. O., Martínez-López, D., Alvarado, S., Corona-Cruz, J. F., & Oñate-Ocaña, L. F. (2013). Association of depression and anxiety on quality of life, treatment adherence, and prognosis in patients with advanced non-small cell lung cancer. *Annals of Surgical Oncology, 20*(6), 1941–1948. https://doi.org/10.1245/s10434-012-2793-5

AZ Quotes (n.d.). Allan Watts. https://www.azquotes.com/quote/308433

Back, A. L., Freeman-Young, T. K., Morgan, L., Sethi, T., Baker, K. K., Myers, S., McGregor, B. A., Harvey, K., Tai, M., Kollefrath, A., Thomas, B. J., Sorta, D., Kaelen, M., Kelmendi, B., & Gooley, T. A. (2024). Psilocybin therapy for clinicians with symptoms of depression from frontline care during the COVID-19 pandemic: A randomized clinical trial. *JAMA Network Open, 7*(12), Article e2449026. https://doi.org/10.1001/jamanetworkopen.2024.49026

Balban, M. Y., Neri, E., Kogon, M. M., Weed, L., Nouriani, B., Jo, B., Holl, G., Zeitzer, J. M., Spiegel, D., & Huberman, A. D. (2023). Brief structured respiration practices enhance mood and reduce physiological arousal. *Cell Reports Medicine, 4*(1), Article 100895. https://doi.org/10.1016/j.xcrm.2022.100895

Barbosa, P. C. R., Cazorla, I. M., Giglio, J. S., & Strassman, R. (2009). A six-month prospective evaluation of personality traits, psychiatric symptoms and quality of life in ayahuasca-naïve subjects. *Journal of Psychoactive Drugs, 41*(3), 205–212. https://doi.org/10.1080/02791072.2009.10400530

Barbosa, P. C. R., Giglio, J. S., & Dalgalarrondo, P. (2005). Altered states of consciousness and short-term psychological after-effects induced by the first-time ritual use of ayahuasca in an urban context in Brazil. *Journal of Psychoactive Drugs, 37*(2), 193–201. https://doi.org/10.1080/02791072.2005.10399801

Barbosa, P. C., Mizumoto, S., Bogenschutz, M. P., & Strassman, R. J. (2012). Health status of ayahuasca users. *Drug Testing and Analysis, 4*(7–8), 601–609. https://doi.org/10.1002/dta.1383

Bartoli, E., Devara, E., Dang, H. Q., Rabinovich, R., Mathura, R. K., Anand, A., Pascuzzi, B. R., Adkinson, J., Kenett, Y. N., Bijanki, K. R., Sheth, S. A., & Shofty, B. (2024). Default mode network electrophysiological dynamics and causal role in creative thinking. *Brain, 147*(10), 3409–3425. https://doi.org/10.1093/brain/awae294

Bateson, G. (2002). *Mind and nature: A necessary unity*. Hampton Press.

Bateson, G., & Bateson, M. C. (2000). *Steps to an ecology of mind*. University of Chicago Press (Original work published 1972).

Bathje, G. J., Majeski, K., Kudowor, K., Opai-Tetteh, D., & Hoffmann, A. (2022). *A meta-synthesis of qualitative studies of psychedelic integration*. *Journal of Humanistic Psychology, 62*(7), 1055–1086. https://doi.org/10.1177/00221678221102478

Baumann, M. H., Xiaoying, W., & Rothman, R. B. (2007). Methylenedioxymethamphetamine (MDMA) neurotoxicity in rats: A reappraisal of past and present findings. *Psychopharmacology, 189*(4), 407–424. https://doi.org/10.1007/s00213-006-0322-6

Beck, A. T. (1979). *Cognitive therapy of depression*. Guilford Press.

Benzenhöfer, U., & Passie, T. (2010). Rediscovering MDMA (ecstasy): The role of the American chemist Alexander T. Shulgin. *Addiction, 105*(8), 1355–1361. https://doi.org/10.1111/j.1360-0443.2010.02948.x

Bonny, H. L. (1969). *The role of taped music programs in psychedelic (LSD) therapy* [Unpublished doctoral dissertation, The Catholic University of America].

Bonny, H. L., & Pahnke, W. N. (1972). The use of music in psychedelic (LSD) psychotherapy. *Journal of Music Therapy, 9*(2), 64–87. https://doi.org/10.1093/jmt/9.2.64

Bonson, K. R. (2018). Regulation of human research with LSD in the United States (1949–1987). *Psychopharmacology, 235*(2), 591–604. https://doi.org/10.1007/s00213-017-4777-4

Bourzat, F., & Hunter, K. (2019). *Conscious medicine*. North Atlantic Books.

Bowler, D. E., Buyung-Ali, L. M., Knight, T. M., & Pullin, A. S. (2010). A systematic review of evidence for the added benefits to health of exposure to natural environments. *BMC Public Health, 10*, Article 456. https://doi.org/10.1186/1471-2458-10-456

Brendan, C., & Belser, A. B. (2022). *Embodied mindfulness for psychedelic integration: Supporting preparation, journey, and integration*. Routledge.

Brown, T. K., & Alper, K. (2018). Treatment of opioid use disorder with ibogaine: Detoxification and drug use outcomes. *The American Journal of Drug and Alcohol Abuse, 44*(1), 24–36. https://doi.org/10.1080/00952990.2017.1320802

Burt, J. B., Preller, K. H., Demirtas, M., Ji, J. L., Krystal, J. H., Vollenweider, F. X., Anticevic, A., & Murray, J. D. (2021). Transcriptomics-informed large-scale cortical model captures topography of pharmacological neuroimaging effects of LSD. *eLife, 10*, Article e69320. https://doi.org/10.7554/eLife.69320

Caddy, C., Giaroli, G., White, T. P., Shergill, S. S., & Tracy, D. K. (2014). Ketamine as the prototype glutamatergic antidepressant: Pharmacodynamic actions, and a systematic review and meta-analysis of efficacy. *Therapeutic Advances in Psychopharmacology, 4*(2), 75–99. https://doi.org/10.1177/2045125313507739

Callaway, J. C., & Grob, C. S. (1998). Ayahuasca preparations and serotonin uptake inhibitors: A potential for severe adverse interaction. *Journal of Psychoactive Drugs, 30*(4), 367–369. https://doi.org/10.1080/02791072.1998.10399712

Callaway, J. C., McKenna, D. J., Grob, C. S., Brito, G. S., Raymon, L. P., Poland, R. E., Andrade, E. N., Andrade, E. O., & Mash, D. C. (1999). Pharmacokinetics of hoasca alkaloids in healthy humans. *Journal of Ethnopharmacology, 65*(3), 243–256. https://doi.org/10.1016/s0378-8741(98)00168-8

Callaway, J. C., Raymon, L. P., Hearn, W. L., McKenna, D. J., Grob, C. S., Brito, G. S., & Mash, D. C. (1996). Quantitation of N, N-dimethyltryptamine and harmala alkaloids in human plasma after oral dosing with ayahuasca. *Journal of Analytical Toxicology, 20*(6), 492–497. https://doi.org/10.1093/jat/20.6.492

Cannon, W. B. (1929). *Bodily changes in pain, hunger, fear and rage: An account of recent research into the function of emotional excitement* (2nd ed.). Appleton-Century-Crofts.

Carhart-Harris, R. L., & Friston, K. J. (2010). The default-mode, ego- functions and free-energy: A neurobiological account of Freudian ideas. *Brain, 133*(Pt 4), 1265–1283. https://doi.org/10.1093/brain/awq010

Carhart-Harris, R. L., & Friston, K. J. (2019). REBUS and the anarchic brain: Toward a unified model of the brain action of psychedelics. *Pharmacological Reviews, 71*(3), 316–344. https://doi.org/10.1124/pr.118.017160

Carhart-Harris, R. L., Bolstridge, M., Rucker, J., Day, C. M. J., Erritzoe, D., Kaelen, M., Bloomfield, M., Richard, J. A., Forbes, B., Feilding, A., Taylor, D., Pilling, S., Curran, V. H., & Nutt, D. J. (2016). Psilocybin with psychological support for treatment-resistant depression: An open-label feasibility study. *The Lancet Psychiatry, 3*(7), 619–627. https://doi.org/10.1016/s2215-0366(16)30065-7

Carhart-Harris, R. L., Erritzoe, D., Williams, T., Stone, J. M., Reed, L. J., Colasanti, A., Tyacke, R. J., Leech, R., Malizia, A. L., Murphy, K., Hobden, P., Evans, J., Feilding, A., Wise, R. G., & Nutt, D. J. (2012). Neural correlates of the psychedelic state as determined by fMRI studies with psilocybin. *PNAS Proceedings of the National Academy of Sciences of the United States of America, 109*(6), 2138–2143. https://doi.org/10.1073/pnas.1119598109

Carhart-Harris, R. L., Kaelen, M., & Nutt, D. (2014a). How do hallucinogens work on the brain? *The Psychologist, 27*(9), 662–665.

Carhart-Harris, R. L., Leech, R., Hellyer, P. J., Shanahan, M., Feilding, A., Tagliazucchi, E., Chialvo, D. R., & Nutt, D. (2014b). The entropic brain: A theory of conscious states informed by neuroimaging research with psychedelic drugs. *Frontiers in Human Neuroscience, 8*, Article 20. https://doi.org/10.3389/fnhum.2014.00020

Carhart-Harris, R. L., Roseman, L., Bolstridge, M., et al. (2018). Psychedelics and the essential importance of context. *Journal of Psychopharmacology, 32*(7), 725–731. https://doi.org/10.1177/0269881118754710

Carod-Artal, F. J. (2015). Hallucinogenic drugs in pre-Columbian Mesoamerican cultures. *Neurología (Barcelona, English Ed.), 30*(1), 42–49. https://doi.org/10.1016/j.nrleng.2011.07.010

Chödrön, P. (2000). *When things fall apart: Heart advice for difficult times*. Shambhala Publications.

Cholden, L. S., Kurland, A. A., & Savage, C. (1955). Clinical reactions and tolerance to LSD in chronic schizophrenia. *The Journal of Nervous and Mental Disease, 122*(3), 211–221. https://doi.org/10.1097/00005053-195509000-00001

Cohen, M. M., Hirschhorn, K., & Frosch, W. A. (1967). In vivo and in vitro chromosomal damage induced by LSD–25. *The New England Journal of Medicine, 277*(20), 1043–1049. https://doi.org/10.1056/NEJM196711162772001

Cohen, S. (1965). LSD and the anguish of dying. *Harper's Magazine, 231*(1386), 69–75.

Collier, B. (1972). Ketamine and the conscious mind. *Anesthesia, 27*(2), 120–134. https://doi.org/10.1111/j.1365-2044.1972.tb08186.x

Corssen, G., & Domino, E. F. (1966). Dissociative anesthesia: Further pharmacologic studies and first clinical experience with the phencyclidine derivative CI–581. *Anesthesia & Analgesia, 45*(1), 29–40.

Critchley, H. D., & Garfinkel, S. N. (2017). Interoception and emotion. *Current Opinion in Psychology, 17,* 7–14. https://doi.org/10.1016/j.copsyc.2017.04.020

da Silva, M. G., Daros, G. C., & de Bitencourt, R. M. (2021). Anti-inflammatory activity of ayahuasca: Therapeutical implications in neurological and psychiatric diseases. *Behavioural Brain Research, 400*(26). Article 113003. https://doi.org/10.1016/j.bbr.2020.113003

Da Silveira, D. X., Grob, C. S., de Rios, M. D., Lopez, E., Alonso, L. K., Tacla, C., & Doering-Silveira, E. (2005). Ayahuasca in adolescence: A preliminary psychiatric assessment. *Journal of Psychoactive Drugs, 37*(2), 129–133. https://doi.org/10.1080/02791072.2005.10399792

Daldegan-Bueno, D., Donegan, C. J., Forsyth, A., Sumner, R. L., Murphy, R. J., Menkes, D. B., Evans, W., Hoeh, N., Sundram, F., Reynolds, L. M., Ponton, R., Cavadino, A., Smith, T., Roop, P., Allen, N., Abeysinghe, B., Svirskis, D., Bansal, M., & Muthukumaraswamy, S. (2024). LSDDEP2: Study protocol for a randomised, double--dummy, triple---blind, active placebo---controlled, parallel groups trial of LSD microdosing in patients with major depressive disorder-. *Trials, 25,* Article 560. https://doi.org/10.1186/s13063-024-08384-3

Dana, D. (2018). *The polyvagal theory in therapy: Engaging the rhythm of regulation*. W. W. Norton & Company.

Danforth, A. L., Grob, C. S., Struble, C., Feduccia, A. A., Walker, N., Jerome, L., Yazar-Klosinski, B., & Emerson, A. (2018). Reduction in social anxiety after MDMA-assisted psychotherapy with autistic adults: A randomized, double-blind, placebo-controlled pilot study. *Psychopharmacology, 235*(11), 3137–3148. https://doi.org/10.1007/s00213-018-5010-9

Davidson, R. J., & McEwen, B. S. (2012). Social influences on neuroplasticity: Stress and interventions to promote well-being. *Nature Neuroscience, 15*(5), 689–695. https://doi.org/10.1038/nn.3093

Dawson, N., McDonald, M., Higham, D. J., Morris, B. J., & Pratt, J. A. (2014). Subanesthetic Ketamine treatment promotes abnormal interactions between neural subsystems and alters the properties of functional brain networks. *Neuropsychopharmacology, 39*(7), 1786–1798. https://doi.org/10.1038/npp.2014.26

de Shazer, S. (1988). Utilization: The foundation of solutions. In J. K. Zeig & S. R. Lankton (Eds.), *Developing Ericksonian therapy: State of the art* (pp. 112–124). Brunner/Mazel.

de Shazer, S., & Berg, I. K. (1997). 'What works?' Remarks on research aspects of solution-focused brief therapy. *Journal of Family Therapy, 19*(2), 121–124. https://doi.org/10.1111/1467-6427.00043

de Shazer, S., Dolan, Y. M., Korman, H., Trepper, T., McCollum, E., & Berg, I. K. (2007). *More than miracles: The state of the art of solution-focused brief therapy*. Routledge.

Doblin, R. (2002). A clinical plan for MDMA (ecstasy) in the treatment of post-traumatic stress disorder (PTSD): Partnering with the FDA. *MAPS Bulletin, 12*(3), 25–29. https://doi.org/10.1080/02791072.2002.10399952

Doblin, R. E. (1991). Pahnke's "Good Friday experiment": A long-term follow-up and methodological critique. *Journal of Transpersonal Psychology, 23*(1), 1–28.

Doblin, R. E. (1998). Dr. Leary's Concord prison experiment: A 34-year follow-up study. *Journal of Psychoactive Drugs, 30*(4), 419–426. https://doi.org/10.1080/02791072.1998.10399715

Doblin, R. E., Christiansen, M., Jerome, L., & Burge, B. (2019). The past and future of psychedelic science: An introduction to this issue. *Journal of Psychoactive Drugs, 51*(2), 93–97. https://doi.org/10.1080/02791072.2019.1606472
Doesburg-van Kleffens, M., Zimmermann-Klemd, A. M., & Gründemann, C. (2023). An overview on the hallucinogenic peyote and its alkaloid mescaline: The importance of context, ceremony and culture. *Molecules, 28*(24), Article 7942. https://doi.org/10.3390/molecules28247942
Domino, E. F. (2010). Taming the ketamine tiger. *Anesthesiology, 113*(3), 678–684. https://doi.org/10.1097/ALN.0b013e3181ed09a2
Domino, E. F., Chodoff, P., & Corssen, G. (1965). Pharmacologic effects of Ci-581, a new dissociative anesthetic. *Manual of Clinical Pharmacology and Therapeutics, 6*, 279–291. https://doi.org/10.1002/cpt196563279
Dore, J., Dwyer, S., Turnipseed, B., Turnipseed, A., Andries, J., Ascani, G., Monnette, C., Wolfson, P., Huidekoper, A., & Strauss, N. (2019). Ketamine assisted psychotherapy (KAP): Patient demographics, clinical data and outcomes in three large practices administering ketamine with psychotherapy. *Journal of Psychoactive Drugs, 51*(2), 189–198. https://doi.org/10.1080/02791072.2019.1587556
Dos Santos, R. G., & Hallak, J. (2021). Ayahuasca, an ancient substance with traditional and contemporary use in neuropsychiatry and neuroscience. *Epilepsy & Behavior, 121*, Article 106300. https://doi.org/10.1016/j.yebeh.2019.04.053
Dos Santos, R. G., Valle, M., Bouso, J. C., Nomdedéu, J. F., Rodríguez-Espinosa, J., McIlhenny, E. H., Barker, S. A., Barbanoj, M. J., & Riba, J. (2011). Autonomic, neuroendocrine, and immunological effects of ayahuasca: A comparative study with d-amphetamine. *Journal of Clinical Psychopharmacology, 31*(6), 717–726. https://doi.org/10.1097/JCP.0b013e31823607f6
Duman, R. S., Aghajanian, G. K., Sanacora, G., & Krystal, J. H. (2019). Synaptic plasticity and depression: New insights from stress and rapid-acting antidepressants. *Nature Medicine, 25*(1), 28–38. https://doi.org/10.1038/s41591-018-0276-3
Elton, C. (2019, September 10). *The interview: MDMA-therapy expert Dr. Rick Doblin*. Boston Magazine. https://www.bostonmagazine.com/health/2019/09/10/rick-doblin/
Erickson, M. H. (1980). *Collected papers of Milton H. Erickson on hypnosis: Volume I–IV* (E. L. Rossi, Ed.). Irvington.
Erickson, M. H. (n.d.). *Quotes by Milton H. Erickson*. Goodreads. Retrieved May 31, 2025, from https://www.goodreads.com/author/quotes/79897.Milton_H_Erickson
Ewing, J. A. (1984). Detecting alcoholism: The CAGE questionnaire. *JAMA, 252*(14), 1905–1907. https://doi.org/10.1001/jama.1984.03350140051025
Fagetti, A., & Mercadillo, R. E. (2022). Experiences with sacred mushrooms and psilocybin in dialogue: Transdisciplinary interpretations of the "Velada." *Anthropology of Consciousness, 33*(2), 385–411. https://doi.org/10.1111/anoc.12163
Ferreira, A. S. M., Martindale, S., & Luke, D. (2024). Change in occupational burnout measures in emergency medical service workers after a psychedelic experience induced by a single self-administered dose of psilocybin mushrooms. *Journal of Psychedelic Studies, 9*(1), 20–30. https://doi.org/10.1556/2054.2024.00368
Ferris, T. (Host). (2018a. May 6). *Michael Pollan (No. 313)* [Audio podcast episode]. In The time Ferris show. Apple Podcasts. https://podcasts.apple.com/us/podcast/313-michael-pollan-exploring-the-new-science/id863897795?i=1000410793152
Ferris, T. (Host). (2018b. November 22). *The Tim Ferris show: Stan Grof (No. 347)* [Audio podcast episode]. In Apple. https://podcasts.apple.com/us/podcast/347-stan-grof-lessons-from-4-500-lsd-sessions-and-beyond/id863897795?i=1000424224389
Flemons, D. (1991). *Completing distinctions*. Shambhala.

Flemons, D. (2002). *Of one mind: The logic of hypnosis, the practice of therapy*. W. W. Norton & Company.

Flemons, D. (2022, July/August). Cultivating empathy. Do we really know how our clients feel? *Psychotherapy Networker*, 48–52. https://www.psychotherapynetworker.org/article/cultivating-empathy

Fond, G., Loundou, A., Rabu, C., Macgregor, A., Lançon, C., Brittner, M., Micoulaud-Franchi, J. A., Richieri, R., Courtet, P., Abbar, M., Roger, M., Leboyer, M., & Boyer, L. (2014). Ketamine administration in depressive disorders: A systematic review and meta-analysis. *Psychopharmacology, 231*(18), 3663–3676. https://doi.org/10.1007/s00213-014-3664-5

Fort, J., & Metzner, R. (1969). LSD, chromosomes and sensationalism. *Psychedelic Review, 10*, 47–51.

Frame, T. (2022). *Psychedelic timeline*. Psychedelic Times. https://psychedelictimes.com/psychedelic-timeline/

Frankl, V. E. (1959). *Man's search for meaning*. Beacon Press.

Frankl, V. E. (2006). *Man's search for meaning*. Beacon Press. (Original work published 1959)

Frecska, E., Bokor, P., & Winkelman, M. (2016). The therapeutic potentials of ayahuasca: Possible effects against various diseases of civilization. *Frontiers in Pharmacology, 7*, Article 35. https://doi.org/10.3389/fphar.2016.00035

Frecska, E., White, K. D., & Luna, L. E. (2004). Effects of ayahuasca on binocular rivalry with dichoptic stimulus alternation. *Psychopharmacology, 173*, 79–87. https://doi.org/10.1007/s00213-003-1701-x

Freud, S. (1958). The dynamics of transference. In J. Strachey (Ed. & Trans.), *The standard edition of the complete psychological works of Sigmund Freud* (Vol. 12, pp. 97–108). Hogarth Press. (Original work published 1912).

Fuentes, J. J., Fonseca, F., Elices, M., Farré, M., & Torrens, M. (2020). Therapeutic use of LSD in psychiatry: A systematic review of randomized-controlled clinical trials. *Frontiers in Psychiatry, 10*, Article 943. https://doi.org/10.3389/fpsyt.2019.00943

Gable, R. S. (2004). Comparison of acute lethal toxicity of commonly abused psychoactive substances. *Addiction, 99*(6), 686–696. https://doi.org/10.1111/j.1360-0443.2004.00744.x

Gamma, A., Frei, E., Lehmann, D., Pascual, R. D., Hell, D., & Vollenweider, F. X. (2000). Mood state and brain electric activity in ecstasy users. *Neuroreport, 11*, 157–162. https://doi.org/10.1097/00001756-200001170-00031

Garcia-Romeu, A., Barrett, F. S., Carbonaro, T. M., Johnson, M. W., & Griffiths, R. R. (2021). Optimal dosing for psilocybin pharmacotherapy: Considering weight-adjusted and fixed dosing approaches. *Journal of Psychopharmacology, 35*(4), 353–361. https://doi.org/10.1177/0269881121991822

Gasser, P., Holstein, D., Michel, Y., Doblin, R., Yazar-Klosinski, B., Passie, T., & Brenneisen, R. (2014a). Safety and efficacy of lysergic acid diethylamide-assisted psychotherapy for anxiety associated with life-threatening diseases. *Journal of Nervous & Mental Disease, 202*, 513–520. https://doi.org/10.1097/NMD.0000000000000113

Gasser, P., Kirchner, K., & Passie, T. (2014b). LSD-assisted psychotherapy for anxiety associated with a life-threatening disease: A qualitative study of acute and sustained subjective effects. *Journal of Psychopharmacology, 28*(1), 63–72. https://doi.org/10.1177/0269881113512900

Gattuso, J. J., Perkins, D., Ruffell, S., Lawrence, A. J., Hoyer, D., Jacobson, L. H., Timmermann, C., Castle, D., Rossell, S. L., Downey, L. A., Pagni, B. A., Galvão-Coelho, N. L., Nutt, D., & Sarris, J. (2022). Default mode network modulation by psychedelics:

A systematic review. *International Journal of Neuropsychopharmacology, 26*(3), 155–188. https://doi.org/10.1093/ijnp/pyac074

Gearin, A. K., & Calavia Sáez, O. (2021). Altered vision: Ayahuasca shamanism and sensory individualism. *Current Anthropology, 62*(2), 139–160. https://doi.org/10.1086/713737

Gillespie, N. (2020, July 1). "People should have the fundamental human right to change their consciousness": Rick Doblin, a leading force in America's psychedelic renaissance, imagines a world of 'mass mental health' facilitated by formerly demonized drugs. *Reason Magazine*. https://reason.com/2020/06/21/people-should-have-the-fundamental-right-to-change-their-consciousness/

Giovannetti, C., Garcia Arce, S., Rush, B., & Mendive, F. (2020). Pilot evaluation of a residential drug addiction treatment combining traditional Amazonian medicine, Ayahuasca and psychotherapy on depression and anxiety. *Journal of Psychoactive Drugs, 52*(5), 472–481. https://doi.org/10.1080/02791072.2020.1789247

Glaser, B., & Strauss, A. (1967). *The discovery of grounded theory: Strategies for qualitative research*. Sociology Press.

Gorman, I., Nielson, E. M., Molinar, A., Cassidy, K., & Sabbagh, J. (2021). Psychedelic harm reduction and integration: A transtheoretical model for clinical practice. *Frontiers in Psychology, 12*, Article 645246. https://doi.org/10.3389/fpsyg.2021.645246

Gould, J., & Austin, P. (Host). (n.d.) Healing war trauma through ayahuasca (No. 96) [Audio podcast episode]. In *The Psychedelic Podcast*. The Third Wave. https://thethirdwave.co/podcast/episode-96-jesse-gould/

Greenberg, R. P., & Fisher, S. (1989). Examining antidepressant effectiveness: Findings, ambiguities, and some vexing puzzles. In S. Fisher & R. P. Greenberg (Eds.), *The limits of biological treatments for psychological distress: Comparisons with psychotherapy and placebo* (pp. 1–37). Erlbaum.

Greer, G., & Tolbert, R. (1986). Subjective reports of the effects of MDMA in a clinical setting. *Journal of Psychoactive Drugs, 18*(4), 319–327. https://doi.org/10.1080/02791072.1986.10472364

Griffiths, R. R., Johnson, M. W., Carducci, M. A., Umbricht, A., Richards, W. A., Richards, B. D., Cosimano, M. P., & Klinedinst, M. A. (2016). Psilocybin produces substantial and sustained decreases in depression and anxiety in patients with life-threatening cancer: A randomized double-blind trial. *Journal of Psychopharmacology, 30*(12), 1181–1197. https://doi.org/10.1177/0269881116675513

Griffiths, R. R., Johnson, M. W., Richards, W. A., Richards, B. D., McCann, U., & Jesse, R. (2011). Psilocybin occasioned mystical-type experiences: Immediate and persisting dose-related effects. *Psychopharmacology, 218*(4), 649–665. https://doi.org/10.1007/s00213-011-2358-5

Griffiths, R. R., Richards, W. A., Johnson, M. W., McCann, U., & Jesse, R. (2018). Psilocybin-occasioned mystical-type experience in combination with meditation and other spiritual practices produces enduring positive changes in psychological functioning and in trait measures of prosocial attitudes and behaviors. *Journal of Psychopharmacology, 32*(1), 49–69. https://doi.org/10.1177/0269881117731279

Griffiths, R. R., Richards, W. A., McCann, U., & Jesse, R. (2006). Psilocybin can occasion mystical-type experiences having substantial and sustained personal meaning and spiritual significance. *Psychopharmacology, 187*(3), 268–283. https://doi.org/10.1007/s00213-006-0457-5

Griffiths, R. R., Richards, W. A., McCann, U., & Jesse, R. (2008). Mystical-type experiences occasioned by psilocybin mediate the attribution of personal meaning and spiritual significance 14 months later. *Journal of Psychopharmacology, 22*(6), 621–632. https://doi.org/10.1177/0269881108094300

Grob, C. S., Danforth, A. L., Chopra, G. S., Hagerty, M., McKay, C. R., Halberstadt, A. L., & Greer, G. R. (2011). Pilot study of psilocybin treatment for anxiety in patients with advanced-stage cancer. *Archives of General Psychiatry, 68*(1), 71–78. https://doi.org/10.1001/archgenpsychiatry.2010.116

Grob, C. S., McKenna, D. J., Callaway, J. C., Brito, G. S., Neves, E. S., Oberlaender, G., Saide, O. L., Labigalini, E., Tacla, C., Miranda, C. T., Strassman, R. J., & Boone, K. B. (1996). Human psychopharmacology of Hoasca, a plant hallucinogen used in ritual context in Brazil. *The Journal of Nervous and Mental Disease, 184*(2), 86–94. https://doi.org/10.1097/00005053-199602000-00004

Grof, S. (1979). *Realms of the human unconscious: Observations from LSD research*. Souvenir Press.

Grof, S. (1980). *LSD psychotherapy*. Hunter House Publishers.

Grof, S. (2006). *When the impossible happens: Adventures in non-ordinary realities*. Sounds True.

Grof, S. (2012). *Healing our deepest wounds: The holotropic paradigm shift*. Stream of Experience Productions.

Grof, S. (2016a). My ketamine journeys or ketamine and the enchantment of the other worlds. In P. Wolfson & G. Hartelius (Eds.), *The Ketamine papers: Science, therapy, and transformation* (pp. 73–85). Multidisciplinary Association for Psychedelic Studies.

Grof, S. (2016b). *The way of the psychonaut*. Multidisciplinary Association for Psychedelic Studies.

Grof, S., & Grof, C. (2010). *Holotropic breathwork: A new approach to self-exploration and therapy*. State University of New York Press.

Grof, S., Hofmann, A., & Weil, A. (2008). *LSD psychotherapy*. Multidisciplinary Association for Psychedelic Studies.

Guerra-Doce, E. (2015). Psychoactive substances in prehistoric times: Examining the archaeological evidence. *Time and Mind, 8*(1), 91–112. https://doi.org/10.1080/1751696X.2014.993244

Halberstadt, A. L. (2015). Recent advances in the neuropsychopharmacology of serotonergic hallucinogens. *Behavioral Brain Research, 277*, 99–120. https://doi.org/10.1016/j.bbr.2014.07.016

Hamill, J., Hallak, J., Dursun, S. M., & Baker, G. (2019). Ayahuasca: Psychological and physiologic effects, pharmacology and potential uses in addiction and mental illness. *Current Neuropharmacology, 17*(2), 108–128. https://doi.org/10.2174/1570159X16666180125095902

Harris, D. S, Baggott, M., Mendelson, J. H., Mendelson, J. E., & Jones, R. T. (2002). Subjective and hormonal effects of 3,4-methylenedioxymethamphetamine (MDMA) in humans. *Psychopharmacology, 162*(4), 396–405. https://doi.org/10.1007/s00213-002-1131-1

Heffter, A. (1897). Uber pellote. *Archive for experimental pathology and pharmacology, 40*, 418–425. https://link.springer.com/article/10.1007/BF01825267

Herculano-Houzel, S. (2012). The remarkable, yet not extraordinary, human brain as a scaled-up primate brain and its associated cost. *Proceedings of the National Academy of Sciences, 109*(Supplement_1), 10661–10668. https://doi.org/10.1073/pnas.1201895109

Hesse, H. (2000). *Siddhartha*. Dover Publications.

Hofmann, A. (1983). *LSD: My problem child: Reflections on sacred drugs, mysticism, and science* (J. Ott, Trans.). J. P. Tarcher.

Hofmann, A., & Ott, J. (1980). *LSD, my problem child*. McGraw-Hill.

Huxley, A. (1963). *The doors of perception, and heaven and hell* (1st Perennial Library ed.). Harper & Row.

Iannelli, E. J. (2020). The most dangerous man in America: Timothy Leary, Richard Nixon and the hunt for the fugitive king of LSD. *Times Literary Supplement, 6116,* 33. https://link.gale.com/apps/doc/A632693110/AONE?u=anon~e62ede51&sid=googleScholar&xid=cd4e8066

Inouye, A. M., Wolfgang, A. S., & Philhower, L. T. (2023). MDMA-assisted dialectical behavioral therapy for borderline personality disorder: A qualitative study of mental health clinicians. *Journal of Psychedelic Studies, 8*(1), 92–105. https://doi.org/10.1556/2054.2023.00281

Joffe, R., Sokolov, S., & Streiner, D. (1996). Antidepressant treatment of depression: A meta-analysis. *Canadian Journal of Psychiatry, 41*(10), 613–616.

Johnson & Johnson. (2025, January 21). *SPRAVATO® (esketamine) approved in the U.S. as the first and only monotherapy for adults with treatment-resistant depression*. https://www.jnj.com/media-center/press-releases/spravato-esketamine-approved-in-the-u-s-as-the-first-and-only-monotherapy-for-adults-with-treatment-resistant-depression

Johnson, M. W., Richards, W. A., & Griffiths, R. R. (2008). Human hallucinogen research: Guidelines for safety. *Journal of Psychopharmacology, 22*(6), 603–620. https://doi.org/10.1177/0269881108093587

JRE Clips. (2018, May 24). *Joe Rogan on ego death* [Video]. YouTube. https://www.youtube.com/watch?v=HCfIXvQ6fxE

Jung, C. G. (1979). *Aion: Researches into the phenomenology of the self* (1st ed.). Princeton University Press.

Kabat-Zinn, J. (1994). *Wherever you go, there you are: Mindfulness meditation in everyday life* (Kindle ed.). Hyperion.

Kabat-Zinn, J. (2005). *Wherever you go, there you are* (10th ed.). Hyperion.

Kabat-Zinn, J. (2012). *Mindfulness for beginners: Reclaiming the present moment—and your life.* Sounds True.

Kabat-Zinn, J. (2013). *Full catastrophe living: Using the wisdom of your body and mind to face stress, pain, and illness* (Rev. & updated ed.). Bantam Books.

Kabat-Zinn, J. (2019). *Mindfulness for all: The Wisdom to transform the world.* Hachette Books.

Kabat-Zinn, J. (2021). The liberative potential of mindfulness. *Mindfulness, 12*(6), 1–9. https://doi.org/10.1007/s12671-021-01608-6

Kaelen, M., Barrett, F. S., Roseman, L., Lorenz, R., Family, N., Bolstridge, M., Curran, H. V., Feilding, A., Nutt, D. J., & Carhart-Harris, R. L. (2015). LSD enhances the emotional response to music. *Psychopharmacology, 232(*19), 3607–3614. https://doi.org/10.1007/s00213-015-4014-y

Kaelen, M., Giribaldi, B., Raine, J., Evans, L., Timmermann, C., Rodriguez, N., Roseman, L., Feilding, A., Nutt, D. J., Kaelen, M., & Carhart-Harris, R. L. (2018). The hidden therapist: Evidence for a central role of music in psychedelic therapy. *Psychopharmacology, 235*(2), 505–519. https://doi.org/10.1007/s00213-017-4820-5

Kanen, J. W., Luo, Q., Rostami Kandroodi, M., Cardinal, R. N., Robbins, T. W., Nutt, D. J., Carhart-Harris, R. L., & den Ouden, H. E. M. (2023). Effect of lysergic acid diethylamide (LSD) on reinforcement learning in humans. *Psychological Medicine, 53*(14), 6434–6445. https://doi.org/10.1017/S0033291722002963

Kast, E. (1966). LSD and the dying patient. *The Chicago Medical School Quarterly, 26*(2), 80–87.

Kast, E. C., & Collins, V. J. (1964). Lysergic acid diethylamide as an analgesic agent. *Anesthesia & Analgesia, 43,* 285–291.

Kekatos, M., & Nissen, N. (2024, June 4). *FDA advisers vote against recommending approval of MDMA as treatment for PTSD*. ABC News. https://abcnews.go.com/Health/fda-advisers-recommending-mdma-treatment-ptsd/story?id=110808948

Khorramzadeh, E., & Lofty, A. O. (1973). The use of ketamine in psychiatry. *Psychosomatics, 14*(6), 344–346. https://doi.org/10.1016/S0033-3182(73)71306-2

Kirsch, I., & Lynn, S. J. (1999). Automaticity in clinical psychology. *American Psychologist, 54*(7), 504–515. https://doi.org/10.1037/0003-066X.54.7.504

Kirsch, I., & Sapirstein, G. (1999). Listening to prozac but hearing placebo: A meta-analysis of antidepressant medication. In I. Kirsch (Ed.), *How expectancies shape experience* (pp. 303–320). American Psychological Association.

Kolbrich, E. A., Goodwin, R. S., Gorelick, D. A., Hayes, R. J., Stein, E. A., & Huestis, M. A. (2008). Physiological and subjective responses to controlled oral 3,4-methylenedioxymethamphetamine administration. *Journal of Clinical Psychopharmacology, 28*(4), 432–440. https://doi.org/10.1097/JCP.0b013e31817ef470

Kolp, E., Friedman, H. L., Krupitsky, E., Jansen, K., Sylvester, M., Young, M. S., & Kolp, A. (2014). Ketamine psychedelic psychotherapy: Focus on its pharmacology, phenomenology, and clinical applications. *International Journal of Transpersonal Studies, 33*(2), 84–140. http://dx.doi.org/10.24972/ijts.2014.33.2.84

Korman, B. A. (2024). Does LSD confer lasting psychological resilience? An investigation of naturalistic users experiencing job loss. *PLOS ONE, 19*(6), Article e0304991. https://doi.org/10.1371/journal.pone.0304991

Korzybski, A. (1931). Supplement III: A non-Aristotelian system and its necessity for rigour in mathematics and physics. http://esgs.free.fr/uk/art/sands-sup3.pdf

Krippner, S., (2016). Remembering Salvador Roquet. In P. Wolfson & G. Hartelius (Eds.), *The ketamine papers: Science, therapy, and transformation* (pp. 92–114). Multidisciplinary Association for Psychedelic Studies.

Krupitsky, E. M., & Grinenko, A. Y. (1997). Ketamine psychedelic therapy (KPT): A review of the results of ten years of research. *Journal of Psychoactive Drugs, 29*(2), 165–183. https://doi.org/10.1080/02791072.1997.10400185

Krupitsky, E., Burakov, A., Romanova, T., Dunaevsky, I., Strassman, R., & Grinenko, A. (2002). Ketamine psychotherapy for heroin addiction: Immediate effects and two-year follow-up. *Journal of Substance Abuse Treatment, 23*(4), 273–283. https://doi.org/10.1016/s0740-5472(02)00275-1

Kryst, J., Kawalec, P., Mitoraj, A. M., Pilc, A., Lasoń, W., & Brzostek, T. (2020). Efficacy of single and repeated administration of ketamine in unipolar and bipolar depression: A meta-analysis of randomized clinical trials. *Pharmacological Reports, 72*, 543–562. https://doi.org/10.1007/s43440-020-00097-z

Kurland, A. A., Unger, S., Shaffer, J. W., & Savage, C. (1967). Psychedelic therapy utilizing LSD in the treatment of the alcoholic patient: A preliminary report. *American Journal of Psychiatry, 123*(10), 1202–1209. https://doi.org/10.1176/ajp.123.10.1202

Kurland, A., Savage, E., Pahnke, N., Grof, S., & Olson, E. (1971). LSD in the treatment of alcoholics. *Pharmacopsychiatry, 4*(2), 83–94. https://doi.org/10.1055/s-0028-1094301

Kustanowitz, E. D. (2024, May 24). *With $2 million raised, MAPS Israel looks to use psychedelics to treat post-Oct. 7 wave of PTSD*. eJewish Philanthropy. https://ejewishphilanthropy.com/with-2-million-raised-maps-israel-looks-to-use-psychedelics-to-treat-post-oct-7-wave-of-ptsd/

L'Amour, L. (1980). *Lonely on the mountain*. Bantam Books.

Lara, D. R., Bisol, L. W., & Munari, L. R. (2013). Antidepressant, mood stabilizing and procognitive effects of very low dose sublingual Ketamine in refractory unipolar and bipolar depression. *Neuropsychopharmacology, 16*(9), 2111–2117. https://doi.org/10.1017/S1461145713000485

Leary, T. (1969). *High priest*. World Publishing.

Leary, T., & Penner, J. (2014). *Timothy Leary, the Harvard years: Early writings on LSD and psilocybin with Richard Alpert, Huston Smith, Ralph Metzner, and others*. Park Street Press.

Leary, T., Metzner, R., & Alpert, R. (1964). *The psychedelic experience: A manual based on the Tibetan book of the dead*. University Books.

Liester, M. B., & Prickett, J. I. (2012). Hypotheses regarding the mechanisms of ayahuasca in the treatment of addictions. *Journal of Psychoactive Drugs, 44*(3), 200–208. https://doi.org/10.1080/02791072.2012.704590

Logothetis, N. K. (2008). What we can do and what we cannot do with fMRI. *Nature, 453*(7197), 869–878. https://doi.org/10.1038/nature06976

Lykos Therapeutics. (2024, August 9). Lykos Therapeutics announces Complete Response Letter for midomafetamine capsules for PTSD. https://news.lykospbc.com/2024-08-09-Lykos-Therapeutics-Announces-Complete-Response-Letter-for-Midomafetamine-Capsules-for-PTSD

Lyubomirsky, S. (2022). Toward a new science of psychedelic social psychology: The effects of MDMA (Ecstasy) on social connection. *Perspectives on Psychological Science, 17*(5), 1234–1257. https://doi.org/10.1177/17456916211055369

Maniaci, G., Daino, M., Iapichino, M., Giammanco, A., Taormina, C., Bonura, G. F., Sardella, Z., Carolla, G., Cammareri, P., Sberna, E., Clesi, M. F., Ferraro, L., Gambino, C. M., Ciaccio, M., Rispoli, L., La Cascia, C., La Barbera, D., & Quattrone, D. (2024). Neurobiological and anti-inflammatory effects of a deep diaphragmatic breathing technique based on neofunctional psychotherapy: A pilot RCT. *Stress and Health, 40*(6), Article e3503. https://doi.org/10.1002/smi.3503

MAPS Israel. (2024). *Education*. https://www.maps-israel.org/healingoct7

Marcus, A. (2020, November 23). *Ayahuasca by Aubrey Marcus and Mitch Schultz* [Video]. YouTube. https://youtu.be/HfM-HhLgDeY

McGirr, A., Berlim, M. T., Bond, D. J., Fleck, M. P., Yatham, L. N., & Lam, R. W. (2015). A systematic review and meta-analysis of randomized, double-blind, placebo-controlled trials of Ketamine in the rapid treatment of major depressive episodes. *Psychological Medicine, 45*(4), 693–704. https://doi.org/10.1017/S0033291714001603

McKenna, T. K. (1992). *Food of the gods: The search for the original tree of knowledge: A radical history of plants, drugs, and human evolution*. Bantam Books.

Melani, A., Bonaso, M., Biso, L., Zucchini, B., Conversano, C., & Scarselli, M. (2025). Uncovering psychedelics: From neural circuits to therapeutic applications. *Pharmaceuticals, 18*(1), Article 130. https://doi.org/10.3390/ph18010130

Menon, V. (2023). Twenty years of the default mode network: A review and synthesis. *Neuron, 110*(2), 180–204. https://doi.org/10.1016/j.neuron.2022.11.007

Metzner, R. (2016). John Lilly and ketamine: Some personal recollections. In P. Wolfson & G. Hartelius (Eds.), *The ketamine papers: Science, therapy, and transformation* (pp. 85–88). Multidisciplinary Association for Psychedelic Studies.

Miller, R. L. (2017). *Psychedelic medicine: The healing powers of LSD, MDMA, psilocybin, and ayahuasca*. Park Street Press.

Milliere, R., Carhart-Harris, R. L., Roseman, L., Trautwein, F.-M., & Berkovich-Ohana, A. (2018). Psychedelics, meditation, and self-consciousness. *Frontiers in Psychology, 9*, Article 1475. https://doi.org/10.3389/fpsyg.2018.01475

Minuchin, S. (1974). *Families and family therapy*. Harvard University Press.

Mitchell, A. J., Chan, M., Bhatt, H., Halton, M., Grassi, L., Johansen, C., & Meader, N. (2011). Prevalence of depression, anxiety, and adjustment disorder in oncological, hematological, and palliative-care settings: A meta-analysis of 94 interview-based studies. *The Lancet Oncology, 12*, 160–174. https://doi.org/10.1016/S1470-2045(11)70002-X

Mitchell, J. M., Bogenschutz, M., Lilienstein, A., Harrison, C., Kleiman, S., Parker-Guilbert, K., Ot'alora G, M., Garas, W., Paleos, C., Gorman, I., Nicholas, C., Mithoefer, M., Carlin, S., Poulter, B., Mithoefer, A., Quevedo, S., Wells, G., Klaire, S. S., van der Kolk, B.,. . . Doblin, R. (2021). MDMA-assisted therapy for severe PTSD: A randomized, double-blind, placebo-controlled phase 3 study. *Nature Medicine*, *27*, 1025–1033. https://doi.org/10.1038/s41591-021-01336-3

Mithoefer, M. C., Feduccia, A. A., Jerome, L., Mithoefer, A., Wagner, M., Walsh, Z., Hamilton, S., Yazar-Klosinski, B., Emerson, A., & Doblin, R. (2019). MDMA-assisted psychotherapy for treatment of PTSD: Study design and rationale for phase 3 trials based on pooled analysis of six phase 2 randomized controlled trials. *Psychopharmacology*, *236*(9), 2735–2745. https://doi.org/10.1007/s00213-019-05249-5

Mobbs, D., & Kim, J. J. (2015). Neuroethological studies of fear, anxiety, and risky decision-making in rodents and humans. *Current Opinion in Behavioral Sciences*, *5*, 8–15. https://doi.org/10.1016/j.cobeha.2015.06.005

Morgan, M. J. (2000). Ecstasy (MDMA): A review of its possible persistent psychological effects. *Psychopharmacology*, *152*(3), 230–248. https://doi.org/10.1007/s002130000545

Muelrath, L. (2018). *Anderson Cooper: 60 minutes special on mindfulness Anderson Cooper*. [Video]. YouTube. https://www.youtube.com/watch?v=ozyr7jVucz0

Multidisciplinary Association for Psychedelic Studies. (2017, August 26). *FDA grants breakthrough therapy designation for MDMA-assisted psychotherapy for PTSD, agrees on special protocol assessment for Phase 3 trials*. https://maps.org/news/media/press-release-fda-grants-breakthrough-therapy-designation-for-mdma-assisted-psychotherapy-for-ptsd-agrees-on-special-protocol-assessment-for-phase-3-trials/

Multidisciplinary Association for Psychedelic Studies. (2019b). *MDMA-assisted therapy code of ethics*. MAPS Public Benefit Corporation. https://maps.org/ethic

Multidisciplinary Association for Psychedelic Studies. (2021, March 22). *MDMA investigator's brochure* (13th ed.). https://mapscontent.s3-us-west-1.amazonaws.com/research-archive/MDMA+IB+13th+Edition+Final+22MAR2021.pdf; https://maps.org/wp-content/uploads/2021/03/MDMAIB13thEditionFinal22MAR2021.pdf

Nestor, J. (2020). *Breath*. Penguin Life.

Nichols, D. E. (1986). Differences between the mechanism of action of MDMA, MBDB, and the classic hallucinogens. Identification of a new therapeutic class: Entactogens. *Journal of Psychoactive Drugs*, *18*(4), 305–313. https://doi.org/10.1080/02791072.1986.10472362

Nisbet, E. K., Zelenski, J. M., & Murphy, S. A. (2011). Happiness is in our nature: Exploring nature relatedness as a contributor to subjective well-being. *Journal of Happiness Studies*, *12*(2), 303–322. https://doi.org/10.1007/s10902-010-9197-7

Pahnke, W. N. (1963). *Drugs and mysticism: An analysis of the relationship between psychedelic drugs and the mystical consciousness* [Unpublished doctoral dissertation]. Harvard University.

Pahnke, W. N. (1969). The psychedelic mystical experience in the human encounter with death. In C. T. Tart (Ed.), *Altered states of consciousness* (pp. 247–274). John Wiley & Sons.

Pahnke, W. N., Kurland, A. A., Goodman, L. E., & Richards, W. A. (1969). LSD-assisted psychotherapy with terminal cancer patients. In R. E. Hicks & P. J. Fink (Eds.), *Psychedelic drugs* (pp. 33–42). Grunne & Stratton.

Pahnke, W. N., Kurland, A. A., Unger, S., Savage, C., Wolf, S., & Goodman, L. E. (1970a). Psychedelic therapy (utilizing LSD) with cancer patients. *Journal of Psychedelic Drugs*, *3*(1), 6375.

Pahnke, W., Kurland, A., Unger, S., Savage, C., & Grof, S. (1970b). The experimental use of psychedelic (LSD) psychotherapy. *Journal of the American Medical Association, 212*(11), 1856–1863.

Pais, A. (1982). *Subtle is the lord: The science and the life of Albert Einstein*. Oxford University Press.

Paltrow, G., & Loehnen, E. (Executive Producers) (2020). The healing trip (Season 1, episode 1) [TV series episode]. In Paltrow, G. (Executive Producer), *The Goop Lab*. Netflix.

Pantoni, M. M., Kim, J. L., Van Alstyne, K. R., & Anagnostaras, S. G. (2022). MDMA and memory, addiction, and depression: Dose-effect analysis. *Psychopharmacology, 239*(3), 935–949. https://doi.org/10.1007/s00213-022-06086-9

Park, C. L. (2010). Making sense of the meaning literature: An integrative review of meaning making and its effects on adjustment to stressful life events. *Psychological Bulletin, 136*(2), 257–301. https://doi.org/10.1037/a0018301

Parrott, A. C., Sisk, E., & Turner, J. J. D. (2000). Psychobiological problems in heavy "ecstasy" (MDMA) polydrug users. *Drug Alcohol Dependence, 60*(1), 105–110. https://doi.org/10.1016/s0376-8716(99)00146-5

Passie, T. (2021). History of the use of hallucinogens in psychiatric treatment. In C. S. Grob & J. Grigsby (Eds.), *Handbook of medical hallucinogens* (pp. 95–118). Guilford Press.

Passie, T., Seifert, J., Schneider, U., & Emrich, H. M. (2002). The pharmacology of psilocybin. *Addiction Biology, 7*(4), 357–364. https://doi.org/10.1080/1355621021000005937

Pennebaker, J. W., & Smyth, J. M. (2016). *Opening up by writing it down: How expressive writing improves health and eases emotional pain* (3rd ed.). Guilford Press.

Perkins, D., Opaleye, E. S., Simonova, H., Bouso, J. C., Tófoli, L. F., GalvÃo-Coelho, N. L., Schubert, V., & Sarris, J. (2022). Associations between ayahuasca consumption in naturalistic settings and current alcohol and drug use: Results of a large international cross-sectional survey. *Drug and Alcohol Review, 41*(1), 265–274. https://doi.org/10.1111/dar.13348

Pinchbeck, D. (2003). *Breaking open the head: A psychedelic journey into the heart of contemporary shamanism*. Crown.

Porges, S. W. (2011). *The polyvagal theory: Neurophysiological foundations of emotions, attachment, communication, and self-regulation*. W. W. Norton & Company.

Proust, M. (1923). *Remembrance of things past* (C. K. Scott Moncrieff, Trans.). Random House. (Original work published 1913–1927).

Psychedelic Newswire. (2020, August 7). *How Israel is taking the lead in medical psychedelics*. https://www.psychedelicnewswire.com/how-israel-is-taking-the-lead-in-medical-psychedelics/

Psychedelic Newswire. (2024). *How Israel is taking the lead in medical psychedelics*. https://www.psychedelicnewswire.com/how-israel-is-taking-the-lead-in-medical-psychedelics/

PubChem. (2025). *Ketamine—PubChem compound summary for CID 3821*. National Center for Biotechnology Information. Retrieved June 23, 2025, from https://pubchem.ncbi.nlm.nih.gov/compound/Ketamine

Raichle, M. E., & Snyder, A. Z. (2007). A default mode of brain function: A brief history of an evolving idea. *NeuroImage, 37*(4), 1083–1099. https://doi.org/10.1016/j.neuroimage.2007.02.041

Ram Dass. (1978). *Be here now, remember*. Hanuman Foundation.

Ram Dass. (Host). (1988). *Promises and pitfalls of the spiritual path* [Audio podcast]. The Library of Consciousness. https://www.organism.earth/library/document/promises-and-pitfalls

Ratey, J. J., & Hagerman, E. (2008). *Spark: The revolutionary new science of exercise and the brain*. Little, Brown.

Riba, J., Anderer, P., Jané, F., Saletu, B., & Barbanoj, M. J. (2004). Effects of the South American psychoactive beverage Ayahuasca on regional brain electrical activity in humans: A functional neuroimaging study using low-resolution electromagnetic tomography. *Neuropsychobiology, 50*(1), 89–101. https://doi.org/10.1159/000077946

Riba, J., Anderer, P., Morte, A., Urbano, G., Jané, F., Saletu, B., & Barbanoj, M. J. (2002a). Topographic pharmaco-EEG mapping of the effects of the South American psychoactive beverage ayahuasca in healthy volunteers. *British Journal of Clinical Pharmacology, 53*(6), 613–628. https://doi.org/10.1046/j.1365-2125.2002.01609.x

Riba, J., Rodríguez-Fornells, A., & Barbanoj, M. J. (2002b). Effects of ayahuasca on sensory and sensorimotor gating in humans as measured by P50 suppression and prepulse inhibition of the startle reflex, respectively. *Psychopharmacology, 165*(1), 18–28. https://doi.org/10.1007/s00213-002-1237-5

Riba, J., Rodríguez-Fornells, A., Urbano, G., Morte, A., Antonijoan, R., Montero, M., Callaway, J. C., & Barbanoj, M. J. (2001). Subjective effects and tolerability of the South American psychoactive beverage ayahuasca in healthy volunteers. *Psychopharmacology, 154*(1), 85–95. https://doi.org/10.1007/s002130000606

Riba, J., Valle, M., Urbano, G., Yritia, M., Morte, A., & Barbanoj, M. J. (2003). Human pharmacology of Ayahuasca: Subjective and cardiovascular effects, monoamine metabolite excretion, and pharmacokinetics. *The Journal of Pharmacology and Experimental Therapeutics, 306*(1), 73–83. https://doi.org/10.1124/jpet.103.049882

Richards, W., Grof, S., Goodman, L., & Kurland, A. (1972). LSD-assisted psychotherapy and the human encounter with death. *Journal of Transpersonal Psychology, 4*(2), 121–150.

Rogers, C. R. (1951). *Client-centered therapy: Its current practice, implications, and theory*. Houghton Mifflin.

Rogers, C. R. (1957). The necessary and sufficient conditions of therapeutic personality change. *Journal of Consulting Psychology, 21*(2), 95–103. https://doi.org/10.1037/h0045357

Roquet, S., Favreau, P., Ocana, R., & Velasco, M. (1971). *The existential through psychodisleptics—A new psychotherapy*. Association Albert Schweitzer.

Roseman, L., Ron, Y., Saca, A., Ginsberg, N., Luan, L., Karkabi, N., Doblin, R., & Carhart-Harris, R. (2021). Relational processes in ayahuasca groups of Palestinians and Israelis. *Frontiers in Pharmacology, 12*, Article 607529. https://doi.org/10.3389/fphar.2021.607529

Ross, S., Agrawal, M., Griffiths, R. R., Grob, C., Berger, A., & Henningfield, J. E. (2022). Psychedelic-assisted psychotherapy to treat psychiatric and existential distress in life-threatening medical illnesses and palliative care. *Neuropharmacology, 216*, Article 109174. https://doi.org/10.1016/j.neuropharm.2022.109174

Ross, S., Bossis, A., Guss, J., Agin-Liebes, G., Malone, T., Cohen, B., Mennenga, S. E., Belser, A., Kalliontzi, K., Babb, J., Su, Z., Corby, P., & Schmidt, B. L. (2016). Rapid and sustained symptom reduction following psilocybin treatment for anxiety and depression in patients with life-threatening cancer: A randomized controlled trial. *Journal of Psychopharmacology, 30*(12), 1165–1180. https://doi.org/10.1177/0269881116675512.

Russ, S. L., Carhart-Harris, R. L., Maruyama, G., & Elliott, M. S. (2019). Replication and extension of a model predicting response to psilocybin. *Psychopharmacology, 236*(11), 3221–3230. https://doi.org/10.1007/s00213-019-05279-z

Salzberg, S. (2011). *Real happiness: The power of meditation*. Workman Publishing.
Santos, R. G., Landeira-Fernandez, J., Strassman, R. J., Motta, V., & Cruz, A. P. M. (2007). Effects of ayahuasca on psychometric measures of anxiety, panic-like and hopelessness in Santo Daime members. *Journal of Ethnopharmacology, 112*(3), 507–513. https://doi.org/10.1016/j.jep.2007.04.012
Saoji, A. A., Raghavendra, B. R., & Manjunath, N. K. (2019). Effects of yogic breath regulation: A narrative review of scientific evidence. *Journal of Ayurveda and Integrative Medicine, 10*(1), 50–58. https://doi.org/10.1016/j.jaim.2017.07.008
Satir, V., Banmen, J., Gerber, J., & Gomori, M. (1980). *The Satir model: Family therapy and beyond*. Science and Behavior Books.
Satir, V., Banmen, J., Gerber, J., & Gomori, M. (1991). *The Satir model: Family therapy and beyond*. Science and Behavior Books.
Schlag, A. K., Aday, J., Salam, I., Neill, J. C., & Nutt, D. J. (2022). Adverse effects of psychedelics: From anecdotes and misinformation to systematic science. *Journal of Psychopharmacology, 36*(3), 258–272. https://doi.org/10.1177/02698811211069100
Schmid, T., & Liechti, M. E. (2021). Set and setting in the Santo Daime. *Frontiers in*
Schopenhauer, A. (1969). *The world as will and representation*. Dover Pub.
Segal, Z. V., Williams, J. M. G., & Teasdale, J. D. (2018). *Mindfulness-based cognitive therapy for depression*. Guilford Press.
Sessa, B. (2017). *The psychedelic renaissance: Reassessing the role of psychedelic drugs in 21st century psychiatry and society* (2nd ed.). Muswell Hill Press.
Shaffer, F., & Meehan, Z. M. (2020). A practical guide to resonance frequency assessment for heart rate variability biofeedback. Frontiers in Neuroscience, 14, Article 570400. https://doi.org/10.3389/fnins.2020.570400
Shannon, S., & Geller, J. (2024). MDMA for PTSD and beyond: A new paradigm brings hope. *Frontiers in Human Neuroscience, 18*, Article 1475013. https://doi.org/10.3389/fnhum.2024.1475013
Shulgin, A. T. (1986). The background and chemistry of MDMA. *Journal of Psychoactive Drugs, 18*(4), 291–304. https://doi.org/10.1080/02791072.1986.10472361
Shulgin, A. T., & Nichols, D. E. (1978). *Characterization of three new psychotomimetics*. In R. C. Stillman & R. E. Willette (Eds.), *The psychopharmacology of hallucinogens*. Pergamon Press.
Shulgin, A. T., & Shulgin, A. A. (1991). *PIHKAL: A chemical love story*. Transform Press.
Singer, M. A. (2015). *The surrender experiment: My journey into life's perfection* (1st ed.). Harmony Books.
Stamets, P. (2005). *Mycelium running: How mushrooms can help save the world*. Ten Speed Press.
Stamets, P. (2020). *Fantastic fungi: How mushrooms can heal, shift consciousness, and save the planet*. Insight Editions.
Stauffer, C. S., Brown, M. R., Adams, D., Cassity, M., & Sevelius, J. (2022). MDMA-assisted psychotherapy; inclusion of transgender and gender diverse people in the frontiers of PTSD treatment trials. *Frontiers in Psychiatry, 13*, Article 932605. https://doi.org/10.3389/fpsyt.2022.932605
Steger, M. F. (2012). Making meaning in life. *Psychological Inquiry, 23*(4), 381–385. https://doi.org/10.1080/1047840X.2012.720832
Stephen, A., & Lui, F. (2021). *Brief psychotic disorder*. Treasure Island Publishing. https://www.ncbi.nlm.nih.gov/books/NBK539912/
Stolaroff, M. J. (1993). *Thanatos to Eros: Thirty-five years of psychedelic exploration*. MAPS.
Strumila, R., Nobile, B., Korsakova, L., Lengvenyte, A., Olie, E., Lopez-Castroaman, J., Guillaume, S., & Courtet, P. (2021). Psilocybin, a naturally occurring indoleamine

compound, could be useful to prevent suicidal behaviors. *Pharmaceuticals, 14*(12), Article 1213. https://doi.org/10.3390/ph14121213

Sumnall, H. R., & Cole, J. C. (2005). Self-reported depressive symptomatology in community samples of polysubstance misusers who report Ecstasy use: A meta-analysis. *Journal of Psychopharmacology, 19*(1), 84–92. https://doi.org/10.1177/0269881105048901

Suzuki, S. (1970). *Zen mind beginner's mind* (1st ed.). Weatherhill.

Tagliazucchi, E., & Carhart-Harris, R. (2014a). Altered states of consciousness: Psychedelics and functional connectivity of the brain. *Frontiers in Human Neuroscience, 8,* Article 173. https://doi.org/10.3389/fnhum.2014.00173

Tagliazucchi, E., & Carhart-Harris, R. (2014b). Enhanced repertoire of brain dynamical states during the psychedelic experience. *Human Brain Mapping, 35*(11), 5442–5456. https://doi.org/10.1002/hbm.22562

Talin, P., & Sanabria, E. (2017). Ayahuasca's entwined efficacy: An ethnographic study of ritual healing from 'addiction.' *The International Journal on Drug Policy, 44,* 23–30. https://doi.org/10.1016/j.drugpo.2017.02.017

Thomas, G., Lucas, P., Capler, N. R., Tupper, K. W., & Martin, G. (2013). Ayahuasca-assisted therapy for addiction: Results from a preliminary observational study in Canada. *Current Drug Abuse Reviews, 6*(1), 30–42. https://doi.org/10.2174/15733998113099990003

Tolle, E. (2001). *The power of now*. Hodder Paperback.

Tomsovic, M., & Edwards, R. V. (1970). Lysergide treatment of schizophrenic and nonschizophrenic alcoholics: A controlled evaluation. *Quarterly Journal of Studies in Alcohol, 31*(4), 932–949. https://doi.org/10.15288/qjsa.1970.31.932

Tupper, K. W. (2009). Ayahuasca healing beyond the Amazon: The globalization of a traditional indigenous entheogenic practice. *Global Networks, 9*(1), 117–136. https://doi.org/10.1111/j.1471-0374.2009.00245.x

U.S. Food and Drug Administration. (2019, March 5). *FDA approves new nasal spray medication for treatment-resistant depression; available only at a certified doctor's office or clinic*. https://www.fda.gov/news-events/press-announcements/fda-approves-new-nasal-spray-medication-treatment-resistant-depression-available-only-certified

U.S. Food and Drug Administration. (2023). *Expedited programs for serious conditions—Drugs and biologics: Guidance for industry*. U.S. Department of Health and Human Services, Center for Drug Evaluation and Research, Center for Biologics Evaluation and Research. https://www.fda.gov/regulatory-information/search-fda-guidance-documents/expedited-programs-serious-conditions-drugs-and-biologics

Van der Kolk, B. A. (2014). *The body keeps the score: Brain, mind, and body in the healing of trauma*. Viking.

van der Meer, P. B., Nijdam, M. J., Vermetten, E., van den Brink, W., & Schoevers, R. A. (2023). Therapeutic effect of psilocybin in addiction: A systematic review. Frontiers in Psychiatry, 14, Article 1134454. https://doi.org/10.3389/fpsyt.2023.1134454

Vollenweider, F. X., Vollenweider-Scherpenhuyzen, M. F., & Babler, A. (1998). Psilocybin induces schizophrenia-like psychosis in humans via a serotonin-2 agonist action. *Neuroreport, 9*(17), 3897–3902. https://doi.org/10.1097/00001756-199812010-00024

Wagner, A. C. (2021). Couple therapy with MDMA—Proposed pathways of action. *Frontiers in Psychology, 12,* Article 733456. https://doi.org/10.3389/fpsyg.2021.733456

Walach, H., & Maidhof, C. (1999). Is the placebo effect dependent on time? A meta-analysis. In I. Kirsch (Ed.), *How expectancies shape experience* (pp. 321–331). American Psychological Association.

Watts, A. (1965). *The joyous cosmology in the chemistry of consciousness*. Pantheon Books.

Watts, R., & Luoma, J. B. (2020). The use of the psychological flexibility model to support psychedelic-assisted therapy: Key insights and clinical considerations. *Frontiers in Psychology, 11*, Article 194. https://doi.org/10.3389/fpsyg.2020.00194

Weil, A. (2022). *Breath: The new science of a lost art* (Updated ed.). Penguin Random House.

Weil, A. (n.d.). *Breathing exercises: 4-7-8 breath* [Video]. DrWeil.com. https://www.drweil.com/videos-features/videos/breathing-exercises-4-7-8-breath/

Wesley, R., Cole, M., & Koek, R. (2016). Ketamine, depression and current research: A review of literature. In P. Wolfson & G. Hartelius (Eds.), *The ketamine papers: Science, therapy, and transformation* (pp. 352–465). Multidisciplinary Association for Psychedelic Studies.

Winkelman, M. (2021). Anthropology, shamanism and hallucinogens. In C. S. Grob & Jim Grigsby (Eds.), *Handbook of medical hallucinogens* (pp. 46–67). Guilford Press.

Winkelman, M., & Sessa, B. (2019). *Advances in psychedelic medicine: State-of-the-art therapeutic applications*. Praeger.

Wong, P. T. P. (2017). Meaning-centered approach to research and therapy. In P. Russo-Netzer, S. E. Schulenberg, & A. Batthyány (Eds.), *Logotherapy and existential analysis: Proceedings of the Viktor Frankl institute* (Vol. 1, pp. 403–417). Springer.

World Health Organization. (2015). *WHO statement on the scheduling of ketamine*. https://www.who.int/news/item/10-03-2015-who-statement-on-the-scheduling-of-ketamine

World Health Organization. (2017, March 29). *WHO model list of essential medicines, 20th list (April 2017)*. https://www.who.int/publications/i/item/EML-20

Woźniak, J., Bogacz, R., Gaik, M., Uram, E., Magda, I., Womperski, K., & Osuch, M. (2023). The use of psilocybin in the treatment of psychiatric disorders—review. *Journal of Education, Health and Sport, 43*(1), 104–115. https://doi.org/10.12775/JEHS.2023.43.01.009

Yalom, I. D. (1980). *Existential psychotherapy*. Basic Books.

Yalom, I. D. (1989). *Love's executioner: And other tales of psychotherapy*. Basic Books.

Yalom, I. D. (2002). *The gift of therapy: An open letter to a new generation of therapists and their patients*. Harper Perennial.

Young, S. (2010). *The science of mindfulness: A guide to pain and suffering*. Mindful Publishing.

Zaccaro, A., Piarulli, A., Laurino, M., Garbella, E., Menicucci, D., Neri, B., & Gemignani, A. (2018). How breath-control can change your life: A systematic review on psycho-physiological correlates of slow breathing. Frontiers in Human Neuroscience, 12, Article 353. https://doi.org/10.3389/fnhum.2018.00353

Zanos, P., & Gould, T. D. (2018). Mechanisms of ketamine action as an antidepressant. *Molecular Psychiatry, 23*(4), 801–811. https://doi.org/10.1038/mp.2017.255

Zur, O. (2007). *Boundaries in psychotherapy: Ethical and clinical explorations*. American Psychological Association.

Index

Note: Page numbers in *italics* indicate figures, **bold** indicate tables in the text, and references following "n" refer to the notes.

For Product Safety Concerns and Information please contact our EU
representative GPSR@taylorandfrancis.com
Taylor & Francis Verlag GmbH, Kaufingerstraße 24, 80331 München, Germany

www.ingramcontent.com/pod-product-compliance
Ingram Content Group UK Ltd.
Pitfield, Milton Keynes, MK11 3LW, UK
UKHW022351190926
475702UK00015B/2222
* 9 7 8 1 0 3 2 8 9 1 8 7 3 *